THE CASE FOR A HUMANISTIC POETICS

The Case For a Humanistic Poetics

Daniel R. Schwarz

upp

University of Pennsylvania Press
Philadelphia

First published in the United States 1991 by the
University of Pennsylvania Press, Philadelphia

First published in Great Britain 1991 by
MACMILLAN ACADEMIC AND PROFESSIONAL LTD
London and Basingstoke

Library of Congress Cataloging-in-Publication Data
Schwarz, Daniel R.
The case for a humanistic poetics / Daniel R. Schwarz.
    p.   cm.
Includes bibliographical references and index.
ISBN 0–8122–3070–1 (cloth). — ISBN 0–8122–1353–X (pbk.)
1. Literature, Modern — History and criticism — Theory, etc.
2. Humanism in literature. 3. Poetics. I. Title.
PN81.S245   1991
801'.95 — dc20   90–23546
                                                       CIP

Printed in Great Britain

In memory of my grandparents:

John and Sadie Rimler;
Otto and Bessie Schwarz

Contents

Acknowledgements

For over twenty years, I have been learning from my Cornell students and colleagues, and I am indebted to them beyond my ability to thank them. I am also indebted to the intellectual stimulation and collegiality provided by the participants in my 1984, 1986, and 1988 National Endowment for the Humanities Summer Seminars for College Teachers, and to my 1985, 1987, and 1989 National Endowment for the Humanities Summer Seminars for High School Teachers. I am grateful to the National Endowment for the opportunity to work with such talented scholar–teachers.

I am particularly thankful for the friendship and insight of M. H. Abrams, Michael Colacurcio, Joanne Frye, Ian Gregor, Tom Hill, Phillip Marcus, Beth Newman, Mary Ann Radzinowicz, and Caroline Webb. I also wish to express my thanks to my students and colleagues at the University of Arkansas (Little Rock), where I spent Spring 1988 as the Cooper Visiting Distinguished Professor.

I also appreciate the cooperation and generosity of my former Macmillan editor, Sarah Roberts-West and her predecessor, Frances Arnold, as well as my current editor Margaret Cannon. Tim Farmiloe, Director of Macmillan, has been supportive and encouraging for well over a decade.

I would also like to thank the editors of *Novel, The Journal of Narrative Technique, The Wordsworth Circle, Contemporary Literature, JEGP, Nineteenth-Century Fiction, Modern Fiction Studies,* and *English Literature in Transition, 1880–1920*; early versions of some material appeared in these journals.

At Cornell, Phillis Molock has provided invaluable secretarial support.

Introduction

The Case for a Humanistic Poetics continues my effort to define a humanistic and pluralistic ideology of reading that takes account of recent theory. This book answers the question that I have often been asked since I have been commenting on theoretical issues, 'What is *your* theoretical position?' Beginning with *The Humanistic Heritage: Critical Theories of the English Novel from James to Hillis Miller* (1986), I have been interested in defining and preserving what is valuable in diverse theoretical approaches. While respecting the contribution of deconstruction, I have been among its sceptics, preferring to consider it as one approach among many. In my practical criticism, most notably in *Reading Joyce's 'Ulysses'* (1987) and *The Transformation of the British Novel, 1890–1930* (1989), I have tried to show how the use of multiple approaches – an informed pluralism – creates a richer reading than exclusive reliance on one approach. I am questioning the hegemony of monolithic ideological thinking that insists that *any* one approach is better or more inclusive than others.

My work establishes a dialogue between recent and traditional theory and between theory and primary texts. Specifically, I try to bisect the distance between reader-response criticism and Aristotelian assumptions about how literary works generate a structure of effects. I read in terms of formal considerations without sacrificing authors, historical contexts, and what actual readers do when they respond to texts. Although the focus of my work has been fiction, much of what I say applies to poetry and drama; as my book-in-progress on Stevens will illustrate, my theoretical position is no less applicable to the reading of poetry. If my examples often derive from Joyce, it is because he provides an example of an author who requires multiple ideologies of reading.

The Case For a Humanistic Poetics was conceived as a whole. While a number of the following interrelated chapters were originally presented as lectures at conferences and later revised and lengthened for publication in journals, all but the first chapter, 'The Case for Humanistic Formalism' – which was the keynote address at the 1987 International Narrative Conference in Ann Arbor – have been substantially revised and their arguments have been developed more thoroughly. Thus a shorter version of the second chapter,

'The Ethics of Reading: The Case for Pluralistic and Transactional Reading', was presented at *Novel*'s Twentieth Anniversary Conference in 1987. In this chapter, I focus on how each reader belongs to numerous interpretive communities and how an ethical reading depends on awareness of how we are reading complex texts. My example is Joyce's 'Araby'. I also propose five stages of the process of reading and a full definition of a transactional model of reading. The third chapter, 'Character and Characterization: an Inquiry', develops a talk I gave at the 1988 Narrative conference at Ohio State. This chapter addresses the necessity for understanding the difference between the mimetic function of *character* and the author's formal choices – conscious and unconscious – that constitute *characterization*. I differentiate the audience response to character in the visual arts from that in literature. In this chapter Joyce's 'The Dead' is a primary example; but, to show the applicability of my theories of reading to poetry, I also refer to the poetry of Wallace Stevens. The original form of Chapter 4, 'The Narrative of Paul de Man: Texts, Issues, Significance', was a lecture that I gave at the 1989 Narrative conference at Madison, Wisconsin. Using the posthumous revelation of de Man's collaborationist and anti-semitic writing, I show that to understand de Man's texts and their significance, we must rely on the continuity of an author's career, historical context, and narrative – the very elements that this major deconstructionist sought to banish from his work. I argue that the *story* of de Man's career questions deconstruction's basic tenets and refocuses our attention on content, narrative, voice, and mimesis. I also explore the relationship between de Man's wartime and later texts, and propose a narrative of repression and displacement to explain his life and work.

My fifth and last chapter, 'Towards a Humanistic Poetics: Contributions and Challenges', addresses recent work that owes its assumptions to and/or contributes to defining a humanistic poetics. Like the chapter entitled 'Modes of Literary Inquiry' in *The Transformation of the English Novel, 1890–1930*, this chapter discusses a number of important and provocative books that speak to the current debates in criticism and to the issues I raise in the earlier chapters. These books enable me both to define significant issues that a humanistic poetics needs to address and to give a sense of the current debates within the profession of teaching literature and reading. In the concluding piece, 'Who's Afraid of *Finnegans Wake*?', I use John Bishop's study of the *Wake* – a deliberately unlikely text – to stress how we necessarily seek to locate coherent character, narrative voice, and anterior reality in even the most resistant texts. I believe that these discussions of critical and theoretical texts add another dimension to what I mean by a humanistic poetics.

1

Humanistic Formalism: A Theoretical Defence

I

While the provocative term 'humanistic formalism' may suggest that I am going to bring you the Old Time religion, what I hope to argue is that a revised humanistic criticism – one that takes account of recent theories – provides a conceptual framework for what is central to our reading, writing and teaching. It behooves traditional Anglo-American humanistic criticism to learn from continental theories, especially deconstruction, even as it defends the ground of its own formalism. Yet it is essential to define the theory and method of a criticism that owes its roots to Plato and Aristotle and that has in its various guises stimulated the serious study of literature in the twentieth century.

In this chapter I shall on occasion privilege polemical bravura over the litmus test of 'for example', in the hope that my other work demonstrates that my interest is in close reading of individual texts. While my focus is on fiction, much of my discussion is applicable to other kinds of narrative. I shall begin this chapter with a brief outline of the tradition I see myself working in before proposing the principles of what I call humanistic formalism.

While Anglo-American critics have not always articulated a philosophic basis for their criticism, they have developed a methodology and principles – even, indeed, an implicit theory – that interpret, analyze, and judge novels effectively. I have spoken at length about this tradition in my book *The Humanistic Heritage: Critical Theories of the English Novel from James to Hillis Miller*. I have cast a wide net to include critics as diverse as James, Forster, Booth, Van Ghent, Watt, Frye, Kermode, Auerbach, and have argued that the Marxism of Raymond Williams and the phenomenology and deconstruction as practised by J. Hillis Miller are in this tradition. Despite some failures, this tradition has explicated the texts of major novelists of the past three centuries and made these texts more accessible to readers. That complicated and problematic modern novels, like *Lord Jim*, *To the Lighthouse*, *The Sound and the Fury*, and *Ulysses*, have become part of the consciousness of educated people and that major English and American eighteenth- and nineteenth-century novels have been better understood and more subtly read is a tribute to the efficacy of this criticism.

The concerns of this tradition have been the accuracy, inclusiveness, and the quality – the maturity and sincerity – of its mimesis, and its mimesis represents how people live in a social community. Perhaps from an historical perspective this criticism should be seen as a response to the British and American novel's interest in content and its moral effects on readers. For this body of criticism believes that, as Gene Thornton puts it, '[A]rt is about something other than art, and subject matter is important precisely because it distracts the viewer's attention from art and focuses it on something outside the [work] – life, the world, God – that is more important than art.'[1] While humanistic novel criticism takes seriously the importance of subject matter, it believes that the doing – technique, structure, and style – is *important* because it reveals or discusses the meaning inherent in the subject.

The differences that separate various strands of Anglo-American criticism seem less significant than they once did. Now we are able to see that New Critics, Aristotelians, the *Partisan Review* group, contextualists, and literary historians share a number of important assumptions – namely that a) authors write to express their ideas and emotions; b) the way man lives and the values for which he lives are of fundamental interest to authors and readers; c) literature expresses insights about human life and responses to human situations, and that is the main reason why we read, teach, and think about literature. While the emphasis varies from critic to critic, we can identify several concepts that define this criticism:

1. The form of a literary text – style, structure, narrative techniques – expresses its value system. Put another way: form discovers the meaning of content.

2. A literary text is also a creative gesture of the author and the result of historical context. Understanding the process of imitating the external or anterior world gives us an insight into the artistry and meaning of the work.

3. A literary text imitates a world that precedes it, and the critic should recapture that world primarily by formal analysis of the

text, although knowledge of the historical context and author are often important. Humanistic criticism believes that there is an original and originating meaning, a centre, which can be approached by perceptive reading The goal is to discover what the author said to *his* intended audience *then* as well as what he says to us now. Acts of interpretation at their best – subtle, lucid, inclusive, perceptive – can bring that goal into sight.

4. Man's behaviour is central to most literary texts, and should be the major concern of analysis. In particular, critics are interested in how and why people behave – what they do, desire, fear, doubt, need. Although modes of characterization differ, the psychology and morality of characters must be understood as if they were real people; for understanding others like ourselves helps us to understand ourselves.

5. The inclusiveness of the novel's vision in terms of depth and range is a measure of the work's quality.

When discussing deconstruction, I shall focus on my colleague Jonathan Culler's *On Deconstruction* because it has become the explanatory midrash for deconstruction, especially for the puzzling works of Derrida and de Man. I would like to play the role of the English Brother William of Baskerville in Eco's *The Name of the Rose* and make a rather pragmatic and Aristotelian inquiry into the mysteries and thickets of deconstruction, acknowledging at the outset that my summary of deconstruction will at times be a whetstone to sharpen my distinctions; like the tolerant Brother William, I am less concerned with heresies than fallacies.

We should begin by recognizing some of the contributions of deconstruction to literary studies. One of deconstruction's virtues is that it reminds us to question unitary stories of reading and monolithic explanations of complex literary texts and issues; as de Man has reminded us: 'The possibility of reading . . . can never be taken for granted.'[2] Deconstruction has been helpful in its stress on the process of reading, on the dialogue between text and reader, and on the need for the reader to stand outside a text. It has helped us understand that moral hierarchies within imagined worlds are in flux, particularly within the spacious worlds of novels where subsequent episodes modify prior ones and vice versa.

Just as structuralism was a response to the alleged impressionism of phenomenology – particularly as practised by Poulet and the Geneva School – deconstruction questions the supposed objectivity of structuralism. Deconstruction reminds us that we cannot use language to summon reality absolutely. Using the English positivist William as his surrogate, Eco puts it nicely in *The Name of the Rose*: 'I had thought each book spoke of the things, human and divine, that lie outside books. Now I realize that not infrequently books speak of books; it is as if they spoke among themselves.'[3] To be sure, we read better when we know what is in other books, particularly the books that the author has read. Intertextuality, the idea that books take their meaning from other books, challenges the assumption that language summons reality and contends that such an assumption is an example of the logocentric fallacy.

Deconstruction stresses that each reading contains the seeds of its own undoing. It privileges the reader rather than the author without quite acknowledging that it does so. Put another way, the text is consubstantial with the reader rather than the author and/or the anterior world on which the text is based. Deconstruction emphasizes that every reader discovers heterogeneous readings in the same text which leads the reader to an irreconcilable paradox or *aporia*. Deconstruction helpfully reminds us that all reading is misreading because no reading can take account of all the possibilities of a text.

Let us turn briefly to the Derridean idea that Western culture has privileged the 'metaphysics of presence' by allowing itself to believe that language can summon or evoke a prior reality. If I, for example, write 'Derrida', he does not appear in the room as a presence; nor does his name mean exactly the same thing to every reader. But it does not follow that his name is merely a series of sounds, a moment of pure textuality, whose significance can derive from its play on 'derision' or 'dadaism' or an inversion of 'arid' or 'Ariadne' (as in, to use a favourite deconstructive trope, 'Ariadne's thread'). Even though words cannot absolutely summon reality, they can approach reality.

In its search for absolutely clean distinctions and definitions, deconstruction often is reductive. While acknowledging that meaning cannot be stable and determinate, we do not need to go the much further distance and concede that meaning is impossible. Just because a text fails to yield one unambiguous reading, it does not follow that most skilled readers cannot agree on the major formal and thematic principles of literary texts. Merely because one can argue that language does not invoke presence, it does not follow that – to recite a shibboleth of recent theory – 'There is nothing outside the text.'[4] Does not our empirical reading experience call into question Riffaterre's assertion that 'Representation of reality is a [merely] verbal construct in which meaning is achieved by reference from words to words, not things'?[5]

In its quest to undermine, to question, and to displace, deconstruction is a kind of radical scepticism. Both deconstruction and scepticism depend on the quite accurate perception that nothing is perfect and that certainty is impossible. Yet does not deconstruction at times seem a modern urban phenomenon in an age of anxiety and disbelief? The deconstructive picaro sees the fly in the ointment, the problem with any idea, and the faults in every explanation; he verbally transforms the spectre of a remote possibility into what might actually happen and makes us aware that the inconceivable might happen just this once. He inverts the meaning of meaning, the significance of significance, by (to use one of their terms) 'valorizing' the marginal, the inessential, the digressive, the false. For example, Culler writes in praise of misunderstanding and misreading: 'Reading and understanding preserve or reproduce a content or meaning, maintain its identity, while misunderstanding and misreading distort it ... We can thus say, in a formulation more valid than its converse, that understanding is a special case of misunderstanding, a particular deviation or determination of misunderstanding.'[6] What Culler is doing is inverting the meaning of the words *understanding* and *misunderstanding*. If we are going to reassign meanings to words and to reinvest the language, then of course we will discover a free play of signifiers, but we will be hard put to make connections with the world outside the text.

II

In the hope that you will *defer* thinking of me as a theoretical Rip Van Winkle, let me define in the remainder of this chapter the basic premises of what I have been calling humanistic formalism.

First, let us consider the concept of humanism. Merely because humanism is a loaded term with a complex history does not mean we should avoid it. Literary study should welcome discussions about human authors, human readers, and human situations in poems and novels; by humanism, I do not mean 'life-affirming', but rather concern with how and why men live, think, act, feel, read, write and speak. When reading or when listening, we respond to the thoughts, feelings, and values of an ego or a consciousness or a presence. We hear a human voice that has tone, timbre, attitudes, gender, and values. Even while disagreeing among its practitioners about the importance of intentionality, humanistic formalism recognizes the folly of the effort to deconstruct the author. Thus it questions Culler's assertion that, 'If, as Barthes claims, "the birth of the reader must be at the cost of the death of the author", many have been willing to pay that price.'[7] I wonder if anyone who has tried to teach *Ulysses* without having read Joyce's prior work or Ellmann's biography could subscribe to such a view. Put baldly, does not a work readily yield a more determinate meaning to those readers who know about the author's other texts, life, and historical context?

A revitalized humanistic criticism would discard such New Critical orthodoxies as the biographical fallacy and the shibboleth 'exit author' and discover how to speak of the author as a formal presence in the text in ways that go beyond equating the omniscient narrator, or implied author with the biographical author. For we need an aesthetic that takes account of how, particularly in such modern texts as *The Rainbow* and *Ulysses*, the author's struggle with his subject becomes a major determinant of fictional form. In the process of reading we respond to an *imitation*, a *representation* of the real creator of the text. He is in the imagined world as a distortion – at times, an idealization, a clarification, a simplification, an obfuscation – of the creating psyche. To paraphrase Patricia Meyer Spacks, '[If authors] create themselves as figures in their [texts], readers choose, consciously or unconsciously, to accept such figures as more or less appropriate to reality.'[8]

Thus humanistic formalism must part company with a parochial formalism – either New Critical or deconstructive – that excludes authors from the critical dialogue. The process of locating a human being within a work recognizes that reading is not merely a verbal game but a shared experience between reader and writer. Do we not seek and respond to a human voice within a text *because* it expresses the energy and values of the author? Voice validates language, gives it shape, connects it with our experiential world. Even when reading letters and newspapers, we ask 'Who is speaking to whom?' 'On what occasion?' and 'For what purpose?' For that reason discussions that ignore authorial voice or reduce speech to a kind of writing should be met with great scepticism.

Because an absolutely complete explanation of the relationship between authors and their characters is not possible, because we cannot provide a mathematical equation for each work, does it follow that we should abandon our inquiry into such matters? While the rhetorical and mimetic function of language cannot be separated, we nevertheless respond to language mimetically as much as we can, because the conventions of meaning and understanding have taught us to do so. As Murray Krieger notes, 'any sense of ultimate verbal absence is shadowed and postponed by our overwhelming sense of its living presence'.[9] To be sure, even when we hear a voice speaking to us and inviting us to enter into and live temporarily in an imagined world, we never forget the text's fictionality, – its 'as if' quality. Yet the energy of a human speaking voice and the story of a realized imagined world deflect most of us, I believe, from perceptions of absence or silence.

Let us turn to *the relationship between fictionality and anterior reality*. To return to *The Name of the Rose*, Eco knows that there is a reality beyond words, even if one cannot quite define or reach it. Brother William's quest for the murderer of real dead bodies is a quest to go beyond signs to discover the anterior reality. As Marianne Moore wrote, we find 'real toads' in our 'imaginary gardens.' Within the abbey of Eco's novel there are texts, but there are also dead bodies – murdered bodies – which make a mockery of immersion in the world of books. As Brother William puts it, 'If the [foot]print exists, there must have existed something whose print it is' (Eco, 381). Or perhaps more to my point, 'The good of a book lies in its being read. A book is made up of signs that speak of other signs, which in their turn speak of things' (Eco, 478).

Perhaps we can distinguish between deconstruction and humanistic formalism by using the metaphors of a mirage and Zeno's paradox. For deconstruction, to believe that an author can approach anterior reality or reveal his own psyche, is a mirage which continually recedes in proportion to the reality that it seemingly approaches. For no sooner do we approach reality, than it is deferred and thus recedes; what we have, we are told, are traces of meaning, not the presence of meaning. By contrast, an apt metaphor for humanistic formalism is Zeno's paradox, for it believes that an author's efforts to present his view of the world or of himself can be seen as akin to bisecting one's way across a room without ever quite reaching the wall.

In his important recent study, *A New Mimesis: Shakespeare and the Representation of Reality*, A. D. Nuttall has defined the principles for his version of a new mimesis. He believes that major topoi – such as recurring moments in the elegiac tradition when the poet speaks of the generations of dead – need be read not simply as recurrences of the same formal conventions but as genuinely felt emotions. He calls for both a 'renewed sense of the variety of reality' and 'a renewed sense of evidence,' as well as what he calls 'the license to ask "Is this true?" or "Is this likely?" when reading fiction'.[10] For Nuttall realism includes 'precise visual description and psychological insight', but it also responds 'to the more fugitive aspects of the real; in particular to shifting *appearances* as distinct from more stable entities.'[11] He is not arguing for the superiority of realistic fiction, but for the premise that 'no form of literature be regarded as wholly insulated from this varying world'.[12] What we need, I believe, is a criticism that understands that 'texts' include not only polysemous signifiers but also *the texture* of the moral and emotional experience it describes.

Some authors wish to approximate reality more than others; traditionally, we have called them realists. By the very nature of its selection and arrangements of its material from all the possible data, realism presents a perspective which is inevitably something of an illuminating distortion. But all authors depend on some recognition on the part of the reader that an act of mimesis is occurring. To invoke my model of Zeno's paradox, even the most realistic texts can approach but never quite reach reality. (The contrasting metaphor for deconstruction is a mirage where reality continually recedes by approximately the same distance that language seems to approach it.)

While all literature has *some* realistic component, I want to stress that realism is not an evaluative term and that we should not assume that the more realism the better. On the contrary, I understand realism as a descriptive term. Moreover, realism is more a process than an end. It involves the attempt to approach an historical or individual world. While ultimately language will not create a world prior to the text, the world evoked by language will have its own verisimilitude. As we read, the reality of the imagined world continually modifies and transforms itself. But the imagined world will always have a continually changing relation both to the anterior world which provided the tentative ground for the imagined world and a continually changing relation to the anterior world in which the reader lives – the world that provides the ground for his or her responses.

Obviously within any literary text some aspects are more grounded in reality than others. For example, the depiction of a character depends upon the selection of one individual from among many possible residents of a city or geographical area, among many possible trades or lifestyles, and among many members of the social class. By convention we understand that a major character – say, in Hardy's *Jude the Obscure*, a young, aspiring, uneducated male from the lower social classes who would rather be a scholar or clergyman than a stone carver – represents or typifies various groups and categories to which he belongs. In other words, under certain circumstances created by the author, readers perceive characters as signs with referents. By contrast, the simple descriptions of objects within a room generally have much less of a signifying function. Representation of humans is of such a different kind of mimesis that it almost becomes different in kind not degree. Representing human beings is both more metaphorical than other kinds of representation because of how we understand characters in their typifying function, and less metaphorical because the creation of people often short-circuits their putative metaphorical function and creates odd kinds of empathy with readers. Moreover, within novels characters are often so individualized and so idiosyncratic that they in fact represent only themselves and undermine the author's patterns of signification; put another way, the infinite variety of complex characters may on occasion deflect them from their signifying function. (As I argue in *Reading Joyce's 'Ulysses'*, Leopold Bloom is an example.)

Realism has been recently called into question on the grounds that there is no possible agreement about what constitutes reality since we as modernists or post-modernists believe that each person perceives in terms of his own experience and psychic needs. This is another version of Conrad's insistence that 'Another man's truth is a dismal lie to me.'[13] We not only all read a different text, but we are aware that even authors who thought they were creating omniscient narrators are really only creating anonymous first-person perspectives since what the omniscient narrator tells us is really only one possible explanation. (As my use of the word 'tells' indicates, I believe that the mimetic model of a story teller, of a person speaking to another through the written word, at times more adequately explains what happens than elaborates theories about differences between speaking and writing.)

Readers and authors do their work in isolation from their fellows and are always lone perceivers; yet rhetorical convention depends upon an author creating a social reality based upon the possibility of implied mutual understanding of author and reader. Rhetorical convention implies that the author is a representative of a larger community; the omniscient narrator, in particular, calls attention to both himself and his or her creator as representative figures. Isn't the reader also a representative of a larger community of readers who are being addressed? Realism depends upon the possibility of creating a hermeneutical circle in which author and reader participate. It depends on the possibility of a shared ontology, an agreed-upon system of language – usually with a varying but relatively low metaphorical quotient. It depends on the belief in an *a priori* world, even if the relation between the anterior world and the imagined ontology continually varies.

In addition to the empirical world, realism addresses dreams, hopes, and plans whose linear narratives may have more in common with the simplified plots of fictions than with the disruptions, abundance, and plotlessness of everyday life. Among other things, what makes *Ulysses* so compelling is its substituting for a traditional monolithic plot a presentation of Bloom's, Molly's, and Stephen's fantasies, hopes, and dreams – often in the form of half-told, dimly acknowledged, and contradictory plot fragments. One reason that twentieth-century writers such as Lawrence and Joyce return to myths for their plots is that our lives seem more and more to lack the kind of coherent forward movement that plots require. As Eliot understood, the mythic dimension orders the futility and anarchy of contemporary history. But does not myth also introduce a level of metaphoricity that breathes new life and gives greater complexity to what may at first seem a rather pedestrian, lifeless or sterile reality?

Humanistic formalism seeks to explore the dialogue between real and imagined worlds with a particular focus on how the imagined world is a work of art created by illuminating distortion, metaphoricity, and signs with varying degrees of determinacy and indeterminacy. Humanistic formalism believes that texts stand in both a metaphorical and a mimetic relationship to the world, the author, and other texts. Its focus is on how texts both represent an anterior world *and* perform their own dance of signification. It addresses the relationship between the imagined worlds of texts and the real or anterior world for which the imagined world is a metaphor, and the relationship between the imagined world and the author for whom the text is an expression – indeed, also a metaphor. It is aware of the ambiguity for both reader and author of what Alex Gelley has called 'narrative crossings' to define the odd movement between fiction and reality.[14] Humanistic formalism respects the old historical contextualism with its concern with cause and effect and the history of ideas, even while it welcomes the new historicism with its focus on the synchronicity of events and the history of power in race, class, and gender. Humanistic formalism welcomes canonical revisions that include writings by minorities, by women, by post-colonial cultures, and by the deprived and disenfranchised. Without necessarily buying into Marxist dogma, it welcomes interest in how texts are produced by socio-economic effects. It sees the need to open its doors and windows to Third World literature and to develop interpretive strategies for literature that, as Nadine Gordimer has written, is concerned less with 'artistic modes and forms' than with the 'substance of living from which the artist draws his vision'.

Now let us consider *the formalism of humanistic formalism*. The formalism component of the term 'humanistic formalism' implies attention to technique and its relation to meaning, for it assumes that content and meaning – story and discourse – are inextricably related. As Mark Schorer taught us, technique is the means of discovering the values implicit in the work of art; themes are realized by technique. What I mean by technique is the conscious and unconscious choices an author makes. Every aspect of form or discourse gives meaning to the imagined world or story and vice versa. The components of a formal narrative include its shape – its beginning, middle, and end and the relations between its parts – its speaking voice, characterization, the imagined audience, its kinds of mimesis, its genre, its style (its diction, syntax, metaphors and metonymies, its rhythms).

The author has created an imagined world, an ontology separate and distinct from the real one; the created world of text is organized according to orderly principles and is apprehensible by orderly principles, although the reader's concepts of order and sense-making may be different from those of the author. The structure of a text is an evolving process in which the reader participates with the author. For the author embodies in his work a structure of affects that arouses expectations and subsequently fulfils, modifies, transforms, postpones, or deflates them. Since each text generates its own aesthetic, we need to inquire into how a particular text signifies. Take *Lord Jim*. Notwithstanding the deliberate efforts to subvert the expectations of traditional narrative by disrupting chronology and doubling every action (a technique that paradoxically calls attention to the fictionality of the text and the inevitability of the events within the imagined world), the narrative that we find in a novel like *Lord Jim* makes a coherent statement about the way life is lived in the imagined world within the text.

Next, let us consider *humanistic formalism's belief in the quest for order and understanding.* Humanistic formalism seeks principles of order. Indeed, it recognizes that our search for order in literary texts is an imitation – an enactment – of the text's search for order. It focuses on both *isness* (what is a work's unifying principle and how does that matter?) and *doesness* (how does a work shape the reader?). As with the genetic code and mathematical formulae, any individual unit of a text is a microcosm of the whole, although deconstruction has taught us to be wary of accepting this as an ov_riding principle. Yet, it may be that criticism that has a teleological bent *results* from literary texts that, as Murray Krieger puts it, 'have wrestled with [their own] teleology to make the teleology [their] organizing principle.'[15]

Humanistic formalism values interpretation to the extent that it accurately reflects the work it is interpreting; thus it establishes a hierarchy in which it is more important that an interpretation be accurate than that it be interesting. Are not my images of mirage and Zeno's paradox also appropriate to contrast deconstruction's view that it is hopeless – a mirage – to believe that we can recuperate the intended text with the humanistic view – again figured by Zeno's paradox – that the critic can approach the conscious and unconscious meaning that the author built into a text? To be sure, the process of bisection towards the goal of accuracy becomes more difficult as we move towards the unapproachable point – the infinity – of complete recuperation. With each succeeding bisection, the process of reaching a meaning intended by the author and one on which diverse readers might agree becomes more difficult; it is as if the process were on an ascending incline or were meeting physical resistance.

Let us now discuss what the humanistic formalist reader does. Literary texts are a constituted reality composed of words; as part of reality, they are – like other experiences – apprehensible; as with other experiences, how they are apprehended depends in part on the apprehender. A text has formal features prior to interpretation. What the essential facts or features of literary texts are will vary from reader to reader depending upon her prior reading experience and the approaches to which she owes critical allegiance. But isn't that true of all reality? For literature, composed of linguistic codes, is different in degree not kind from other experiences – experiences like baseball, bridge and academic conferences which have their own rules and codes. If a geologist and a botanist were to explore the same place, would they not focus on different phenomena?

Readers create stories of reading, but these stories are shaped by inherent qualities of literary works as well as by each reader's unique sense-making. Our criticism needs to account for both what the text does to the reader and what the reader, who is reporting her reading, is doing to the text. The linguistic symbols that compose a text condition the reader, but the reader also creates his own linguistic response when he reads and that response varies with his attention, attitudes, memory, experience, and knowledge. As Nietzsche puts it in *On the Genealogy of Morals*:

> Whatever exists ... is again and again reinterpreted to new ends, taken over, transformed; all events in the organic world are a subduing, a becoming master, and all subduing and becoming master involves a fresh interpretation, an adaption through which any previous 'meaning' and 'purpose' are necessarily obscured or even obliterated.[16]

Or, as Borges put it, quoting from a certain 'Chinese encyclopedia' of his invention:

> Animals are divided into a) belonging to the empire, b) embalmed, c) tamed, d) suckling pigs, e) sirens, f) fabulous, g) dogs at liberty, h) included in the present classification, i) which act like madmen, j) innumerable, k) drawn with a very fine camel's hair brush, l) et cetera, m) which have just broken jugs, n) which from afar look like flies.[17]

In both the above quotations, the thrust is that we interpret and organize the world – that is, we read the text of the world – as we need and wish to do.

E. D. Hirsch, one of the more eloquent defenders of the mimetic function of literature and one of the most thoughtful about how literature means, writes in *Validity in Interpretation* that 'Validity implies the correspondence to a meaning which is represented by the text', and '[T]he only compelling normative principle that has ever been brought forward is the old-fashioned ideal of rightly understanding what the author meant.'[18] Do not good readers stand outside the work and think about what the author means to contemporary readers as well as what the work means to the original audience? As we read in terms of our own historical and personal position, we are aware of changes and similarities between the author's *Zeitgeist* and ours. We try to recuperate the original text – both the world which shaped its creation as well as the world it represents (which may as in Eco's contemporary and savvy tale about the fourteenth century be quite different); but as time passes the attempt to do so – to understand what the author meant – becomes more difficult. Yet, paradoxically, to the extent that books liberate us from a sense of the tick-tock of time in our world and put us inside an imagined world where we are immersed in the narrative time of that world and of the people who inhabit it, is not reading also ahistorical?

Deconstruction and its cousin, reader-response criticism, have introduced the valuable idea that interpretations are stories of our reading experience – that is, interpretations are shaped by our particular personality and historical situation. Furthermore, it has warned us that these stories of reading, although they may pose as objective commentaries, are really, like all writing, to some degree at least, a disguise for idiosyncratic troping. But its practitioners have often not sufficiently stressed the infinite gradations of metaphoricity within a complex work, nor how our reading involves a continual process of determining the precise gradations of literalness and figurativeness. As readers we organize even the most literal and realistic language into narrative units of reading experience; these units always have something of a metaphorical component because they represent our understanding of the absent world and of the absent author who breathed life into that world and represents herself in it. As we read and determine the ever shifting relationship between literal and metaphorical, does not our reading process resemble the author's original organization of her experience?

Let us consider *the function of literary theory and literary criticism*. It may be time to propose the term Theoretical Fallacy for the phenomenon of speculating about texts from such a remote distance and at such an abstract level of discussion that the theories do not help the reader understand what is within texts. In *On Deconstruction*, Culler writes, 'The notion that the goal of analysis is to produce enriching elucidations of individual works is a deep presupposition of American criticism.'[19] I proudly share that benighted notion, and believe that we must demand of theory that it be useful to literary interpretation and to bridge the gap between theory and practice.

Should not literary theory stress how it contributes to readings of literary texts and helps us to understand how the texts we read behave and how we behave when we read? Should it not address methods of reading literary texts and help us to think conceptually about how literary texts cohere? The purpose of theory is to give principles and concepts to criticism, but the test of theory is that it produces powerful interpretations of complex texts and gives us fresh readings of major authors. At times, one feels in reading the practitioners of deconstruction that they are insufficiently interested in works of literature. Or, as Eco's nominalist Brother William puts it, '[T]rue learning must not be content with ideas which are, in fact, signs, but must discover things in their individual truth' (Eco, 382). Our criticism needs to tell a story of what happens in the fictional world; it needs to report or represent what it feels like to be part of that world; we should be wary of approaches that in the name of rigour speak disdainfully of 'recuperation' or 'naturalizing'. I believe that the best criticism accounts for the most aspects of the imagined world and takes account of multiple perspectives – sociological, philosophical, psychological, and linguistic.

In his later study *The Aims of Interpretation*, Hirsch writes, 'Meaning . . . refers to the whole verbal meaning of a text, and "significance" to textual meaning in relation to a larger context, i.e. another mind, another era, a wider subject matter.'[20] But can meaning be separated from significance? As soon as one describes what is inherent in the text it *becomes* 'significance'; the 'isness' or meaning of a work cannot be separated from its 'doesness' or significance. To use Hirsch's distinctions, literary criticism should not be content with meaning, but needs to concern itself with significance. Thus humanistic formalism is interested in how the work includes and conveys the author's social, moral, and political goals and visions. Humanistic criticism believes that human authors create works that reflect experiences that people have and that readers respond with interest to human situations. It knows that we can only *seek* to understand, and that understanding must be partial and incomplete. It is not embarrassed to locate themes or to 'recuperate' characters from the polysemous signifiers; it understands how 'readings,' *all* readings, are partial and metaphorical – including 'the theme is . . .'. It sees criticism as a dialogue between contending and competing perspectives, but acknowledges the value of such a dialogue. It speaks in the spirit of 'This is true, isn't it?'

Humanistic formalism emphasizes the referentiality of fictional characters in terms of *motives* as well as *function*. Humanistic formalism assumes that we read to complement our own experience; or as Paul Ricoeur notes, 'to understand a text is at the same time to light up our own situation, or, if you will to interpolate among the predicates of our situation all the significations which make *welt* of our *unwelt*.'[21] The reader *sees* into the imagined world, perceives, understands, and has her perspective widened, even as she responds to the work's formal arrangement. The qualities for reading and understanding texts and for reading and understanding our own lives and those of others are similar, and thus we can tentatively speak of the continuity between perceptive reading and perspicacious living.

In *On Deconstruction*, Culler writes: '[T]o deconstruct a discourse is to show how it undermines the philosophy it asserts, or the hierarchical oppositions on which it relies, by identifying in the text the rhetorical operations that produce the supposed ground of argument, the key concept or premise.'[22] But why does *identifying* its rhetorical operations undermine a discourse? If one identifies the rhetorical operations in *Emma* or *The Rape of the Lock*, isn't one finding what reinforces or supports the philosophy it asserts? For most works, identifying the rhetorical operations will show how a coherent, organic work is produced. But even if one identifies tensions within the rhetorical operations – tropes that pull in diverse directions – are we really moving in a direction necessarily different from the old formalism? Finally, the act of identification is only the prelude to imposition of some pattern of reading or interpretation, even if it is a pattern of reading that challenges prior readings. As the excesses of the New Criticism taught us, cataloguing tropes for their own sake has little real value; I can recall reading in critical articles and books in the early 1960s such banal sentences as the following: 'In this poem, there are four kinds of color imagery (blue, green, red, and white) and three kinds of animal imagery.'

One problem with the concept of textuality is that it releases the critic from the responsibility of describing what a work says; when language is merely the interplay of signifiers, canniness and wit become the goals rather than truth or mimesis. Those who lost families in the Holocaust or their friends in the Viet Nam war – indeed women and minorities who have suffered oppression – will find it puzzling to have experience reduced by deconstruction to a rhetorical figure: ' "experience" is divided and deferred – already behind us as something to be recovered, yet still before us as something to be produced.' (Culler, p. 82) What I find most striking about Culler's version of deconstruction in *On Deconstruction* is its failure to deal with both political and social causes and effects and with human behaviour – its causes, personal motives, and its consequences. By contrast, a revived humanistic criticism welcomes the new historicism, with its focus on the history of power in class, race, and sex relations; it also values the boid historical contextualism of a book like Michael Colacurcio's brilliant *The Province of Piety*, which shows how recreating the mind and world of Hawthorne is essential to approaching Hawthorne's determinate and stable meanings. It finds more common ground with the feminist criticism that seeks to render women's experience, such as Joanne Frye's excellent *Living Stories, Telling Lives; Women and the Novel in Contemporary Experience*, than with approaches that emphasize textuality at the expense of representation.

For humanistic formalism, the critic's task is to discover meaning and significance within the imagined world, often by focusing on how the author has created a structure of effects for the reader. Each reading is a quest towards the goal of an accurate reading, even though it is a goal which we can only approach but never reach. But we can make very substantial progress toward that goal. The critic's task is to recover meaning and report it intelligibly to other readers who have shared with her or him the experience of reading a work. The critic seeks to explain literature in terms of experience that authors, fictional characters, and readers might hypothetically share. Such a criticism believes that words signify and that Joyce's words in *Ulysses* can create an imagined world of Dublin, 1904, which temporarily displaces the reader's consciousness of her real one. For humanistic criticism, reading – entering into the imagined world of another – is itself pleasurable.

Humanistic formalism does not believe that the critic creates the pleasures of a work; no, the pleasure of reading comes from a transaction, a dialogue between the reader and the work. Ultimately, while responsive to the indeterminacy of the polysemy of language, humanistic formalism stresses the signified over the signifier. It sees the importance of the text's silences, gaps, and opacities in terms of what they signify about the imagined world outside the text. For it seeks to include what Culler calls 'the strange, the formal, the fictional' – but it sees them in terms of its concept of the representational. Humanistic formalism stresses the necessity for including the strange (experiences, particularly psychological ones, that defy ordinary experience or reflect the dimly acknowledged needs of characters and authors); the formal (the aesthetic organization of experience); and the fictive (imaginary experience which, in the form of dreams, fantasies, and plans for the future, is part of human life).

Humanistic formalism calls into question deconstruction's insistence on the arbitrariness of signs in the only sense that such a concept matters to literary criticism. It assumes that in specific circumstances readers share similar recognition of signs and thus may possibly respond in somewhat similar ways. Of course, the more readers share the same cultural background as the author, the more they will share her/his experience and the less arbitrary will appear the author's signs. Readers who have been reading similar novels and critical texts in the same field will share a greater recognition of the signs I have written on this page. Thus the arbitrariness of signs is not absolute but rather a function of the reader's experience, the author's intent, and, of course, historical circumstances, which render some signs far more arbitrary to a contemporary audience than they were for the original reader. For example, Conrad would have expected contemporary readers of 'The Secret Sharer' to understand the British maritime code; he would not have expected them – as many of his readers today do – to extenuate Leggatt or to be reluctant to pass judgement about the captain's providing refuge for an escaped murderer. Nor would he have expected us to be taken in by Marlow's empathetic reading of Jim's abandoning the native passengers and crew in *Lord Jim*. Put another way, are not Woody Allen's movies more determinate for those who know New York American-Jewish culture?

Finally, *humanistic formalism stresses pluralistic reading*. Humanistic formalism reads and writes interpretive criticism in a probing, interrogative spirit rather than in the declarative, unitary narrative of 'I've cracked a poem or story' spirit. Valuing nuances of tone in literature, its criticism values nuances and subtle discrimination. Valuing pluralism and diversity, it wants a dialogue with other approaches. For our readings need to be open, dialogic, and aware of the possibilities of other readings. Pluralistic reading enables us to see the diverse possibilities of a work and to better understand the possibilities of a text's meaning and significance. In its pluralism, humanistic formalism includes – or at least alters the possibility of – all other approaches; for it rejects the 'rigour' of relying on one mode of reading to provide a paradigm which each text fulfils. Thus it rejects unitary theoretical explanations that magnetize each text into an either/or polarity. As readers we can and should belong to multiple interpretive communities, and rather than choose between either/or of possible readings, we can and should enjoy multiplicity and diversity in our readings. In its healthy and open pluralism, humanistic formalism is inclusive rather than exclusive. It sees interpretation as a series of hypotheses rather than a final product. For as we answer each question and pursue each line of inquiry, we become aware that each explanation is partial. Thus it sees the critic not as a prophet; rather it wishes to return to the more modest Socratic question-and-answer structure in order that we leave rhetorical space for other explanations.

Recently, Don Bialostosky has argued that we need a dialogic criticism which 'will not try to decide among [the] competing claims or synthesize their opposing beliefs but will try to imagine and enter their unrealized conversation.'[23] To an extent, my book *The Humanistic Heritage: Critical Theories of the English Novel from James to Hillis Miller* is an effort to do this by imagining what the voices of diverse critics would be saying to one another if they were discussing traditional English novels from Defoe through Joyce. As if imagining a synchronic dialogue, I considered how fourteen critics might discuss the same group of novels. As Bialostosky puts it, 'Those who take turns speaking and listening, representing others and being represented by them, learn not just who these others are but who they themselves may be, not just what others may mean but what they themselves may mean among others.'[24]

We need to acknowledge the impossibility of quite reaching one determinate meaning, while creating a flexible dialogic field in which plausible meanings may contend – a field from which we may propose theoretical hypotheses derived from close reading.

The more we can maintain a dialogue between contending inter-pretive communities, the more the theoretical explosion will produce powerful readings rather than parochial and remote debates; by powerful readings, I mean not merely unitary narratives produced by self-assessed wizards or super readers on whom the text's sense depends, but the pluralistic reading of the more humble figure of an exegetical reader, whose compelling interrogatives take account of diverse approaches. As T. S. Eliot reminds us in *Little Gidding*, 'We shall not cease from exploration/and the end of all our exploring/will be to arrive where we started/and to know the place for the first time.' If we propose our readings and seek to demon-strate what it is that we find in the text, we are able to imagine the response of other readings. If we can be aware of why we disagree and of what assumptions or predilections take us in diverse paths, we will be in a position to have a dialogue about the problems of reading each text. Should we not try to become what Don Bialostosky calls a dialogic critic, that is, a critic who 'not only . . . respond(s) to . . . diverse voices . . . but [invents] the responses they have made to one another'?[25] Thus in *Reading Joyce's 'Ulysses'*, I have tried to establish how, within a contemporary reader, a dialogue takes place between, on the one hand, reading *Ulysses* as a polysemous text that disseminates its linguistic phenomena but fails to achieve coherence and order, and, on the other hand, reading it as a traditional novel that has the kind of organic unity that we find in elaborate literary texts, the genetic code, and complex mathematical formulae.[26]

III

To conclude: I am calling for a revised humanistic criticism that insists on the inseparability of such formal matters as rhetoric and narrative codes from the content, meaning, and significance of imaginative literature. Rather than using literature as an occasion for speculation about the *text*'s implications for semiotics, Marx-ism, or deconstruction, this revised humanism would seek to understand the essential experience of participating in imaginative worlds. While continuing to emphasize interpretation of literary works, my revised humanistic criticism – which I am calling humanistic formalism – would require of literary theory that it develop concepts about how texts behave and how readers respond. Perceiving reading as an active quest to discover what words mean and signify within the imagined world, humanistic formalism seeks to understand how these words function within their own ontology and how the rhetorical effects – usually, but by no means always, consciously built into the world by the author – affect the reader in her or his world. Humanistic formalism unembarrassedly asks, 'What happens to characters within an imagined world?' 'What is the nature of the voice that speaks to us; specifically, what are her or his attitudes, values, and feelings, and how does the artist convey them?' 'What do we learn from the representation of human behaviour within that world?' 'What is the relation of form – including structure as process (especially beginning and ending); mode of narration; patterns of language – to meaning?' 'What does the imagined world reveal about the author and the actual, historical world in which she or he lived?' Since humanistic criticism assumes that texts are by human authors for human readers about human subjects, a humanistic criticism is interested in how and why people think, write, act, and ultimately live.

Notes

1. Gene Thornton, 'P. H. Polk's Genius Versus Modernism', *New York Times' Leisure*, 12 February 1982, pp. 25–6.
2. Jonathan Culler, *On Deconstruction* (Ithaca, New York: Cornell University Press, 1982), p. 224.
3. Umberto Eco, *The Name of the Rose*, trans. William Weaver (New York: Warner Books, 1983), p. 342.
4. Murray Kreiger, *Theory of Criticism: A Tradition and Its System* (Baltimore: Johns Hopkins University Press, 1983), p. 213.
5. Quoted by Wayne Booth, *Critical Inquiry* 3:3 (Spring 1977) p. 408; from Michael Riffaterre, 'Interpretive and Descriptive Poetry: A Reading of Wordsworth's "Yew-Trees,"' *New Literary History*, 4 (Winter 1973), p. 230.
6. Culler, p. 176.
7. Culler, p. 31.
8. Introduction to *The Author and his Work*, ed. Louis L. Martz and Aubrey Williams (New Haven and London: Yale University Press, 1978), p. xii.
9. Krieger, p. 224.
10. A. D. Nuttall, *A New Mimesis: Shakespeare and the Representation of Reality* (New York: Methuen, 1983), p. 182.

11. Nuttall, p. 186.
12. Nuttall, p. 193.
13. November 2, 1895 letter to Edward Noble in Georges Jean-Aubrey's *Joseph Conrad: Life and Letters*, 2 vols (Garden City: Doubleday, 1927).
14. Alex Gelley, *Narrative Crossings: Theory and Pragmatics of Prose Fiction* (Baltimore: Johns Hopkins University Press, 1987).
15. Krieger, p. 213.
16. Quoted in 'Introduction to *The Reader in the Text*,' eds. Susan R. Suleiman and Inge Crosman (Princeton, New Jersey: Princeton University Press, 1980), p. 17.
17. Quoted in Richard Poirier, *The Performing Self: Compositions and Decompositions in the Languages of Contemporary Life* (New York: Oxford University Press, 1971), p. 43.
18. E. D. Hirsch, *Validity in Interpretation* (New Haven and London: Yale University Press, 1967), pp. 10, 26.
19. Culler, p. 22.
20. E. D. Hirsch, *The Aims of Interpretation* (Chicago: University of Chicago Press, 1976), pp. 2–3.
21. Paul Ricoeur, 'The Model of a Text: Meaningful Action Considered as Text,' in *Social Research: 50th Anniversary* 51:1 (Spring 1984), p. 192. The essay is reprinted from *Social Research*, 38:3 (Autumn 1971).
22. Culler, p. 86.
23. Don Bialostosky, 'Dialogues as an Art of Discourse in Literary Criticism,' *PMLA*, 105:5 (October 1986), p. 792.
24. Bialostosky, p. 792.
25. Bialostosky, p. 792.
26. Admittedly, in *Reading Joyce's 'Ulysses'* I see the dialectic as finally being resolved in favor of mimesis, plot, and theme.

2

The Ethics of Reading: The Case for Pluralistic and Transactional Reading

My project is to define a humanistic poetics as an ideological and theoretical alternative to deconstruction even while calling into question the hierarchical role that ideology and theory have been playing in literary discussion. This project began with my book *The Humanistic Heritage: Critical Theories of the English Novel from James to Hillis Miller* (1986), in which I sought to define the theoretical underpinnings of Anglo-American criticism, and continues in my *Reading Joyce's 'Ulysses'* (1987) and *The Transformation of the English Novel, 1890–1930* (1989). Within my larger project of defining a theoretical base for humanistic formalism, I shall in this chapter focus on the reader.

Here and elsewhere I call for a revised humanistic criticism that insists on the inseparability of such formal matters as rhetoric and narrative codes from the content, meaning, and significance of imaginative literature. While continuing to emphasize interpretation of literary texts, my revised humanistic criticism – what I call humanistic formalism – would require of literary theory that it develop concepts about how texts behave and how readers respond. Humanistic formalism seeks to understand how texts function within their own ontology and how the rhetorical effects – usually, but by no means always, consciously built into the text by the author – affect the reader in her or his world. It regards reading as an active quest to discover what words mean and signify within the imagined world. Humanistic formalism unembarrassedly asks, 'What happens to characters within an imagined world?' 'Who is speaking to whom and for what reason?' 'What is the nature of the voice that speaks to us? Specifically, what are her or his attitudes, values, and feelings, and how does the artist convey them?' 'What do we learn from the representation of human behavior within that world?' 'What is the relation of form – including structure, mode of narrative, patterns of language (syntax, diction, rhythm, metaphors and metonymies) – to meaning?' 'What does the imagined world reveal about the author and the actual, historical world in which she or he lived?'

I. INTRODUCTION

For many of us, educated in English departments between 1950 and 1970, it seems as if we are, in Arnold's words ('Stanzas from the Grand Chartreuse'), 'Wandering between two worlds, one dead/The other powerless to be born'. We are caught between two worlds; one is interpretive humanistic criticism, not dead, but called into question by the challenge of recent theory. The other is deconstruction, fully born but unsatisfactory to many of us for three reasons: its failure to understand or account for the entirety of a text; its tendency to read reductively so that all texts seem much the same; and its polemical tone and at times arrogant stance which looks down on other approaches from a steep and icy peak.

Perhaps we can, as suggested in Chapter 1, distinguish between the two approaches by using the metaphors of a mirage and Zeno's paradox. For deconstruction, it is a mirage to believe that an author can approach anterior reality or reveal his own psyche; for no sooner do we approach reality than it is deferred and thus recedes; what we have is traces of meaning, not the presence of meaning. By contrast, an apt metaphor for humanistic formalism is Zeno's paradox, for humanistic formalism believes that an author's efforts to present his view of the world or of himself can be seen as akin to bisecting one's way across a room without ever quite reaching the other side. Moreover, the images of mirage and Zeno's paradox are appropriate to contrast deconstruction's view that it is hopeless – a mirage – to believe that we can recuperate the intended text, with the humanistic view – again figured by Zeno's paradox – that the critic can discover the conscious and unconscious meaning that the author built into a text. The process of bisection becomes more difficult as we move towards the unapproachable point – the infinity – of complete recuperation. With each succeeding bisection, the process of reaching a meaning intended by the author and one on which diverse readers might agree becomes more difficult; it is as if the process were on an incline or were meeting physical resistance.

II. THE USE AND ABUSE OF LITERARY THEORY

In this age of literary criticism and literary theory, the ethics of reading require us to be honest about what criticism and theory do. For many of us the problem in English studies today is how to apply the work of the theoretical explosion to close reading of texts. Put another way, we want to maintain a balance between the interpretation of texts – studies that seek to recreate or represent a text – and speculation about how language behaves. How can we describe the dialogue between reader and text without acknowledging that each reader brings diverse experiences – notably, but not exclusively, the other texts he has read – to the text? Do we not need interpretive criticism that maintains the uniqueness of each text and indeed values the interpretive process more than the teleological goal? Critical explanations should be perceived as an ongoing dialogue; talk of 'cracking a poem', of arriving at a final interpretive destination, deprives us of the very spirit of reading as intimate sharing of consciousness. We should eschew criticism that fulfils the teleology of one dominant concept – whether it be irony, tension, ambiguity, or more recently, 'aporia', 'absence', and 'phallo-centricism'. We should be wary of valuing the challenges of unity and meaning in the form of gaps, fissures, and enigmas – as if *not to mean* and *not to signify* were better than *to mean* and *to signify*.

When we enter into an imagined world, we become involved with what Nadine Gordimer calls 'the substance of living from which the artist draws his vision', and our criticism must speak to that 'substance of living'.[2] In Third World and postcolonial literature this involvement is much more intense. Thus the recent interest in postcolonial and Third World literature – accelerated by Soyinka's Nobel prize – challenges the tenets of deconstruction. Literature written at the political edge reminds us what literature has always been about: urgency, commitment, tension, and feeling. Indeed, at times have we not transferred those emotions to parochial critical debate rather than to our response to literature? While it may not be completely irrelevant to talk about gaps, fissures, and enigmas, and about the free play of signifiers in the poetry of Wally Serote ('Death Survey') and Don Mattera ('Singing Fools'), we must focus, too, on their status as persecuted blacks in South Africa and on the pain and alienation that they feel in the face of persecution. In the piece from which I quoted above, Nadine Gordimer has written – and Joyce might have said the same thing about Ireland: 'It is from the daily life of South Africa that there have come the conditions of profound alienation which prevail among South African artists.' When discussing politically engaged literature, we need to recuperate historical circumstances and understand the writer's ordering of that history in his imagined world. We need to know not merely what patterns of provisional representation are created by language but the historical, political, and social ground of that representation. We need to be open to hearing the often unsophisticated and unironical voice of pain, *angst*, and fear.

When we read literature we journey into an imaginary land, while at the same time remaining home. Reading is a kind of imaginative travelling; unlike real travelling, it allows us to transport ourselves immediately back 'home'. Travel is immersion; home is reflective. How we take our imaginative journeys depends on how we are trained to read: what we as readers do with the available data – how we sort it out and make sense of it. Although the text has a kind of stability because it cannot *change*, our ways of speaking about texts are always somewhat metaphoric. In our interpretive criticism we cannot fully represent a text. When we describe or interpret a text we inevitably order and distort it. Our language is metaphorical – or as de Man would have it, allegorical. But the metaphoricity of our efforts to represent a text in part mirrors the metaphoricity of the author's efforts to mirror the world. Since interpretive criticism does not – cannot – provide transparent or literal language for understanding texts, interpretive criticism creates in part its own text.

Theoretical discourse is far more metaphoric than interpretive exegesis – or at least what exegesis wished to be when it was a nominalistic report of the imagined world evoked by a text. We should understand that theories are metaphors, and like all metaphors they need to show the relationship between the 'image' (in this case, the conceptual framework proposed for a group of texts) and the 'thing imaged' (here, the individual texts). We should remember that when theoretical discourse tries to represent the texts about which it is generalizing, it becomes more metaphorical – and hence more rhetorical and disfiguring – than interpretations. In other words, each stage of telling is inevitably a disfiguration, not an imitation. Or as Stevens puts it in 'The Man With the Blue Guitar', '[T]hings as they are/are changed upon the blue guitar.' For is not the 'blue guitar' the basic impulse of the imagination – and of its surrogate in literature, namely language – to be metaphorical, disfiguring, and performative?

Literary theory seeks to offer hypotheses about how literary texts behave, what they do to readers, what readers do to them, and how language means; it seeks to find rigorous principles akin to those of science to explain what happens in literature. To the degree that literary theory is as rhetorical as it is descriptive, it cannot claim to have the status – as it often implies – of a scientific hypothesis explaining how texts behave. Yet to the degree that it is descriptive and pragmatic, it may help us understand individual texts. Theories, like genres, propose models; they become useful, I believe, when we examine the models in detail and find the ways that the models both adhere to and do not quite fit the theory, causing us to rethink the theory to accommodate new data. Theory always imposes its own ordering text. Because language distorts and disfigures even as it generalizes, theory is to interpretations as interpretations are to literary texts and as literary texts are to the anterior world. Yet all too often theory depends on our need and desire to have a unitary narrative in the form of a pattern or hypothesis to explain our diverse reading experiences of actual texts. Because we read in multiple ways, even contradictory ways, we need many tentative and often contradictory hypotheses – or theories – to accommodate one specific reading experience. If theoretical formulations do not seem to represent actual relationships to texts, if they do not seek a dialogue between specific and abstract, then their language becomes truly signifiers without signifieds; or in other terms, they become dead metaphors because they are detached and separate from what they are imaging.

III.　READING PLURALISTICALLY

It is unfortunately true that we are in a period where, for many, commitment to a dominant interpretive strategy shapes stories of reading every text – that is, the critic brings the same strategy to each text and finds the same things. Paradoxically, the very deconstructive criticism that objects to critical *telos* in unitary narratives of a text's meaning finds its own *telos* in both its readings and its theory. But need that be so? Should we not have an array of strategies which we use depending on the text and, to a lesser extent, on our interests? Should we not allow the text to shape our readings? Put another way, as readers we are members of diverse interpretive communities which should be in a unique dialogic relationship with each text. I am much more interested in the socio-economic implications of *Nostromo* than I am, say, of 'The Secret Sharer', where my concerns are more weighted to the psychology of the young captain as revealed by his first-person narration.

Should interpretive strategies create texts, or can we imagine a process by which a critic is sufficiently eclectic that he draws upon his familiarity with a range of interpretive strategies, choosing those that are most appropriate for each text and author? We need to learn how to enter into a dialogue with diverse approaches, to see their point of view, to understand that interpretive communities become narrow enclaves unless they conceive themselves as part of larger intellectual communities. What is appealing to me about Bakhtin is the implicit acknowledgement of pluralism within a novel's style and imagined world:

> The novel as a whole is a phenomenon multiform in style and uniform in speech and voice. . . . The novel can be defined as a diversity of speech types (sometimes even diversity of language) and diversity of individual voices, artistically organized. . . . Authorial speech, the speeches of narrators, inserted genres, the speech of characters are merely those fundamental compositional unities with whose help heteroglossia [*raznoercie*] can enter the novel; each of them permits a multiplicity of social voices and a wide variety of their links and interrelationships (always more or less dialogized). These distinctive links and interrelationships between utterances and languages, this movement of the theme through different languages and speech types, its dispersion into the rivulets and droplets of social heteroglossia, its dialogization – this is the basic distinguishing feature of the stylistics of the novel.[3]

The same multiplicity of contending voices not only is inherent in critical dialogue about a text, but is and *should* be present in the criticism of any one critic.

Just as an author 'rents' multiple linguistic systems to create what Bakhtin calls heteroglossia, the reader 'rents' diverse interpretive strategies – or perspectives – depending upon his prior experience. But we each belong to multiple interpretive communities; and as we read, we draw upon our participation and experience in several interpretive communities. Not only do those interpretive communities change as well as modify and subvert one another, but our relationship to them varies from text to text. How we read the texts – and the world – depends on an ever-changing hierarchy of interpretive strategies. These hierarchies constitute our reading of texts – and the world – even as they are constituted by it. That is, as we read, our interpretive strategies are challenged and modified even as they modify what we read. When reading criticism we need to be aware of the theoretical and methodological assumptions that produce a reading and examine whether we belong to the community of readers who share those assumptions.

Our ethics of reading needs to account for the subjectivity inherent in our reading. For may not subjectivity idiosyncratically deflect us from the decision about which interpretive communities we shall use? Need we be self-conscious about the distinctiveness of our position as to the text that we are describing or responding to? If someone were to read my interpretive criticism or come to my classes, he would be aware of my propensity for seeing texts in historical, mimetic, and formal terms – especially my propensity as a pragmatic Aristotelian to hear the voice of narrators and to stress the relationship between *doesness* and *isness*. And what about my personal background and experience? My biases and shortcomings? Do I not have a greater professional and personal stake in some texts than in others?

What I am suggesting is that the reader as *übermensch* or as super-reader is a disguise for the human reader with all his tics and quirks, as the recent de Man revelations remind us. Thus if we wish to enter into a dialogue with other approaches, we need to understand the deflection caused by our subjectivity and that of the interpretive critics we read. It may be worth the effort to induce from each interpretive text a persona of the critic to see if we can explain his subjectivity and thus understand his underlying perspective, approach, values, methods, and theory. That is, we must read critical texts as if they too were spoken by a human voice to a human audience, and – as if we were hearing a first-person narration – we must attend to what is missing or distorted.

Since my ethics of reading depends upon the litmus test of 'for example', I want to propose the kinds of inquiry that would constitute a dialogic or pluralistic reading of Joyce's 'Araby', a work chosen because it is short, well-known, frequently taught, and understood in many different ways. If we see 'Araby' as belonging to a sequence of stories that thematizes the moral paralysis of Dublin; as a product of the socio-economic reasons for that paralysis; as the third story of the sexual initiation of a young boy in a series beginning with 'The Sisters' and 'An Encounter'; as an earlier version of Joyce's *A Portrait of the Artist as a Young Man*; as a confession that carries heavy autobiographical freight; as a polemic urging us to see what happens when we are limited and defined by systems of perceptions not our own; as an elegy for boyhood; as a satire on the inhibiting and debilitating effects of a Catholic education; as an artistically organized structure of linguistic effects; as a dramatic monologue; and as an instance of early modernism in several ways (including its turn-of-the-century fascination with masks, its biographical relationship to the author, and its demands upon the reader to weave the meaning of the text) – if we see 'Araby' in all these ways, then we *begin* to define what kind of story we are dealing with.

When reading 'Araby', each of us becomes a member of a number of different audiences:

1. The 1895 audience to whom Joyce imagines that the adolescent speaker is narrating his story – a story based on the young Joyce's visit to an actual bazaar in 1894. This narrative audience, whom the speaker addresses, is an implied audience within an imagined world who knows the customs, politics, routines of Dublin, and even the popular culture of Dublin, including its songs and folk legends.

2. The 1904 historical audience that the author had in mind as he wrote the story.

3. The 1990 contemporary audience. Those of us who teach Joyce are conditioned by the interpretive history of 'Araby' and our varying knowledge of Joyce's life and text. Does the reality of a text include not only its interpretive history, but our memory of our last rereading – i.e. *our* interpretative history? When we discuss books or poems, do we not present the shape we put upon it? When we 'speak' of our reading to a class or colleagues we draw upon our own anterior experience; as we *reread* we modify our understanding because our intertextual and real experience have changed. But, in a process akin to pentimento, past readings peek through; what we did to the text and it did to us in our prior readings shape each new reading, just as we live in the texture of past association when we meet an old friend.

The students coming to a text for the first time will respond differently, moreover, depending on age group, socio-economic group, nationality, education level; their response can be further broken into fragments depending on interest and learning – including knowledge of Catholicism and Ireland. In fact, each of us has her own particular response – subjective, disfigured, a function of who we are when we read and how that uniquely shapes our response to each word. Finally, the largest interpretive community – the largest interpretive entity or unit – is each reader: that is, you or me.

As readers, we create a version of events other than the one the author wrote; in varying degrees, we weave the texture of an open text – open in a sense that it requires our sense-making to complete it – especially with modern texts such as Joyce's which are more open to varying interpretations. But an open text need not be indeterminate merely because a reader needs to *interpret* it. Acts of interpretation depend on answering a series of hypothetical questions that determine the ground of the inquiry and become the cause of interpretive effects. One might conceive the reader at the centre of a series of concentric circles – each representing an interpretive strategy. Depending on the literary text and what interests that reader, the ordering of the circles from closest to most distant varies. My ideal reader is a pluralist who centres herself at a radial centre of concentric circles of diverse interpretive communities and draws upon the appropriate circles for each text and each reading, even while understanding that what is appropriate for her reading would not necessarily be appropriate for another's reading or even her next reading. With each rereading the circles of interpretive strategies that the reader brings closest to her radical centrepoint will change.

A pluralistic interpretation of Joyce's 'Araby' might address the following interrelated questions, and as it found answers, would then – depending on the reader's interests – establish a hierarchy of issues:

1. What is the *point of view*? Who is speaking to whom and for what purpose? Who is telling the story, and on what occasion? What is the speaker's relation to Joyce? What does Joyce expect of the reader? My own reading of 'Araby' argues for a triple perspective. An indeterminate time has passed between the boy's original experience and his retrospective first-person telling of that experience. Joyce expects us to share his ironic

perspective towards a retrospective teller who is myopic and limited in his understanding, embedded in the ecclesiastical language he would disavow, and, as a very young artist, infatuated with what he believes is poetic and literary language. The young speaker's interior verbal world – excessive, colourful, elegant – contrasts poignantly with his inability to *speak* to Mangan's sister. Indeed, does not the *lack* of dialogue between the speaker and Mangan's sister poignantly comment on the rest of his world which seems full of talk – the talk of priests, his uncle and aunt, his friends – that does not speak to his soul? For the boy, as for Stevens in 'An Ordinary Evening in New Haven', 'the words of the world are the life of the world'.

2. What is the genre? What kind of text are we reading? As discourse, 'Araby' needs to be generically defined in terms both of the dramatic monologue and what Adena Rosmarin has recently called, in her magnificent study *The Power of Genre*, the mask lyric. As a story, it needs to be seen as having aspects in miniature of confession, *künstlerroman* and *bildungsroman*. It also may be seen in terms of Joyce's generic distinction between lyrical, dramatic, and epical as presented in *A Portrait of the Artist*.

3. What does 'Araby' reveal as an *expression* of Joyce's life? In what way does Ellmann's monumental biography become part of our intertextual response to the story?

4. How is 'Araby' a socio-economic text produced by Ireland's historical circumstances – in Joyce's view, by Ireland's twin servitude to the Catholic Church and England? How is 'Araby' a satire on Catholicism which – along with England – is the social and political antagonist of the story? Isn't Joyce using the boy to demonstrate the values of a representative pre-adolescent in Dublin and showing what forces – notably Catholicism and British domination of Ireland – shape the boy's epistemology and language, even as the speaker performs for us the consequences of that upbringing?

5. How is 'Araby' a study of sexual repression? Can it be discussed in psychoanalytic terms?

6. How is 'Araby' a chapter in the evolving collection called *Dubliners*? How do we link the speaker to the younger first-person narrators of the two prior stories, 'The Sisters' and 'An Encounter'? Because of the continuity among the three stories, does he not become a shadowy version of a portrait of the artist

as a *very* young man? In that vein, how are these three stories part of a fictional sequence, including *A Portrait of the Artist* and *Ulysses*, about a young man's growing up in Dublin? How do we link his sexual repression with the frustrated and guilty sexuality of the title character of the subsequent story, 'Eveline'?

7. How is 'Araby' part of Joyce's cityscape – his representation of Dublin – and how does that look forward to, and become part of, his later depictions of Dublin's characters in *Ulysses*, and *Finnegans Wake*?

8. How is 'Araby' a 1904 text that depends on historical and literary allusions which have to be recuperated by historical scholarship? (Harry Stone's excellent essay in the Viking Critical Edition of *Dubliners* does this as do the footnotes in that edition.) As a 1904 text, 'Araby' is an historically determined production written by a specific author at a particular time. One critical task is to reconstruct the expectations that existed when the story originally appeared and to understand the distinction between that response and a contemporary response. Of course, Joyce had no one 'horizon of expectation', but rather had several in mind at the same time: Dublin's drowsing citizens whose consciences and consciousness needed arousing; the Catholic hierarchy; the Irish artistic and intellectual elite, including Yeats; the British public; and perhaps a prospective publisher for his story.

9. How does 'Araby' enact a dialectical linguistic drama in which realistic, descriptive language describing the pedestrian world of Dublin struggles with the language of the romance world? Within the boy's mind the language of sexual desire, religious education (especially the ritual of confession), Irish songs, and literary naturalism not only struggle with one another, but also with his own desire and efforts as a putative artist to invent stylized and mannered forms to render his past experience. The boy's romance language – the language borrowed from his reading rather than his experience – is transformed and undermined by the pedestrian world of Dublin and the obsessive hold of the Church.[4]

10. How does 'Araby' fulfil the conventions of the modern short story – including endings that are the fulfilment of prior hints; dense verbal textures in which the linguistic subject reinforces the theme and action, as well as the compression of storytime (several weeks) into a few pages to be read within a twenty-

minute reading? How does 'Araby' look back to the naturalism and realism of nineteenth-century fiction?

11. How is 'Araby' a story of what happens to the ideal reader – although we realize an ideal reader is a fiction – as he or she moves from the beginning to the end, making sense of the story as he or she responds to the structure of effects that results from the voice, organization, conventions, and linguistic patterns?

12. In what way is the text an experience, like other experiences, which resists full understanding, but iterates the boy's quest for understanding – a quest which is the subject of the boy's adventure and of his retelling? As readers, we find what we look for: our readings may be creative, open, and part of our realization of the world; or they may be narrow, stilted, unimaginative, and controlled *completely* by the text. The adolescent speaker's reductive reading of his experience teaches us what happens when we read in either extreme way.

13. Finally, my pluralistic reading would induce a story of *my* personal experience of reading 'Araby': my identification as an adolescent with the boy's love of language and prepubescent sexual anxiety, my visit to Dublin a few years ago, and my twenty-four years of pleasure of teaching and speaking about the story. As teacher and critic should I not try to explain how and why I am touched at every stage of my life by the story of a young boy whose quest for love and language mirrors, parodies, and tropes aspects of my own quest?

Let us pursue our discussion of 'Araby' as our paradigmatic text. Each major work enacts its own ideology of reading which the reader inculcates as he moves from page to page. Each work has its own narrative code of repetitions, half-repetitions, parallel episodes, parallels with striking differences; this code creates contexts for readers' responses within imagined worlds. The reader must not only read logically and sequentially, but intuitively and spatially. As we read *Dubliners*, we see the totality of Dublin life and the evolving patterns that hold Joyce's visions of the city together even when aspects of that pattern are in the different stories. We see the stories in a spatial configuration as if they were stars in a constellation held together by what I call the magnetism of significance. The episodes cohere into a mindscape of Dublin and enact the repetitious cycle of blunted aspiration and frustration, of crass materialism, of sexual repression, of drunkenness, of moral idiocy.

The reader, too, is the object of Joyce's artistry, the figure whose lapsed soul must be restored to his imagination, who must re-discover his humanity in order that Dublin will become healthy and whole. Joyce wants to teach imperfect Irish readers to make sense of Dublin by showing them what *Dublin* really is. What Giuseppe Mazzotta has written in *Divine Comedy* is true of *Dubliners*: 'The *Divine Comedy* dramatizes in a fundamental way the activity of interpretation – it recounts the effort of the poet–exegete to read the book of the world.'[5] Joyce is reading the book of Dublin for us. Like Dante we are pilgrim–spectators, and Joyce is Virgil showing us the inferno of contemporary Dublin. The reader, guided by the narrator-guide, sees the landscape of Dublin and is urged to think of the possibility for renewal. The reader in his sense-making must not only establish hierarchies among his critical approaches, but hierarchies among the details. Language means differently and one must understand the differences between *leitmotifs* and important recurring metaphors, metonymies and minor linguistic details. Our reading iterates the characters' efforts to make sense of the world, but it must go beyond theirs. *Dubliners* teaches the reader to abandon Dublin-think and Dublin-speak if he is to find meaning. Because the reader's sense-making involves fulfilled expectations and under-stood patterns, his activity is at odds with the frustrated quests of most of the figures in *Dubliners*. But because the speaker's telling reveals that he is only at a resting-place and that he has the resources of language and imagination to resume the struggle to discover meaning in his quest, the reader may have more in com-mon with the speaker in 'Araby' than with the other protagonists.

We should think of *Dubliners* as both an evolving series of stories and as a kaleidoscope where each story takes turns as the centre-piece in the pattern. Do we not read *Dubliners* metonymically – responding to recurring patterns of language and structure – and metaphorically – with reference to a world outside the text? The principle metonymic reading of 'Araby' depends on placing it in the context of a sequential reading of *Dubliners*, but as we read each story, doesn't it become a centrepoint of a concentric circle of episodes, including our memories of other stories in *Dubliners*? And it also becomes a centrepoint in the consciousness of our memory of other Joyce works; other works of the period; intellec-tual and cultural history of Ireland; and the modernist movement in England and its counterparts in Europe, including develop-ments in painting and sculpture.

That 'Araby' is the third of a series of stories in which boys wander through Dublin looking for meaning, in which sexuality seems debased and corrupt, creates a context for our response. Yet the stylistic signature of the speaker is different from the first-person speaker's alienated detachment from his subject in 'The Sisters' – where spaces between anecdotes enact his anaesthetized condition – and the relatively straightforward account of 'An Encounter' where the speaker's obsession with the homosexual flagellant is in stark contrast with the distancing of 'The Sisters'. Unlike the other characters in the first three stories, the boy in 'Araby' is a magician with words. Yet his speech, like the pervert's in 'An Encounter', finally 'circles round and round in the same orbit' as if he cannot leave the Church's epistemology. Just as he is constrained by his English and Catholic masters in action, he iterates his past experience. Indeed, doesn't he flagellate himself as – to recall a key phrase from 'An Encounter' – a 'rough and unruly' boy who has, as he puts it in his reminiscence, been 'driven and derided' by vanity at the end of 'Araby'? He 'whips' himself for having a 'sweetheart'. Indeed, at the end of 'Araby' isn't he accusing himself of simony – the worldly traffic in spiritual things of which the priest in 'The Sisters' was supposedly guilty?

The engaged first-person speakers of the first three stories create an identification, an empathy, that makes the ironic detachment of the following stories – 'Eveline', 'After the Race', 'Two Gallants' – all the more striking. 'Eveline', as a version of the aged spinster in 'The Sisters', is not only a warning of what Mangan's sister might become, but of what the boy might become, did he not have the resource of imagination to create his own world.

For 'Eveline' – the title character's name denotes her reflexive self-imprisonment – retells 'Araby' in the third person. Not only is the speaker much older, but she lacks the imaginative power of the speaker of 'Araby' – a power which always has the potential to transform the drab world of Dublin. The final image of her leaning on the rail is a metonym for imprisonment by the Catholic epistemology and by Irish traditions and conventions, both of which define pleasure and self-gratification as sinful, and which, because of that definition of sin, create damaged psyches which feed on repression, sublimation, and projection. In the face of systems of cognition embedded in her psyche, Eveline becomes catatonic when she has a chance for escape: 'She set her white face to him passive, like a helpless animal. Her eyes gave him no sign of love or farewell or recognition.' At this crucial moment she recoils to religion ('her lips moved in silent prayer'), her promise to her mother ('she prayed to God to direct her to show her what was her duty'), whose unintelligible Irish speech – 'Derevaun Seraun! Derevaun Seraun!' – reminds us that Joyce was very sceptical even in 1904 of Yeats and the Irish Renaissance and that he felt that Ireland's future lay with the European community. Didn't he have Stephen say in the opening chapter of *Ulysses*: 'I am the servant of two masters. Said Stephen, an English and an Italian . . . and a third there is who wants me for odd jobs'?

Texts teach us how to read them. Depending on our prior reading experience and other interests, they teach us somewhat differently. But the nuances of dialogue and description, the ordering of events, the way the work opens and closes, the modes of characterization, the choice, narration and the relationship of the narrator to the author, his characters, and the audience create the readers' responses. Let us take the elusive beginning of 'Araby': 'North Richmond Street, being blind, was a quiet street except at the hour when the Christian Brothers' School set the boys free. An uninhabited house of two stories stood at the blind end, detached from its neighbours in a square ground. The other houses conscious of decent lives within them, gazed at one another with brown imperturbable faces.'

The paragraph (a) provides a physical correlative to moral paralysis stifling Dublin; (b) enacts the speaker's desire to postpone and defer the difficult telling of an embarrassing story about prepubescent sexuality and subsequent guilt; (c) enacts his adolescent and imaginative tendency to ascribe power to external things and to be intimidated by his environment. The 'houses' are anthropomorphized ('conscious of decent lives', 'gazed') and 'the street sets the boys free' from the school's bondage. At the same time, the speaker's act of using words is a creative experience that reflects the anterior reality prior to this experience of telling. Because we write and speak to others, because our speech acts and writing are basic to our lives, we take words as *real*. We live within the world of novels in a different way than we listen to music or see paintings because words themselves evoke the illusion of life. Words in literature are not merely marks, traces, indeterminate signifiers. Isn't the self-conscious dramatized voice of Conrad and James an effort to exploit speech and create a form that recognizes telling as action? Isn't the ventriloquy of styles in *Ulysses* a recognition that unitary stories of reading are incomplete? 'Araby' is an example of such a controlled, self-dramatizing perspective. As readers, we impose formal coherence on our experience – whether aesthetic, religious, political, or social – even as we understand that they are fictions evoking reality in a metaphorical or 'as if' sense. They discover for us – even as we discover in them – an order that we need and that our lives lack. We leap to discover teleological organizing principles, even as we step back and doubt these principles.

In reductive terms, 'Araby' is a dialogue between two perspectives, the realistic and romance, and two kinds of language – the literal and the metaphorical – as well as between reason and passion and between the vertical value-oriented life and the horizontal time-oriented life. Joyce chooses words which imbue the story's plot with a subtext or supratext. The opening paragraphs contain language – 'blind', 'musty', 'littered', 'useless', 'enclosed' – which for the rereader metonymically becomes associated with the culture which is stifling the boy's growth. The 'brown imperturbable faces', living 'decent lives', represent the coarse, materialistic paralyzed life of Dublin; in Yeats's words, these are the faces of those 'that fumble in a greasy till' ('September 1913'). The boy's sexual and romance fantasies are a response to this life, and the words he uses as he retrospectively recalls what has happened align themselves as an alternative, not merely in their sensuous, mysterious connotation but in their circumlocutious syntax, incantational intonation, and performative quality: 'The career of our play brought us through the dark muddy lanes behind the houses where we ran the gauntlet of the rough tribes from the cottages to the back doors of the dark dripping gardens where odours arose from the ashpits to the odorous stables where a coachman smoothed and combed the horse or shook music from the buckled harness.' The speaker revels in sounds, smells, touches, and disrupts the expected patterns of syntax to savour and linger over the words which evoke them.

The speaker's (and reader's) discovery of 'I' – the tentative discovery of 'I' – with which he begins the last three longish paragraphs of 'Araby', struggles with the earlier paragraphs in which 'I' was submerged and distanced. Who would guess from the story's first paragraph, or even the second or third paragraph, how his secret feelings would emerge as the central focus? The telling itself mimes the tendency to submerge sexuality, feelings of self: 'North Richmond Street, being blind . . .' is the language of an official tour guide. 'The former tenant of our home' submerges the apparent orphan state of the boy – the felt loss of his parents whether from death, desertion, or consignment of him to relatives – and seems to begin a paragraph focusing on the loss of a tenant. Isn't the next paragraph also dominated by his belonging to the enclave defined by his aunt and uncle and his playmate? Gradually the speaker reveals that Mangan's sister – whose name he cannot articulate even now – is the focus of his attention. 'I imagined that I bore my chalice safely through a throng of foes. Her name sprang to my lips at moments in strange prayers and praises which I myself did not understand. My eyes were often full of tears (I could not tell why).' As he recalls these events, he transforms them into sensuous, romantic images; yet he cannot escape the religious epistemology on which he was educated, even as he seeks to find refuge in the medieval romance of Scott's novels. Moreover, savouring words and creating excessive sentences that do not quite work, he is Joyce's ironic portrait of the artist as a very young man: 'I did not know whether I would ever speak to her or not or, if I spoke to her, how I could tell her of my confused adoration. But my body was like a harp and her words and gestures were like fingers running upon the wires.'

Rather than sing of his love in terms of his personal feelings, the boy ironically chants the religious language that has been written on his consciousness and conscience. Mangan's sister is enclosed by the silver bracelet and spikes, images of the enclosure of Irish culture – particularly the Church. Note how light creates a halo over her bowed head, as if to make her an ironic saintly virgin: 'The light from the lamp opposite our door caught the white curve of her neck, lit up her hair that rested there, and falling, lit up the hand upon the railing.' Her bondage metonymically extends to him: 'When she spoke she turned a silver bracelet round and round her wrist. . . . She held one of the spikes, bowing her head towards me.' In anticipation of the ending, his excessive and hyperbolic language is disproportionate to the data. 'What innumerable follies laid waste my working and sleeping thoughts. . . . I wished to annihilate the tedious intervening day.' Yet the trip to the bazaar confirms the tedium he would annihilate.

At the close, the speaker of 'Araby' bitterly recalls his own experience and iterates his self-disgust for deviating from his religious training; but Joyce asks the readers to see that his self-damnation is ironically poignant and self-defeating – and finally an indictment if not a damnation of a culture that represses sexuality and feeling. Aren't we overwhelmed by the poignant self-castigating voice of the conclusion of 'Araby'? 'Gazing up into the darkness I saw myself as a creature driven and derided by vanity; and my eyes burned with anguish and anger.' Because of his ecclesiastical education, the speaker reads *in the darkness* – the darkness of his own mind – that he is guilty of one of the seven deadly sins, namely vanity or pride. It is those words or ghosts, and the images they summon, that physically affect him – 'burn his eyes'; for to him they have the reality of physical things; just as the Catholic code imprisoned Mangan's sister, the words torture him. Even as we intrude a trace of sceptical reading that casts a shadow of doubt over whether the speaker means his self-condemnation, we are moved by the boy's pain. Do we not respond to the boy's traumatic response to disappointment – a response which takes the form of using the very linguistic system that he had sought to disavow? Ultimately isn't his response an enactment of the terrible force of language, of teaching, transformed into obsession? Isn't he as paralyzed as the dying priest in 'The Sisters'?

Finally, the woman who speaks 'out of a sense of duty' is deflecting his dreams and evoking his internalized fears that, by abandoning his work for his quest for love, he is sinning. The darkness and silence are the closed text – the text written on him by convention and Catholicism – and the erasure of his feelings. The phallic jars remind us of the sexuality that he is missing and 'her wares' remind us how sex has become a commodity in the modern world. 'The Arab's Farewell to his Steed' is another sexual thrust, reminding us how the English modernists (i.e. Forster, Conrad, Lawrence) turn faraway places (India, Italy, Malay, Mexico, and New Mexico) into libidinous sexual ones. In a sense 'Araby' is about the detumescence of adolescent sexual expectations – expectations associated by the boy with otherness of place ('The Arab's Farewell to his Steed', 'Cafe Chantant').

Sexuality – repressed by Catholicism – has expanded infinitely in the guise of romance and the bazaar (Eastern enchantment) to challenge the limits and confines of the rest of his world. Under the power of childhood sexual obsession – 'her image' and the quest to fulfil his mission – he cannot 'read' his experience as we must do to understand the story. Our synchronic reading sees that he has become, without reading it, a poignant Dante – Dante on a quest for his Beatrice – or a priest obsessively serving the blessed Virgin. The boy's metaphors for the quest and for the fair have died and become transformed in his memory of experience; his words that refer not to the train-ride but to the fair, and finally to the catatonic state of mind in which the boy is left. The 'magical' name 'Araby' is demystified, deprived of its metaphorical potential by his experience; retelling, he stresses the 'deserted train', the 'intolerable delay', the 'ruinous' – not ruined – 'houses', the 'bare carriage'. Apparently, cultural mediocrity can even rob one of the magic of words. And does this not provide us with an allegory for reading? As heroic readers, we must resist bringing our pre-existent marks – our critical biases – to texts, or to choose another metaphor, we must avoid using our fingers to look for pre-existent shapes as if we wished our interpretive criticism to be a kind of braille in which we look for recognizable formulae with our critical fingers.

Let us think of the boy's telling as an imaginative structure woven as an antidote to a literal, physical structure, a house that stands into the blind street and that is filled with musty, stifling air creating an enclosed, claustrophobic space: the lights go out in the final scene and the house is left in darkness. And the house as physical structure which – standing with the other drab, dusty, musty houses on a blind street – is a metaphor for Dublin; put another way, each story of *Dubliners* is a room in a house in Dublin. Until the end when he is overwhelmed by guilt and frustration, the boy is telling or building his own alternative 'house' in the interior world of his mind to stand in contrast to the paralysis of Dublin. In contrast to 'old useless papers', his uncle's vapid words, the pedestrian language of the English accents, the popular songs which are evoked by the text are the vitality, sensitivity, precocity, and sensuality of his response. But the retrospective view enacts how his house – his 'text' – has been overwhelmed by silence and darkness. On a blank page on which the boy writes his imaginative text – his house – and erected his empire – he has been ironically colonialized; for retrospectively we see that his pages had markings through which – in a process akin to pentimento – the past peeked; put another way, as he builds his imaginative 'house', his originality and imagination give way to tracing pre-existing letters. For the retrospective teller is trapped in metaphorical systems that constitute and produce him – that write its text on him even while he would write a romantic text. That the boy's imagination can turn on lights to living words, imagination, and life lingers in our mind. For finally, as Stevens puts it in 'An Ordinary Evening in New Haven', 'The words of the world are the life of the world'; for the boy lives in the world of his imagination and he can create 'ghostlier demarcations' and 'keener sounds'.

At times, interpretive critics may merely remind us of what we know; as when I told you that the boy's disillusionment in 'Araby' relates to the English accents at the bazaar and to the demystification of sex into stale, vapid flirtation. But rhetoricity can be helpful to hermeneutics. If I stress that the phrase 'I never said such a thing' from the dialogue that the boy overhears could be taken as the epigraph for the story, the phrase that metonymically stands for what the boy cannot say about his psychosexuality – for the ironic gap between the grim reality of Dublin and his dreams – I should catch your attention. And if I propose that 'thing' becomes a metonymic substitution for sexuality – for after all, isn't sexuality the subject not only of the conversation among the English, but of the boy's entire discourse – won't you perhaps agree that the English have appropriated sexuality by cheapening the word-world in which for the boy sexuality exists? Isn't he left to stare into darkness for new words? Indeed, do we not realize that the Church had already taken possession of his words when he compares the 'darkness' and 'silence' to a 'church after a service' or compares the coins on a tray at the bazaar to 'money on a salver'?

In the adolescent speaker's mind, clerical and literary styles struggle with the usual conventions and the popular songs and poems, and he learns from life in Dublin, including his uncle's pub culture. The clash of voices and styles is inherent in 'Araby'. The boy's romance style, his affected literary style, his genuine love of the sounds and textures of words, the ecclesiastical style inculcated at the Christian Brothers' School, and his desire as a young artist to see his experience in universal and metaphoric terms, struggle with one another as he seeks his voice; his languages clash with the lower middle-class English speech, the half-attentive, intoxicated speech of his uncle as well as the conventional response of his aunt (both of which are aspects of the 'adult' world) and the naturalistic style where metaphors are deprived of their meanings – the style with which the story opens and which reasserts itself as he experiences the blighted expectation of his quest. In addition to the dialogue of styles, past and present inform one another, clash, modify one another and yet cannot be separated. Just as his former self sought to fulfil his mission and return with a present to the girl, the speaker at an indeterminate distance of time seeks to define what happened to himself – and he fails.

According to Bakhtin, each linguistic system responds differently to 'socio-linguistic world views' (360). 'The novelistic hybrid is an *artistically organized system for bringing different languages in contact with one another*, a system having as its goal the illumination of one language by means of another. The carving-out of a living image of another language' (361). 'Hybridization' – 'a mixture of two social languages within the limits of a single utterance' – is essential to the technique of 'Araby'. In hybridization, 'only one language actually presents utterance, but is rendered in light of another language' – i.e. the boy in 'Araby' responding to his sexual needs and fantasies, describing the bazaar in terms of religious language, or his love for Mangan's sister in terms of romance; Stephen's speaking in *Ulysses* of his mother's death in terms of Swinburne and Yeats (Bakhtin, 362). If we recall the ability of the Irish god Cuchulain to inflate and deflate at will in the face of danger, and think of the teller's self-inflation and deflation, the *playful* symbol of the bicycle pump will be clear.

If Bakhtin is fundamentally correct that various linguistic systems 'encounter one another and co-exist in the creative consciousness of people who write novels,' the reader must try to define those languages. But of course readers may not *know* what styles they read; as time passes, it becomes harder to see what styles the original audience responded to. For 'North Richmond Street, being blind' no longer implies a 'dead end' street; 'salver' – the plate for collecting coins in a Catholic church – is to some an obsolete word. Were it not for carefully footnoted editions and essays such as Stone's that retrieve past references, the reading of texts would begin to change, but since the text is always there for scholars to rediscover, it remains the same – just as other archaeological data lie there awaiting discovery. Recently discovered pre-Christian, Roman or Jewish ruins clearly existed in Jerusalem, although no one had yet found them. My point is that a text pre-exists its perception and constitutes a reality beyond the subjectivity of readers.

IV. THEORIES OF READING

Let us examine several ideologies of reading on the current critical mindscape.

1. *Aristotelian criticism* asks questions about genre, plot, and mimesis; it is concerned with what a text does, how it persuades us and elicits emotions. It reasons *a posteriori* from effects to causes. The implied reader, created by the implied author, is created by the structure of effects that the author embodies in the text. Aristotelians ask the generic question 'what kind of' to understand effects and reason back to causes. Generic criticism, like structuralism, seeks to define 'underlying and self-regulating' explanatory rules for a group of works. But generic criticism is more tentative, more hypothetical than structuralism. When we speak of a text in terms of genre, we are providing a categorical explanation that cannot be fully represented as a literal fact, but rather as an 'as if' hypothesis to which we refer as we note similarities and differences between the literary work under discussion and the hypothetical category. Generic criticism, then, is a metaphor for other metaphors. Put another way, generic criticism seeks to define works as instances or images of a paradigm, even as it seeks to discover distinctions from that paradigm by looking at a text's formal patterns and comparing it with other not-dissimilar works. This is another way of saying genre is deductive and inductive. The value of answering the question 'what kind of' is that it shapes our expectations as readers. We respond differently to an elegy than to a dramatic monologue. In practice, Aristotelian criticism may propose rigid categories and terms with which to define reading; even for some of us sympathetic to the Aristotelian approach, these categories and terms at times belie the fluidity and flexibility of reading.[6]

2. *New Criticism* is a formalism that emphasizes the *isness* of the work, how the parts within the imaginary ontology relate to the whole. It relies on close reading of linguistic patterns; at its best it is aware of the diversity in texts – as its conceptual principles of ambiguity, tension, paradox, and irony indicate. It stresses, like other formalisms, the inextricable relation between form and content. But at times it seeks to resolve these diverse elements into a whole. Readers of Kenneth Burke, Wayne Booth and other Aristotelians, Mark Schorer and Dorothy Van Ghent

know that a humanistic poetics – influenced by New Criticism and the work of I. A. Richards and Empson – is aware of language. Indeed, the New Criticism saw the text as a self-contained linguistic system, even as it sought to banish biography, intention, and historical explanations.

3. *Speech act theory* sees literary works as speaking gestures in response to a particular situation, occasion, and audience. It sees the act of speaking in terms of a hierarchy of subordinate acts: a) the locutionary or propositional act – that is, the act of saying; b) the illocutionary act or force – what we do *in* saying; c) the level of perlocutionary act – what we do *by* saying.

4. *Historicism* believes that one must recover the contexts to recover the text. While the words in a text remain the same, what they mean to readers will change. Contextualism seeks to recover the mind of the author and the *zeitgeist* in which he wrote. Thus we must take account of the factual underpinnings – the grounds and origins – of texts. To recapture a text we must do literary archaeology, some of which may be labelled 'pre-critical'. For example, in 1904, when *Ulysses* takes place, the Boer war was still on the minds of publicly and politically-conscious Dubliners, and Joyce's reference to that war and South African history – references that he made for the purpose of establishing a parallel between the Afrikaners and the Irish, as victims of imperialism – would have been noticed by a 1904 Irish reader. Joyce pressed the parallel between the Boer war and the British efforts to dominate and repress Ireland, and drew a parallel between Dewitt and Parnell. It turns out that the Boer war occupied a central place in Irish newspapers of the 1900–1904 period. But in 1922, these references were barely noticed by (or recuperated by) Joyce's readers, and now, few American readers would be aware of their importance were it not for recent research by Barbara Temple-Thurston, a young South African scholar who took her Ph.D. in America. Each reading – and teaching – of a major work is a dialogue between this reading and/or teaching and prior ones; now that I know about the South African reference, my mind responds differently, just as it does when I respond to a person in light of new facts.

New Historicism stresses interrelationships between literary and other cultural phenomena rather than simple cause and effect. It looks synchronically at parallel phenomena. It is more concerned with the history of power as it pertains to class, gender, and race than with the history of ideas. It looks not only at what is included, but at what is omitted from an imagined world – how the lower classes lived, why women play minor roles, etc.

5. *Reader-response criticism* asks, as Fish put it,

> What is the reader doing? What is being done to him? For what purpose? [These are] questions that follow necessarily from the assumption that the text is not a spatial subject but the occasion for a temporal experience. It is in the course of answering such questions that a reader-response critic elaborates 'the structure of the reading experience,' a structure which is not so much discovered by interrogation but demanded by it. (If you begin by assuming that readers do something and the something they do has meaning, you will never fail to discover a pattern of reader activities that appears obviously to be meaningful.)[7]

For Fish reading is a temporal experience, the meaning of a passage is made by our reading, and the unit of analysis is less the sentence or passage – or what Fish calls the 'deliberative act': 'my unit of analysis is formed (or forms itself) at the moment when the reader hazards interpretive closure, when he enters into a relationship of belief, desire, approval, disapproval, wonder, irritation, puzzlement, relief with a proposition.'[8] According to Gerald Prince: '[The reader's] physiological, psychological, and sociological conditioning, his predispositions, feelings, and needs may vary greatly and so may his reading: his knowledge, his interests, and his aims determine to a certain extent the conventions, assumptions, and predispositions he takes to underline the text, the kinds of connections he is particularly interested in making, the questions he chooses to ask, and the answers he brings to them.'[9] The reader is a kind of mental athlete who not only does things to texts and meanings, but who is imaged as acting. The reader is a play or film director who transforms the script (the text) by reading into the text his own vision of how it should really be.

6. *Structuralism* discovers codes embedded in a text. Using the linguistic model of Saussure, it sees the text as a construct of self-sufficient and self-regulating elements. In the guise of scientific objectivity, it is purportedly more analytic than interpretive. Structuralism can focus on genres, plots, and

stylistics. Stylistics is often a subdivision of structuralism and seeks to explain what happens in linguistic terms, often in terms of proposing self-regulating structures available to a savvy reader. It may be that structuralism's ability to propose a morphology of themes, plots, historical backgrounds has been neglected in favour of linguistic structuralism.

7. *Deconstruction.* The reader as Penelope weaves and unweaves a tapestry of his own meanings. It develops Saussure's insight that language depends on differences between signs, rather than objective relationships between signifiers and signified. It sees the act of reading as breaking up the apparent units and meaning of a text. For deconstruction, it is an illusion to think one can discover a unifying theme or an authorial presence within a text. It stresses the polysemy of texts and sees texts as, in Barthes' words, 'a galaxy of signifiers, not a structure of signifieds'.[10]

Let us acknowledge the contribution of deconstruction. Deconstruction has taught us to acknowledge gaps and enigmas in a work's teleology and to recognize the marginal aspects that challenge unitary stories of reading. Deconstruction has reminded us that it needs to be aware of what happens to the text as a warp and woof of language. Yet deconstructive reading is one of many theoretical possibilities; it only stands in relation to all possible modes of reading as broccoli stands to all the world's vegetables. For it is only one of many kinds of readings that attend to linguistic phenomena.

8. *Phenomenological* criticism. As Iser puts it: 'The convergence of text and reader brings the literary work into existence' (*The Implied Reader*, quoted in Suleiman and Crosman, 22). The reader responds to the phenomena of a text in terms of his own experience, but also acknowledges the reality of the text's codes, convictions, and mimesis. In Suleiman's words, reading is a 'sense-making activity, consisting of complementary activities of selection and organization, anticipation and retrospection, the formulation and modification of expectations in the course of the reading process' (Suleiman and Crosman, 22–3).

V. TRANSACTIONAL THEORY OF READING

I would like to propose the concept of transactional reading to stress how reader and text meet in the seam of the reading experience. In my view, text and reader are engaged in a trans-action where each does something to the other.[11] Peter Ruppert has put it nicely in his *Reader in a Strange Land*: 'In a dialectical model of the reader/text relationship, neither reader nor text is a stable entity or a finished product; each constitutes, rather, an active component in a mutual transaction that produces discord, disagreement, and transformation.'[12]

The equivalent to squaring the hermeneutical circle is to bisect the distance between, on the one hand, reader-response criticism which argues that the reader creates the text and which is epito-mized by Stanley Fish; and, on the other, Aristotelian principles which assume that texts shape readers and are epitomized by Wayne Booth and his followers. What Fish and Booth both do is focus on the structure of affects generated by the text and the process of the sense-making that continually goes on in the reader's mind. Both are interested in *doesness*, in reading as action, but whereas for Booth it is the text that transforms, modifies, qualifies, and reformulates the reader's emotions and values, for Fish it is the reader who does these things to the text. For Booth, language represents non-linguistic aspects such as theme, plot, character, and structure. While Fish claims that the language is itself the focus, in practice he too is reading through language to what it represents.

Traditional Aristotelian criticism argues that the author – or the implied author – speaking to an implied reader, *produces* the effects based on prior causes built into the text by the author in his *making* of the fiction. Such criticism moves from author as maker to the made object – the text – to what the text or made object does. The traditional paradigm is:

(from the) anterior world ⟶ the author (makes) the text
(or imaginary universe) $\xrightarrow{\text{(which produces effects on)}}$ the reader.[13]

Reader-response criticism argues that ultimately readers produce the text and infer a hypothesis of the author: it moves backwards from reader to text to author. When Fish reads seventeenth-century poetry, he is something of a closet Aristotelian in his concern with the structure of effects and its relationship to the enactment of a plot and the genre of the text. Fish reverses the method of inducing *doesness* from the text and ultimately the author; he induces the text from what it does to the reader and then induces the author from the text he creates. So we can graph Fish:

the reader $\xrightarrow{\text{(unmakes/creates)}}$ the text (or imaginary universe) $\xrightarrow{\text{(from which he induces)}}$ the author as well as the anterior world that the author attempts to describe.

Since in practice both include a dialogue between reader and text, Aristotelian criticism and most reader-response criticism are transactional.

Let me distinguish what I am calling transactional reading from the theoretical underpinnings if not the practice of reader-response criticism. For Fish, '[I]nterpretation is the source of texts, facts, authors, intentions' (Fish, 16). But I would argue that interpretation is the way we organize and give shape to both the experience of reading texts and what they do as a class of objective phenomena. As a reader, Fish believes that he does not recuperate texts, but rather *makes* texts. Fish wants to focus on the temporal flow of the developing responses of the reader to the words as they succeed each other on the page; the critic describes his experience of that process. As Fish puts it, '[T]he meaning of an utterance . . . is its experience – all of it – and that experience is immediately compromised the moment you say something about it' (65). For Fish, '[I]nterpretive strategies are not put into execution after reading; . . . they are the shape of reading, and because they are the shape of reading, they give texts their shape, making them rather than . . . arising from them' (13). But while interpretation, cognition, and perception are inseparable from reading, are they not also part of the reflective process that succeeds reading? Even if we accept Fish's view that 'the formal features . . . are the *product* of the interpretive principles for which they are supposedly evidence', and that 'formal units are always a function of the interpretive model one brings to bear', does that mean they – the units – are not 'in the text' (12–13)? What we see in the experiential world depends on our perspectives, but what we do *not* see is still there and perhaps the very thing that others will see. For Fish, criticism cannot be demonstrative, but only persuasive.[14] Yet, I would argue, stories of reading – like all telling and writing – are partly demonstrative and partly persuasive or performative. Cannot a discussion of the *isness* and *doesness* of the text, its original author, and its historical context be *demonstrative* rather than merely rhetorical?[15]

Transactional reading is, for me, a crucial component of the informed pluralism essential to humanistic formalism. In my transactional model the reader is a savvy figure – part picaro, part hero – who lives by his wits, intuition, and humour as he moves through time engaged in the process of sense-making. But he is also a reflective figure who lives at the centre of concentric circles of epistemologies – interpretive communities, if you will – and moves outward from a passage to read synchronically. For the odyssey of reading requires both a wily, shrewd, canny, linear reader as well as a reader who resists temporal narratives of reading, and who sees the multiplicity of meanings generated by literary texts and the primitive mystery of combinations of words. The transactional reader does not take signs for wonders; she establishes in the adventure of reading a hierarchy of meanings, even while understanding that such a hierarchy varies depending upon her interests and values at the time of reading. Such a reader has the openness, flexibility, and humility to allow the text its occasion, and gives it space to perform its meaning. Open to new experience, she is not intimidated by the possibility that texts will not fit pre-existent patterns. She is willing to use diverse interpretive strategies for different texts, and she has no pre-existing formula for reading.

While a transactional approach does not arrive at one valid meaning, it permits a dialogue between phenomena discovered in the text and the reader's sense-making; it also seeks to demonstrate how that sense-making derives from a dialogue of interpretive strategies within the reader's mind. It is in those passages where determinacy comes into question and ambiguity exists, that the most interpretive cognition and analysis are required of our transactional reader. The reader weaves patterns of meaning from implication, imagines unseen motives not articulated in dialogue, interprets more knowingly than characters or narrator, and supplies unwritten threads of plot to tie discrete episodes together. Do we not make our world from our responses to experience and do not authors write because they assume that we do so?

My transactional model stresses both the private nature of our story of reading and the public nature of our sharing knowledge generated by the text. It seeks to give account of the multiple and contradictory kinds of reading that are part of the critical process of reading, a process that has disruptions and short circuits. Fish argues that stability exists not in texts, but in interpretive communities defined by literary, political, and cultural determinants. But I believe that it is just as correct to say that communities of words – i.e. literary texts – make readers. All Fish is really saying is that a text – or a tree – depends on human cognition; the text or tree cannot look at me. This is, of course, Stevens's point in 'The Idea of Order in Key West' – our imagination responds to experience and makes ghostlier demarcations and keener sounds – and a major point of the entire Romantic movement of which reader-response criticism is so much a part.

If texts are the products of interpretive acts, interpretive acts are the products of texts. Doesn't an author encode a response? Doesn't she use her words to structure her effects? Do not texts produce effects in readers? The problem with speaking exclusively of what the reader does to the text is that it deflects attention from the way readers respond to an imagined world created by the words and the anterior world which gives it shape. It tends to stress moments of disunity rather than see patterns of unity. Do we not read to *know*, to learn about behaviour? Do we not need to account for why one kind of imitation interests more readers than others; what attracts us to some imagined ontologies more than others; of what are pleasing fictions constituted; why we need organization and unity; why necessity and probability *are* aesthetically pleasing; and why we wish to allegorize universals from details?

Let us for a moment consider codes. Just as we respond to baseball games, social behaviour, and academic conferences by reference to codes based on prior knowledge of the purposes, goals, and practices of those activities, our responses to texts depend on the conventions and customs of the prior texts that we have read. What is important to stress is that texts contain the potential for provoking our knowledge developed from prior reading. Authors build a narrative code into their texts, a code that instructs the reader how to respond to each text; when the reader adds a supplement of his reading experience, the decoding becomes a transaction. Yet the perception of the author's code varies with readers and changes with time. When Eliot defined 'objective correlative', was he not talking about narrative coding? 'The only way of expressing emotion in the form of art is by finding an "objective correlative"'; in other words, a set of objects, a situation, a chain of events which shall be the formula of that *particular* emotion; such that when the external facts, which must terminate in sensory experience, are given the emotion is immediately evoked.'[16] Wasn't Eliot speaking of the inadvertent *effects* of polysemous signifiers when he complained that 'Hamlet (the man) is dominated by an emotion which is inexpressible, because it is in *excess* of the facts as they appear' (Eliot, 125)? By contrast, performative passages like the ending of 'The Dead' or the scene in which Lawrence has Ursula confront the horses in *The Rainbow* rhetorically urge a feeling rather than present it; we might call this a subjective correlative where the signifiers laterally move through the reader's consciousness without creating a code. In both cases, the text and reader meet in a kind of no-man's land, an uncharted space where the reader uses words to draw a map.

Does not my transactive model make us realize that reading is both temporal and spatial? Let me propose that we may have gone too far in emphasizing the temporality of readings and suggest tentatively a spatial apostasy. On the one hand, we read temporally, moving through the text linearly. But on the other hand, after finishing a text, we contemplate its whole and reinterpret the temporal process. Moreover, our pauses within the temporal reading can become speculative and synchronic quests for understanding that disrupt the immersion of reading. When we decode a text within our reading transaction, we think of the meaning of its iterations (as when we see Jim's jump in the context of his failure on the *Patna*). When we think of a text in terms of its allusions to prior works (*Ulysses* and *The Waste Land*), don't we read a text as if it were a spatial configuration as well as a temporal event? The concept of synchronicity – so important to textuality and to the concept of metaphor where something is summoned to join the imagined world that has been absent – is spatial. The temporality of reading is complemented by a spatial dimension; the reader is in a place within the text as he reads; his mind conceives of the events or situations as a space and place; his mind moves outward from the text to make various kinds of associations, to connect himself with the text, to ponder about what will happen or recall what has happened, and to link the work to other works by the same author and different authors. To be sure, because of the length of time required for reading, fiction is a more temporal process than reading lyric poetry. But because it more completely evokes an external world with a detailed physical geography and a population of characters, it is more spatial. As we read, we visualize, I believe, an imagined world, with its senses and touches, and that, too, is spatial. Also, when the ending becomes an apocalypse reordering what precedes, our memory of the completed text is conflated into a pattern with a strong spatial component. Do we recall a novel more as a completed and somewhat static whole than as a process of testing, discarding, modifying, and reshaping meaning? Isn't that recollection spatial?

Let me tentatively propose five stages of the hermeneutical activities involved in reading and interpretation. Even while acknowledging that my model is suggestive rather than rigorous, I believe that we do perceive in stages that move from a naive response or surface interpretation to critical or in-depth interpretation and, finally, to understanding our readings conceptually in terms of other knowledge. My stages are:

1. *Immersion in the process of reading and the discovery of imagined worlds.* Reading is a place where text and reader meet in a transaction. As we open a text, we and the author meet as if together we were going to draw a map on an uncharted space. We partially suspend our sense of our world as we enter into the imagined world; we respond in experimental terms to the episodes, the story, the physical setting, the individualized characters as humans, the telling voice. In 'Araby' we live in the world of 1895 Dublin, see it from an adolescent's point of view, and experience his quest for meaning and understanding. While it has become fashionable to speak dismissively of such reading as 'naive', or the result of the 'mimetic illusion', in fact how many of us do not read in that way with pleasure and delight? Who of us would be teaching and studying literature had he not learned to read mimetically?

2. *Quest for understanding.* Our quest is closely related to the diachronic, linear, temporal activity of reading. The quest speaks to the gap between 'what did you say?' and 'what did you mean?' In writing, as opposed to speech, the speaker cannot correct, intrude, or qualify; she cannot use gestures or adjust the delivery of her discourse. Because in writing we lack the speaker's help, we must make our own adjustments in our reading. As Paul Ricoeur notes, 'What the text says now matters more than what the author meant to say, and every exegesis unfolds its procedures within the circumference of a meaning that has broken its moorings to the psychology of its author.'[17]

We complete the sign of the imagined world by providing the signified, but no sooner do we complete a sign than it becomes a signifier in search of a new signified. In modern and postmodern texts, our search for necessary information may parallel that of many major characters. Where we cannot rely upon the teller or have sufficient information, the quest for necessary information will be much more of a factor than in traditional texts. In this stage we are actively unravelling the complexities of plot; we also seek to discover the principles or world-view by which the author expects us to understand characters' behaviour in terms of motives and values.

The text of 'Araby' invites – indeed, demands – an ironic reader who shares with Joyce an objective view of the adolescent teller; because of his cynicism, hyperbole, verbal extravagance and syntactical disruptions, we understand that this is not the normative style of *Dubliners*. Until recently, I would have claimed that 'Araby' is a prose version of a dramatic monologue, but Adena Rosmarin has taught us that such a first-person confessional work might better be called a 'mask lyric'. For Joyce does not expect us to judge the speaker by a set of values he lacks and of which he is unaware, but expects us rather to share emphatically the speaker's vision. By thinking of unreliable speakers in modern fiction as having much in common with dramatic monologues, we explain the story in terms of a recognized genre. Yet isn't Joyce's speaker – the younger, retrospective, imperceptive, sensitive poet who is in love with language – also a version of the author? Indeed, collectively Joyce's works are striking examples of how the author enters into the text of modern British literature.[18]

3. *Self-conscious reflection.* Reflection speaks to the gap between 'what did *you* mean?' and 'what does *that* mean?' Upon reflection, we may adjust our perspective or see new ones. What the interpretive reader does – particularly with spare, implicatory modern literature – is fill the gaps left by the text to create an explanatory text or *midrash* on the text itself. As Iser puts it, 'What is said only appears to take on significance as a reference to what is not said; it is the implications and not the statements that give shape and weight to the meaning.'[19] While the reader half-perceives, half-creates his original 'immersed' reading of the text, he retrospectively – from the vantage point of knowing the whole – imposes shape and form on his story of reading. He

discovers its significance in relation to his other experiences, including other reading experiences, and in terms of the interpretive communities to which he belongs. He reasons posteriorly from effects to causes. He is aware of referentiality to the anterior world – how that world informs the author's mimesis – and to the world in which he lives. He begins – more in modern texts, but even in traditional texts – to separate his own version of what is really meant from what is said.

Here Todorov's distinction between signification and symbolization is useful. 'Signified facts are *understood*: all we need is knowledge of the language in which the text is written. Symbolized facts are *interpreted*: and interpretations vary from one subject to another' (Suleiman and Crosman, 73). A problem is that, in practice, what is understood by one reader may require interpretation by another. What is a pre-interpretive fact within a first-person discourse like 'Araby'?[20] The more interpretive work she finds to do, the more the reader *acts*. Even as we discover the meaning of implications, we are aware of challenges to unitary reading.

4. *Critical analysis*. The principal metonymic reading of 'Araby' depends on placing it in the context of a sequential reading of *Dubliners*, but as we read each of the stories, does not each become the centrepoint of a concentric circle of episodes, including our memories of other stories in *Dubliners*? And it also becomes a centrepoint in the consciousness of our memory of other Joyce texts; other texts of the period; intellectual and cultural history of Ireland; and the modernist movement in England and its counterparts in Europe, including developments in painting and sculpture.

For example, in 'The Sisters' the boy 'felt that I had been far away in some land where the customs were strange – in Persia'. To the reader of 'Araby', the dream of escape inevitably ties him to the younger boy of the prior story. What these recurring references do is modify our reading to understand the boy in 'Araby' as an evolving figure who *continually* meets paralysis and disappointment. 'Araby' becomes the third unit in a narrative code and 'Eveline' is the fourth. We begin then to think of 'Araby' in terms of its place in *Dubliners*. We place the text into an historical, authorial, generic, or theoretical context. As Paul Ricoeur writes, 'To understand a text is to follow its movement from sense to reference, from what it says to what it talks about' (Ricoeur, 214). In the process, we always move from signifier to signified; for no sooner do we understand what the original signifiers signify within the imagined world than these signifieds in turn become signifiers for larger issues and symbolic constructions in the world beyond the text.

While the reader responds to texts in such multiple ways and for such diverse reasons that we cannot speak of a correct reading, we can speak of a dialogue among plausible readings. Drawing upon our interpretive strategies, we reflect on generic, intertextual, linguistic and biographical relationships that disrupt linear reading; we move back and forth from the whole to the part. My responses to my reading are a function of what I know, what I have recently been reading, my last experience of reading a particular author, my knowledge of the period in which he wrote as well as the influences upon him and his influence on others. My responses also depend on how willing I am to suspend my irony and detachment and enter into the imagined world of the text as well as on how much of a text my memory retains.

Isn't the self-dramatizing speaker, with his highly-charged metaphorical imagination and his love of language – its sounds, sights, textures – a portrait of a very young artist? If one reads 'Araby' aloud, one can hear how the speaker savours the sensuality of language and realizes that he has transferred his sublimated sexuality to his telling. Indeed, his image of the physical, intimidating crowd contrasts with his own abstract, solitary, idealized and platonic need for love. How oddly he describes his view of Dublin life in terms of his clerical education – 'the shrill litanies of shop-boys', the 'nasal chanting of street singers'. 'Araby' – the name of the bazaar – is the soul, the chant, of Desire: 'The syllables of the word *Araby* were called to me through the silence in which my soul luxuriated and cast an Eastern enchantment over me.' And the narrator recaptures the excitement of this magic even as he retells it. The telling, like the bazaar, is the antidote to the pedestrian world that imprisons him and Mangan's sister. It is his response to sights, sounds, and texture of words which may save him, despite his veering round to darkness at the end – the reference is to Sue's renunciation of freedom in *Jude the Obscure*. For doesn't the speaker's plight remind us of how, in late nineteenth- and early twentieth-century British literature, inhibiting social conventions stifle the soul's urge to be free? Isn't that the subject not only of *Jude* but of *A Room with a View*, *Heart of Darkness*, *Mrs Dalloway* and *To the Lighthouse*, as well as so much of Eliot's and Yeats's poetry?

5. *Cognition in terms of what we know.* Drawing upon our interpretive strategies, we reflect on generic, intertextual, linguistic, and biographical relationships that disrupt linear reading; we move back and forth from the whole to the part. As Ricoeur writes: 'The reconstruction of the text as a whole necessarily has a circular character, in the sense that the presupposition of a certain kind of whole is implied in the recognition of the parts. And reciprocally, it is in constructing the details that we construe the whole' (Ricoeur, 204). We return to the original reading experience and text and subsequently modify our conceptual hypotheses about genre, period, author, canon, and themes. We integrate what we have read into our reading of other texts and into our way of looking at ourselves and the world. Here we consciously use our categorizing sensibility – our rage for order – to make sense of our reading experience and its way of being in our world. In the final stage, the interpretive reader may become a critic who writes his own text about the 'transaction' between himself and the text.

That 'Araby' reflects Joyce's boyhood in Dublin in 1894 is part of 'cognition in terms of what we know'. Indeed, isn't our understanding of what Rosmarin calls a mask lyric increased by knowing about Joyce and the world in which he lived? Expressive issues include the relationship between 'Araby' and the first two stories in *Dubliners*, between the boy and Stephen Dedalus in *Portrait* and *Ulysses* – including the way that 'Araby' can be understood in terms of Joyce's aesthetic theories in both works – and between Joyce and the evolving persona of the volume *Dubliners*.

Let us pursue the relationship between the boy and Joyce, and see briefly how the boy is a surrogate for Joyce. Were it not for Ellmann's biography – and, of course, the letters – 'Araby' would read differently; but if we know that it is biographically and historically grounded in anterior reality, that knowledge becomes part of our pluralistic response from the first reading. Joyce tells us that these first three stories are of 'my childhood' (he is much more ambiguous about the biographical origins of the subsequent stories in *Dubliners*). His narrator's self-indictment, his escapism, his fascination with the sounds of words – 'Her name was like a summons to all my foolish blood' – reflect Joyce's own history. Harry Stone has written of the importance of the literary allusions; and while we might differ on how he makes sense of these sources, he has shown that they are essential to biographical and historical contexts.[21] And if we know the bazaar took place in Dublin on 14–19 May 1894, when Joyce was thirteen, we can hypothesize that the story may have taken place in the springtime of the boy's thirteenth year. If we know also that in late 1894 Joyce lived at North Richard Street, a dead-end near the Christian Brothers' School, we have a specific locale for the story.

The boy's hyperbolic language is meanwhile at odds with a stifling respectability which has ground his life to dust ('decent lives', 'safely housed'), in part because respectability itself had been revealed as a sham to young Joyce as his father's fortunes declined and as alcoholic scenes became embedded in his memory. Can the reader who does not know Joyce's vision of Dublin here and elsewhere – the pervasive idleness and sloth of adults – quite understand the resonance of the word 'work' in the cliché: 'All work and no play makes Jack a dull boy'? So, yes, eroticism and sublimated sexuality are part of the texture, but so is the cityscape of Joyce's imagined Dublin, a cityscape that reflects a Dublin in which Joyce lived and walked.

Paradoxically, when we speak of a work as an expressive tale, we talk about it as an historically determined product. Didn't Joyce write from self-imposed exile about the political and social realities of Dublin? Isn't 'Araby' a story that comes from the depth of conscience and commitment? Just as I believe referents in art are necessary, so are referents in criticism. Criticism must take account of how literature is an historically determined product, how both the author and the reader are products of the worlds in which they live. To quote Mary Louise Pratt, '[J]ust as textual reception can be shown not to be the private personal exercise in semantic promiscuity that it was feared to be, so it can be shown that textual production is not simply a matter of individual authors acting out inscrutable intentions, personal prejudices, and private anxieties. Just as the subject who reads a text must be seen not as an autonomous, self-consistent essential self but as constituted by its social reality, so must the same be said for the subject who produces a literary text.'[22] In treating literary interpretations as historical human productions, both the New Historicism and Marxism have more in common with what I call humanistic formalism than with criticism that ignores representation. Indeed, I would agree with Pratt that 'what the theory of socially constituted reality says is that what people actually do and the interpretations they produce are attached to *everything* outside themselves, to the whole of their social and material life' – although I might not agree with her about the definition of 'socially constituted reality' (Pratt, 46).

While within my paradigm the above stages of reading occur in order, in fact we continually move back and forth through the stages. Cognition in terms of what we know is less a part of actual reading than immersion in the text, but most reading experience includes all five levels interacting simultaneously. In other words, my paradigm has both a synchronic and diachronic dimension. Different texts not only elicit different components of each phase, but each reader will respond differently depending on her interests. Within our own minds, *each* reader of a text is different because *we* are different; indeed, one difference when we reread is that we have more experience with the text than when we originally or last read it. Our first reading cannot be said to precede our critical activity any more than we can say that the events in our lives are separable from our first efforts at understanding. Even in our first reading we move from immersion in a text to interpretive reflection, particularly for complex texts and/or for those texts in which we have a personal or professional investment. Not only when we teach and write about texts, but when we reread them, we should be self-consciously aware of the stages and evolution in our responses to texts.

V. THEORETICAL IMPLICATIONS: TOWARDS A PLURALISTIC THEORY OF INTERPRETATION

I have been arguing that 'Araby' is about the problem of a way of telling and reading – about the continuity between perceiving experience and reading texts, between reading and writing. In 'Araby', while the Church's monologic perspective, and its imposition of that perspective on its acolytes, excludes, narrows and limits the young speaker, he resists that perspective enough to give the reader a sense of what is missing, even though he finally submits to that perspective in the story's closing lines. Like his contemporaries Conrad, James, and the Cubists, Joyce favoured multiple perspectives – witness *Dubliners* and *Ulysses*. Finally, 'Araby' shows language, perspective, sexuality to be problematic; it asks rather than answers questions and by asking questions invites a critical methodology that would do the same.

To think of fictions only as textual events rather than representations diminishes them. I am doubtful that we ever suspend our representational sense of reading and forget that we are listening to a human voice. Test 'Araby' on a class of educated readers and they respond in terms of a young boy's psychological and sexual maturation in an inhibiting culture. For does not the boy align the work of his life – his classroom world – with life itself? Does not the alternative play-world of his adolescent desire become inevitably synonymous with his hopeless romantic quest? My undergraduates see 'Araby' in terms of what we might call a thematic genre or an experiential archetype. Can we sensibly discuss fiction without reference to character and plot? As I have shown, Hillis Miller, in his deservedly praised *Fiction and Repetition*, reveals the difficulty in doing so as he enacts his own private *aporia* between deconstructive and humanistic criticism in his discussion of major English novels.[23]

My own approach depends on self-consciousness about theory and method, with the understanding that interpretations – powerful, sensitive readings – are still a primary business of literary criticism. By powerful readings, I mean readings that take account of a text's unity and the factors that challenge it; readings with an awareness of how texts are metaphorical in relation to anterior worlds and authors; readings that show a sense of which audience the writer had in mind; readings that realize how each of us reads uniquely and self-consciously; readings that have knowledge of relations to other texts by the same author as well as to authors in the same culture; readings that convey generic decisions made by the author and an awareness that what makes genre interesting is both similarity to and difference from models; readings that are attentive to patterns of syntax, diction and tropes; readings that understand the characters' and speaker's grammar of personal motives; readings that respond to how historical cause and effect shape characters, implied author, and implied reader; readings that have a complex understanding of how political, social, and economic reality produces effects that not only shape the author's creative process but also the responses of his original and all subsequent readers.

What are the ethics of reading? Should we not teach our students how the pleasure and purpose of reading complements experience? Can we not show our students how reading teaches us how to *see* – how to read human situations, including how to respond to various uses of language? Because of their ontological status as fictions, novels can be used as reference points to learn about ourselves. By reading we extend our knowledge of ourselves and of the real world; novels enable us to see ourselves by showing us versions of not-ourselves and versions of ourselves. Because novels are representative of recognizable experience, they explore, test, question, and, at times, confirm ourselves. 'Araby', of course, is about interpretation – that is why, as you have surely realized, it has been my example; because the speaker is locked into a monologic way of seeing, he has to 'read' his disappointment as a way of resolving his complex prepubescent emotions into an acceptable *telos*. That is Joyce's point. We learn from 'Araby', among other things, the danger of seeing our experience as a replica of prior experience. The boy has been taught to believe sexuality is sinful and sees himself as a kind of St Augustine figure who must turn his back on sexuality and turn to spirituality if he is to avoid damnation.

A humanistic poetics affirms a criticism that is honest about its theoretical and methodological assumptions and is dialogic in tone. An ethical reader speaks as if there were a response, another way of looking at things, and implies that when he stops his own demonstrative and rhetorical performance, he will listen and give space to a different view. The ethical reader seeks to understand the perspective of other readers. He is tactful, judicious, modest, wide-ranging, open, and pluralistic in his response to texts and to other critical views. Yet he is aware of the mysteries of language, the possibility of indeterminacy, disorder, and misunderstanding. He is wary of proposing flamboyant and hyperbolic readings in the name of being interesting. Regarding self-knowledge as a value, an ethical humanistic reader seeks to discover how and why authors create imagined worlds that mime real ones. An ethical teacher acknowledges his responsibility in teaching students what literature is *about* without sacrificing a focus on formal issues. Ethical teaching recalls why each of us began to be interested in literature in the first place, and insists on maintaining the excitement of responding to content. Finally, the ethical reader imagines himself in the role of an odyssean figure seeking meaning rather than in the position of *vates* or super-reader. He feels a responsibility to try to recreate both the text *and* the anterior world on which the text is based. Indeed, does not an ethical reader understand a moral responsibility to try to recreate the text as it was written for its original audience, as well as to define what that text means to us now?

Notes

1.   Bialostosky, Don, 'Dialogics as an Art of Discourse in Literary Criticism', *PMLA*, 105:5 (October 1986), 788–97.
2.   Gordimer, Nadine, 'The Arts in Adversity: Apprentices of Freedom', *New Society* (24, 31 December 1981).
3.   According to Bakhtin,
       the internal stratification of any single national language into social dialects, characteristic group behavior, professional jargons, generic languages, languages of generations and age groups, tendentious language, languages of the authorities, of various circles and of passing fashions, languages that serve the specific sociopolitical purposes of the day, even of the hour (each day has its own slogan, its own vocabulary, its own emphases) – this internal stratification present in every language at any given moment of its historical existence is the indispensable prerequisite for the novel as a genre. The novel orchestrates all its themes, the totality of the world of objects and ideas depicted and expressed in it, by means of the social diversity of speech types [*raznorecie*] and by the differing individual voices that flourish under such conditions (M. M. Bakhtin, *The Dialogic Imagination*, ed. Michael Holquist [Austin: University of Texas Press, 1981], pp. 261–3).
4.   Bakhtin's concept of heteroglossia is particularly useful to discuss the dialogues among styles in 'Araby.' As Bakhtin notes:

       Languages do not *exclude* each other but rather intersect with each other. . . . All languages of heteroglossia, whatever the principles underlying them and making each unique, are specific points of view on the world, forms of conceptualizing the world in words, specific world-views, each characterized by its own objects, meanings, and values. As such they all may be juxtaposed to one another, mutually supplement one another, contradict one another and be interrelated dialogically. As such they encounter one another and co-exist in the consciousness of real people first and foremost in the creative consciousness of people who write novels. As such, these languages live a real life: they struggle and evolve in an environment of social heteroglossia. Therefore they are all able to enter into the unitary plane of the novel, which can unite in itself parodic stylizations of generic languages, various forms of stylizations and illustrations of professional and period-bound languages, the languages of particular generations, of social dialects and others (as occurs, for example, in the English comic novel). They may all be drawn in by the novelist for the orchestration of his themes and for the refracted (indirect) expression of his intentions and values (291–2).

5. Quoted by Mary Reynolds, *Dante and Joyce* (Princeton: Princeton University Press, 1981), p. 220.
6. Thus, to an Aristotelian such as James Phelan, a response to 'Araby' would inquire to what extent the characterization is mimetic, didactic, and synthetic (a term he has proposed to explain how characters 'are *also* artificial constructs – that is, part of the narrative discourse). See James Phelan, *Reading People, Reading Plots: Character, Progression and the Interpretation of Narrative* (Chicago: University of Chicago Press, 1989).
7. Fish, Stanley, *Is There a Text in This Class?* (Cambridge, MA: Harvard University Press, 1980).
8. Fish, Stanley, 'Facts and Fiction: A Reply to Ralph Rader', *Critical Inquiry*, 1 (1975), 888–9. Quoted in James Phelan, *Words From Worlds: A Theory of Language in Fiction* (Chicago: University of Chicago Press, 1981), p. 17.
9. 'Notes on the Text as Reader', Susan Suleiman and Inge Crosman, (eds) *The Reader in the Text: Essays on Audience and Interpretation* (Princeton: Princeton University Press, 1980), p. 229.
10. Roland Barthes, quoted in Suleiman and Crosman, p. 19.
11. As Iser in his essay 'Interaction Between Text and Reader' has written: 'Communication in literature, then, is a process set in motion and regulated not by a given code, but by a mutually restrictive and magnifying interaction between the explicit and implicit, between revelation and concealment. What is concealed spurs the reader into action, but this action is also controlled by what is revealed, the explicit in its turn is transformed when the implicit has been brought into light. Whenever the reader bridges the gaps, communication begins' (Suleiman and Crosman, p. 111).
12. Ruppert, Peter, *Reader in a Strange Land: The Activity of Reading Literary Utopias* (Athens: University of Georgia Press, 1986), p. 42.
13. Todorov has provided the following graph:

1. The author's account   4. The reader's account
   $\downarrow$ $\uparrow$
2. The imaginary universe _____ 3. The imaginary universe
   evoked by the author $\longrightarrow$ constructed by the reader

14. Fish writes, 'That is why, as I said, the stakes in a persuasion model are so high. In a demonstration model our task is to be adequate to the description of objects that exist independently of our activities, we may fail or we may succeed, but whatever we do the objects of our attention will retain their ontological separateness and still be

what they were before we approached them. In a model of persuasion, however, our activities are directly constitutive of those objects, and of the terms in which they can be described, and of the standards by which they can be evaluated. The responsibilities of the critic under this model are very great indeed, for rather than being merely a player in the game, he is a maker and unmaker of its rules' (*Is There a Text in This Class?*, p. 367).

15. We should note that Fish shares the binary fallacy with deconstruction – that is, he assumes that if something is not absolutely irrevocably true, it must be false.

16. Eliot, T. S. 'Hamlet and His Problems', *Selected Essays, 1917–1932* (New York: Harcourt Brace, 1960), pp. 121–6.

17. Ricoeur, Paul, 'The Model of the Text', *Social Research*, 51:1 (Spring 1984), 185–218.

18. Schwarz, Daniel R., ' "I Was the World in Which I Walked": The Transformation of the British Novel,' *University of Toronto Quarterly*, 51:3 (Spring 1982), 279–97; reprinted in *The Transformation of the English Novel, 1890–1930* (London: Macmillan; New York: St. Martin's, 1989).

Crosman, p. 111.

20. As I have argued elsewhere, indeed, even pre-critical facts provided by an omniscient narrator involve selection and arrangement; we must interpret his psyche and character from what he includes, emphasizes, evades, and omits. See my 'The Narrator as Character in Hardy's Fiction', *Modern Fiction Studies*, 18 (Summer 1972), 155–72; reprinted in *The Transformation of the English Novel, 1890–1930*.

21. Stone, Harry, ' "Araby" and the Writings of James Joyce', in *Dubliners*, ed. Robert Scholes and A. Walton Litz (New York: Viking Press, 1969), pp. 344–68.

22. Pratt, Mary Louise, 'Interpretive Strategies/Strategic Interpretations: On Anglo-American Reader Response Criticism', in *Postmodernism and Politics*, ed. Jonathan Arac (Minneapolis: University of Minnesota Press, 1986), pp. 26–54.

23. Schwarz, Daniel R. *The Humanistic Heritage: Critical Theories of the English Novel from James to Hillis Miller* (London: Macmillan; Philadelphia: University of Pennsylvania Press, 1986).

3

Character and Characterization: An Inquiry

I

On the ground floor in the Johnson Museum at Cornell stand two statues – the one by Jason Seley entitled *Herakles in Ithaka I* (Herakles is the Greek name for Hercules), the other by Alberto Giacometti entitled *Walking Man II* (See Figures 1 and 2). Seley's figure takes its meaning from the prototype of strength, Hercules; this epic figure of strength, this figure whose name is synonymous with physical prowess, is rendered in the medium of post-modernism, or perhaps we should say post-industrialism: discarded automobile bumpers. At first the ten-foot tall Herakles made of shiny automobile bumpers seems to call into question the statue of Hercules as a heroic figure; shiny as if hand-polished, and gleaming in the light, the bumpers seem to suggest the armament of a warrior. But gradually we understand Seley's bumpers as a post-modern medium which lends dignity to the huge nude male figure, for even as he acknowledges the expected imposing physical presence of his Hercules, Seley expands the concept of 'beauty' to include intellectual and emotional stature.

While Seley's heroic figure has the masculinity of his Greek prototype, it takes its identity from the setting of the university in Ithaca, New York where I teach – Cornell University. His *Herakles in Ithaka* leans on a staff and is a contemplative figure with a Rodinesque head (recalling Rodin's *The Thinker*) which is slightly larger than it would be even in a man of ten feet. Because he stands on a podium, we must look up to see him. That the eyes under his protuberant eyebrows are hollow shows us that he cannot see; rather his insight comes from a strength within, a strength indicated by his contemplative face, his physical prowess, and his sensitive hands, one opened behind his back and the other

65

Figure 1   Jason Seley, *Herakles in Ithaka I* (1980–81)

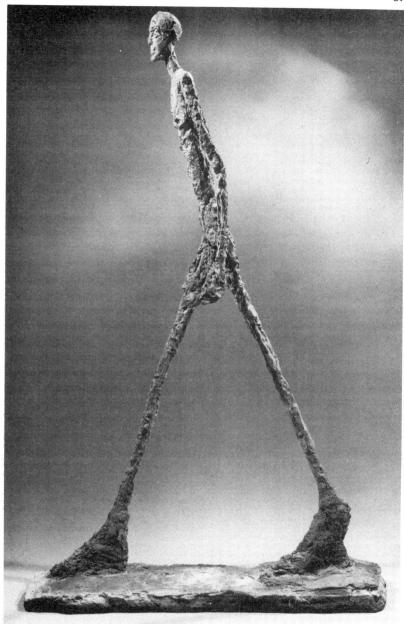

Figure 2   Alberto Giacometti, *Walking Man II* (1959–60)

pointing downward as if to remind us more of a university lecturer than a man of violence. Indeed, his intellectual command, self-control (in legend, Hercules had a volatile temper) and pacificism imply an Ovidian transformation of the mythic prototype. The male genitals seem to have a prominent place until we notice that this Hercules is something of an androgynous figure which has protuberant breasts; underneath his penis are testicles, but upon close examination we see that these flattish testicles also resemble a vagina.

By contrast, Giacometti's tiny, emaciated, post-Holocaust man stands for the indomitable spirit which cannot be squelched by history. Does not the figure recall not only the athleticism of Rodin's 1877 *Walking Man* but photographs of those people discovered when concentration camps were opened? Produced in 1959–60 at a time when Europe was conscious of African famines and nuclear war, and at the zenith of the Ban the Bomb movement, the statue needs to be understood as a powerful humanistic testament in the face of historical catastrophe. Yet if the tiny head shows how little control man has over his fate and shows how difficult it is for the figure to cope with the physical conditions of human life, it also shows how man's will and mental capacity survive and endure in the face of horrifying external circumstances. In bronze whose texture looks like papier-mâché, the thin, gaunt figure with his arms held close to his side has a face whose features are distorted beyond recognition; yet the figure looks forward and retains its courage, integrity, and nobility, qualities which are reinforced by the proud square shoulders. The roughness of the texture of this traditional bronze contrasts with the polished smoothness of Seley's unconventional bumpers. Pushing off his lifted back foot as if he *will* walk, *will* endure if not prevail no matter what resistance he must confront, while the front foot is firmly placed for the next step, the Giacometti figure stands as an historical statement of man's ability to survive in the face of overwhelming odds.

I begin with these two sculptures – both of which reflect the artists' own self-images, their self-characterization – for several reasons. For one thing, it gives us an opportunity to look at characterizations which – unlike the characters in literature – can be visually apprehended. We do not see literary characters in quite the same way, because no matter how graphic their physical descriptions, each of us uses his *own* imagination to complete the picture. Nor do we visualize the story-teller who presents these characters, although that figure looms large in our response to fiction. For another thing, these sculptures enable us to see the complex dialogue between our mimetic and didactic responses when an author characterizes humans, a dialogue that echoes the author's original creative process when presenting the individualizing or typifying aspects of humans. Moreover, these sculptures remind us that in the visual arts the object can be perceived in space at a glance; while future perceptions may modify our original impression, we can keep the entire image in our mind. By contrast, as we turn pages, our mental images change, modify, transform, and we forget – or remember incorrectly – what has preceded. Reading is much more dependent on the capriciousness and selectivity of memory. Yet, as we have seen, even in the three-dimensional sculptures the process of our sense-making joins with Seley's and Giacometti's images to create a meaning – or rather to set in motion a never-ending but progressive quest toward meaning. When responding to figures that represent humans, we do so in terms of the human qualities *and* what they metaphorically represent.

Obviously within any work some aspects are more grounded in reality than others. I wish to examine the imitation of humans in literature, even while recognizing that it is an oversimplification to isolate character from other aspects of literature. Readers always perceive characters as signifiers with referents. By contrast, the simple descriptions of objects within a room generally have much less of a signifying function. Representation of humans is different from other kinds of mimesis in important ways. The depiction of a character depends upon the selection of one individual from among many possible residents of a city or geographical area, among many possible professions, among many members of a social class. By convention we understand that a major character – say, in Hardy's *Jude the Obscure* – a young, aspiring, uneducated male from the lower social classes, who would rather be a scholar or clergyman than a stone carver – represents or typifies various groups and categories to which he belongs.

We hear a stereophonic voicing within every text. Should we not acknowledge that within every text the narratee or embedded audience is not a single entity but a complex mélange of diverse audiences which are imagined and addressed differently in every passage by the narrator? Thus, not only is 'we readers' a fiction even when discussing the original putative audience, but even more so when considering the poly-auditory nature of the contemporary pluralistic reader who belongs to diverse, competing, interpretative communities which struggle for his attention. When I speak, in this chapter, of 'we', I am trying to isolate a code which is not white, male, academic-specific, even while acknowledging the partial fictionality of the attempt. It may be because of our poly-auditory responses to texts that complex characters seem to elude our desire to sum them up or define their significance.

Characters live within and are defined by the intensive and purposeful world of novels; in part they originate for readers as *characterizations* produced by authors for a complex mixture of aesthetic, thematic and rhetorical readers. Characterization is a formal term – a term of discourse – while character belongs to content or story. As Martin Price notes,

> The scale of a work of art always seems smaller than that of life if only because what it presents is more intensively ordered, more transparently significant, more readily encompassed and studied, more sharply framed and closed than any segment of actual experience.[1]

We cannot conceive Bloom or Emma as separable from the world that produces him or her; thus critics as diverse as Aristotle and Barthes have sought to see character in terms of plot or spheres of action.

Representing human beings is both more metaphorical than other kinds of representation because of how we understand characters in their typifying function, and less metaphorical because the creation of people often short-circuits their putative metaphorical function and creates odd kinds of empathy with readers. Moreover, within novels characters are often so individualized and so idiosyncratic that they in fact represent only themselves and undermine the author's patterns of signification; put another way, the infinite variety of complex characters may deflect them from their signifying function when the author does not take pains to give limiting stylistic clues that provide a context for the reader's response. A characterization is a trope – a figure or vehicle for a character formally realized by an author in an aesthetic structure. What is being troped is how humans live and the signified of the trope includes the narratee, the author, the audience for whom the work was written, our contemporary audience – most notably us. It stands for the nominalism of particularity and the universality of the general. The very descriptions and dramatizations of this human *figure* (I use the term in its meaning as individual and trope) are often the power of a text – its ideology, politics, and cultural system. When we anthropomorphize a text to describe what it does – or anthropomorphize what 'history' does or produces, are we not paradoxically displacing our interest in humans to descriptions of what these abstractions do *because* of our human interest?

Focus on characters in imagined worlds implies an interest in something other than ourselves; it means relinquishing our power over the text. Theoretically, interest in humans may seem formally sloppy because it means surrendering some rigour and admitting we read to hear a human voice speaking words in a speech act. Particularly in the English tradition, as Margery Sabin has noted, we hear the idiomatic voice of speech in both narrator and dialogue.[2] Full acceptance of the Derridean master term 'writerly' preempts our hearing those voices. Can we read *The Rainbow* or *Women in Love* without hearing Lawrence's prophetic, yet rhetorically bullying voice as he *speaks*? When I read *Ulysses* I hear a dialogue among diverse voices, voices – usually but not always – controlled by Joyce's ventriloquy. Surely the characters of *Ulysses* include the speakers of 'Sirens', 'Cyclops', 'Nausicaa', 'Circe', and 'Oxen of the Sun'. As Edward Pechter remarked: 'Acquiring power over the text will seem a costly achievement, since what it sacrifices is the potential power of the text – the power to open up new areas of experience, unfamiliar ways of being in the world.'[3] One of my focuses as a reader and a teacher is to discern and find ways of speaking of those 'new areas of experience, unfamiliar ways of being in the world'.

The concept of characterization – of the idea that formal authorial and mimetic tools organize character – challenges the Derridean master term 'writerly' because it wants us to conceive the character in terms of presentation, depictions, and the *telling* of tales about humans. Although we want to see characterization in terms of thematics – of patterns of meaning enacted by the structure of language – we also need to see characterization in terms of fictionality *and* in terms of its rhetorical role in a structure of effects. Should we not perceive character pluralistically – in terms of its mimesis, as part of an expressive relationship in which character is a surrogate for an author as Stephen is for Joyce, as part of an historical context, and in terms of its linguistic function within a text? Do we not respond differently to characters who are obvious functions of the author's autobiographical history? Character is an extended personification or prosopopeia, a sign endowed with human attributes; it is also originally a word – a proper noun – which the text invites us to think of as speaking or feeling. Yet, as an extended set of words, it requires a context to give it metaphorical and metonymical life. Even if Bloom or Gabriel or Emma are merely letters that form sounds, are they not also contextually and metonymically shaped referents? Are they not metaphors, representations for something anterior to the text? It may be, as Iser notes, that 'the polysemantic nature of the text and the illusion-making of the reader are opposed factors',[4] but in practice those aspects are always modifying one another.

It seems clear that illusion takes precedence when human behaviour is being described. To again quote Iser,

> In the oscillation between consistency and 'alien associations,' between involvement in and observation of the illusion, the reader is bound to conduct his own balancing operation, and it is this that forms the esthetic experience offered by the literary text.[5]

Even in the most obscure texts like *Finnegans Wake*, we insist in our sense-making upon finding representation – upon the illusion of reality – as one of our ordering principles. Let us consider, too, that if, however, we become *only* interested in character – if we become lost in the illusion of the text and seem to ignore other aspects (linguistic play, reversal of our expectations), then we lose the dialogue between fictionality and mimesis that is important to our aesthetic response. As Iser puts it,

> The act of recreation is not a smooth or continuous process, but one which, in its essence, relies on *interruptions* of the flow to render it efficacious. We look forward, we look back, we decide, we change our decisions, we form expectations, we are shocked by their nonfulfillment, we question, we muse, we accept, we reject; this is the dynamic process of recreation. This process is steered by two main structural components within the text: first, a repertoire of familiar literary patterns and recurrent literary themes, together with allusions to familiar social and historical contexts; second, techniques or strategies used to set the familiar

against the unfamiliar. Elements of the repertoire are continually backgrounded or foregrounded with a resultant strategic over-magnification, trivialization, or even annihilation of the allusion. This defamiliarization of what the reader thought he recognized is bound to create a tension that will intensify his expectations as well as his distrust of those expectations. Similarly, we may be confronted by narrative techniques that establish links between things we find difficult to connect, so that we are forced to reconsider data we at first held to be perfectly straightforward.[6]

What is it about characters that short-circuits the visual and insists on their metaphoricity? We may remember one chrystallizing trait such as Jaggers's pointed finger in *Great Expectations* or the obesity of Verloc in *The Secret Agent*. The characters we know best by sight are often relatively two-dimensional or minor figures like Dickens's Smallweeds, Smollett's Lismahago, Conrad's Professor. But complex characters rarely coalesce as visual images. That is why, when reading or recollecting a text, we have no physical image of the narrator and authorial presence, even though we know a great deal about their values, attitudes, and psyche. Yet, paradoxically, we know characters best from their *voices*, either in our hearing of the narrator's own voice, or in his presentation of other characters' words through dialogue. One reason we don't visualize major characters in fiction is that we see through *their* eyes; the more we see life through their eyes, the less we see them. Another is that we are always judging and evaluating in response to data provided by the text. When we read we become immersed in the text and have an illusion of being there, but we simultaneously are aware that lives of the characters are lives lived by someone who is not ourselves.

When we become interested in the imaginary people within the author's world or the teller or the imagined audience or the reader or the author or even the anterior reality that gave rise to a text, we are soon discussing aspects of human life that pertain to character. Do we not do a disservice to our students, ourselves, and literature when we say that it is naive to discuss motives, values, and emotions of characters and when we replace the life and energy of our human responses with our theoretical perspectives? Wherever one begins in discussing a work of fiction or indeed a film or play or a narrative poem, the *character* of the subject, the author, the reader, and the represented social group at some point moves to the centre stage of discussion. I am talking about the experience of real readers – not imaginary ones. For at times I believe that current criticism has spoken of imaginary readers whose response to textuality and the free play of signifiers has the approximate relation to the reading experience of most of us that descriptions of griffins and unicorns have to do with our perceptual experience of actual life.

I want to stress the continuity between reading texts and reading lives. We should acknowledge, too, that when we respond to fictional characters, we think of the personality of characters – their public personae and quality of their psyche – their anxieties, frustrations, and obsessions, and the quality of the individual's moral strength and reputation. In one sense, when we speak of a person's character, we mean the quality of a person, his text as we perceive it; when we say that Gary Hart's character is the issue, we mean that something may be wanting, some qualities of judgement, self-control, integrity, self-knowledge. But in imagined worlds such judgements are shaped by context, by a structure of affects. But why do we accept behaviour similar to Hart's in Woody Allen's *Manhattan*? Why are some of my feminist colleagues and non-sexist males sympathetic to Arnold Singer's relationship with a beautiful female high school student, his effort to run down his wife's former lover, and to various excesses of his sexual life? Just as Woody Allen has done to a thinly disguised version of himself, the media in 1988 carnivalized Hart's life and called attention to the materiality of personal life. Yet, for some of us, our poly-auditory nature permits Allen his excesses and condemns Hart's. But in the context of our culture – as opposed to, say, the Canadian culture where Trudeau's sexual behaviour has never become the decisive issue – Hart's public aspirations demand a particular standard. It is well to remember that because this qualitative issue – what kind of character does a person have? – is part of our response to our aesthetic and life experience, we cannot speak of character as if it were only a formal element in fiction.

Let us take the opening of *Lord Jim* and consider how we respond:

He was an inch, perhaps two, under six feet, powerfully built, and he advanced straight at you with a slight stoop of the shoulders, head forward, and a fixed from-under stare which made you think of a charging bull. His voice was deep, loud, and his manner displayed a kind of dogged self-assertion which had nothing aggressive in it. It seemed a necessity, and it was directed apparently as much at himself as at anybody else. He was spotlessly neat, apparelled in immaculate white from shoes to hat, and in the various Eastern ports where he got his living as ship-chandler's water-clerk he was very popular.

Our image is of a man whose slight deformity and arrogant manner betray an inner inadequacy. As we read, we continually return to this odd description to fill in the questions it raises: why a 'slight stoop of the shoulders, head forward, and a fixed from-under stare'? What is the cause of his 'dogged self-assertion which had nothing aggressive in it'? How does this self-image shape how others read him and he reads others? Why this emphasis on his *neatness* and *cleanliness*? That Jim carries the baggage of former experience arouses our interest; it is the very mixture of the ordinary and recognizable with the quirky and idiosyncratic that moves us forward. Yet our powerful curiosity to figure out *why* Jim is presented in this way takes our minds back to the passage.

It may be that character is the most metaphoric ingredient of fiction; we think of it as representing larger patterns of behaviour *because* we need to. Moreover, we do not think of depictions of humans as *other*; we see them as metaphors for ourselves. Just as narrators are metaphors for authors – are they not vehicles for absent human tremors? – characters are metaphors for their creators, for narrators, and for readers. And authors are metaphors for historical periods which they represent and image. Does not our understanding of complex characters undermine or decon-struct or resist totalization of descriptive master terms, such as the man in the macintosh in *Ulysses* as 'a sign without a referent' or – to reach for the opposing pole – *Emma* as a 'sincere, authentic, but proud character'?

Our desire for unity makes us privilege how characters make sense in their narratives as well as the plotting that makes a coherent narrative. What characterizes fiction is that we perceive the details in larger-than-life terms. Thus in 'The Dead' we look beyond the immediate few hours in Gabriel Conroy's life to ask what it means. Characterization depends on mimesis – but mimesis of what? How characters might behave in certain situations – say in certain socio-economic conditions or communities? Or of how a character responds within the conventions demanded by the literary form, as when the speaker of *Lycidas* grieves in a stylized way – stipulated by the demands of a pastoral elegy – for the loss of a friend. But our response may also be produced by cultural convention; is not the concept that death is the birth of the eternal soul a trope for most readers? Our readings depend on a dialogue with the past, and an important part of the dialogue is understanding that what an author intended as a representation of experience may become for us a trope for something else. Isn't 'The Dead' about that very process by which the past has disseminated into rhetorical trope for a diversity of characters – Gabriel, Miss Ivors, Gretta – a trope that each reshapes according to his or her own needs and self-interests? At crucial times in *Ulysses,* Bloom depends on the cultural traditions of Judaism (or his figurative and quirky version of it), Irish life in Dublin, and Freemasonry to define his responses; recuperating how Joyce represents those contexts is part of our reading experience.

Why is character so central to us? Is it not because it is a displacement of our self – our realization that just as we have a conscious and unconscious life, so do others? Is it not that we seek to understand general patterns and causes – historical, sociological, and psychological – from specific human experience? We privilege character in how we respond to forward thrust and narrativity of plot. As Peter Brooks reminds us in a book that compellingly argues for the *a priority* of plot:

> Our lives are ceaselessly intertwined with narrative, with the stories we tell and hear told, those we dream or imagine or would like to tell. We live immersed in narrative, recounting and reassessing the meaning of our past actions, anticipating the outcome of our future projects, situating ourselves at the intersection of several stories not yet completed.[7]

Let us consider the relationship between plot and character. Brooks tells us that 'Plots are not simply organizing structures, they are also intentional structures, goal-oriented and forward-moving' (Brooks, 12); so, too, are the plots each character tells himself, even if he does not live them. If plot is the syntax of narrative, characterization is the subject of that sentence and character is the verb. Defining plot as 'the principles of interconnections and intention which we cannot do without it moving through the discrete elements – incidents, episodes, actions – of a narrative; that is the narrative element that gives a story shape, movement, and teleology', Brooks notes, 'The plotting of the individual or source or institutional life story takes on a new urgency when one can no longer look to a sacred masterplot that organizes and explains the world' (Brooks, 5–6). Because we now believe less in plots than we used to, we tend to be more interested in extrapolating meaning from individual experience. In that way, the story of Leopold Bloom and Clarissa Dalloway as they live one day of their lives – as we follow them through one day – becomes at first its own archetype of the story of ordinariness and lack of plenitude. Aren't their odysseys ours? As we read the text isn't the seeming plotlessness of their lives what we fear? Does not the plotting of texts – postponement, fulfilment, delays, circling back, iteration of prior patterns, reorganization of data, description of patterns, forward thrusts and lurches – echo the way we make sense of our lives?

Our interest in character defines, in part, our compulsion to read and understand. Just as interest in narrators comes from a curiosity to hear how others *tell*, our interest in characters depends on our interest in the very act of plotting, planning, shaping, and modifying. Our desire for sense-making is fulfilled by something completed. In 'The Storyteller', Walter Benjamin writes, 'Death . . . is the sanction of everything the story can tell' – and yet that fulfilment is never complete and one reason that we seek to reread.[8] We look to the linearity of narrative – in fiction and cinema – to explain what has preceded, to give it new meaning, and we find fulfilment in that process; we might call this the *plenitude* of narrative. In privileging plot over character, Aristotle did not have in mind the modern novel where our focus always returns to the teller. When Brooks writes: 'Narratives . . . lay bare the nature of narration as a form of human desire: the need to tell as a primary human drive that seeks to seduce and to subjugate the listener, to implicate him in the thrust of a desire that can never quite speak its name . . . never can quite come to the point . . . but that insight on speaking over and over again its movement toward that name,' we note that he is addressing less the narratology of plot than the character of the reader (Brooks, 61).

When critics isolate characterization from language, setting, or plot, or when they see character only as a function of the action of a narrative – when they see characters simply as agents of action or agents acted upon – they often reduce character to either a verbal display (in the manner of deconstruction) or extricate it from the form of the fictive world, thus blurring more than necessary the distinction between art and life. Once we say all the right formal things – 'character is manifested or externalized in language by the fiction of a narrator within an imaginary ontology' or 'characters are incomplete signifiers and the reader completes them' – we must acknowledge that characterization depends upon our interest in the cause and effect in human behaviour, in the grammar of motives. Put another way, our desire for 'stories' of people weaves patterns of meaning that focus on human behaviour. We understand characters in terms of traits and predispositions which recur in their behaviour and from which we can predict their actions; we look for patterns because we fear randomness and unpredictability in human behaviour. Indeed do we not call randomness and unpredictability by the names criminality, perversity and madness?

Does not the power of telling derive from our desire for understanding – and the stakes are raised when the telling is, as it always is, about humans? The reason we begin to speak about texts as autonomous is that we are drawn to texts by their power of disclosing a world, but that power appeals to our need for controlling our world – ourselves and others – and our need to disclose our means of control. Rhetorical power mimes our urge for control. If, as Ricoeur notes, texts 'display a *welt* which is no longer an *unwelt*',[9] they do so for us readers for whom acts of understanding – and control – are compelling.

It is because readers are drawn to dramatization of fellow humans that characterization in fiction takes precedence, or seems to, over other ingredients. Isn't this why we read novels? Are we not aware of the continuity between the narrative – our hopes, dreams, and fantasies – and of the intensive and purposeful lives of fictional characters? Do we not see fictional characters as living beings whose *fictionality* paradoxically gives them ghostlier demarcations and keener sounds than our own? Isn't part of our reading a means of locating ourselves within an alternative world, of perceiving through the eyes of someone not ourselves, of living as if we were another? Do we need to read differently when the continuity of our lives may be less than that of the characters about whom we read? Yet, at times we choose to read because of the *discontinuity* between our lives and those we read about; on those occasions we read simplified and exaggerated kinds of fiction such as detective stories, science fiction, and romance. As Eco implies in *The Name of the Rose*, in his use of the character Salvatore who speaks all languages and none, our recent obsession with perversities of language – polyglot, neologistic, asyntactical – seems to be an apt image for confusion about the way language works.

Characterization is a function of two important qualities of novels: temporality and spatiality. Characterization depends upon perceiving fictional humans in a spatial–temporal locus that helps define them (Bakhtin calls this locus the chronotype). Characterization cannot be separated from other aspects of the imagined world. The imagined worlds of novels are drawn with considerable verisimilitude and give the illusion of presenting an actual place; often sense of place is created less with realism in mind than with a structure of effects to which the reader will respond. The fog of *Bleak House* and *The Secret Agent* not only obscures visualization, but gradually becomes a trope that affects the reader's perception of city life. Notwithstanding Joyce's hope that *Ulysses* would depict the city of Dublin, what we have inevitably is an extended trope that allegorizes the quality of life and the kinds of values for which men lived in Dublin in 1904. For representation is more than representation of absent reality; for one thing, it cannot be inclusive. For another, any representation becomes contextualized by the reality of the perceiver's prior experience. As readers, our *knowledge* is of controlled effects generated by texts as much as it is of the anterior reality that gave rise to texts.

Our consideration of character must be attentive to the role of time in three separate aspects: (1) human experience as rendered in the novel; (2) the telling experience; and (3) the reading experience. Consciousness of time is part of an author's creation, the character's humanity within the imagined world, and the reader's response. As Meyerhoff wrote in *Time and Literature*, 'what we call the self, person, or individual is experienced and known only against the background of the succession of temporal moments and changes constituting his biography'.[10] A characterization is the cartography of identity as defined by changing conditions in a character's life. That nineteenth-century novels often read the world in terms of an optimistic upward teleology shapes our response, just as the endings of devolution (*Women in Love*) and inconclusiveness (*Ulysses*) shape our responses. Yet do we not read differently depending on the views of time and history that we bring to our reading? If we see time as linearly evolving upward – a teleological progression towards a goal – our response to characters' progress will be different than if we see time as a linearly devolving view or a cyclic one. Thus our modern scepticism may be less responsive than a Victorian audience to the implications of Esther's marriage in the ending of *Bleak House*.

In our reading, as in our lives, we want to believe in change, and even will take signs for wonders in proposing transformation and growth; witness much of the criticism of 'The Dead' and *Ulysses*. Characters can develop and change through the time of the narration or they can remain relatively static as episodes bring out various aspects of their relatively stable traits. More than in other literary forms, the time frame in which novels take place and in which novels are read – or consumed – has the capaciousness to allow the plausibility of growth and evolution. The myth of growth appeals to us because of our desire for an upward movement. We have not only secularized the Christian notion of spiritual growth, but modern psychology and its popular offsprings stress the possibility of growth. Yet when growth and change are implied within twenty-four hours, as in *Ulysses* and the classical tragedies, the reader may be resistant to such mimesis. Is not so-called unity of time an allegorical concept when it leads us to accept character development and transformation in a short period of time? Indeed, since we cannot read *Ulysses* in a mere twenty-four hours, our reading time counterpoints and qualifies the time of the action.

We might note, too, how the concept of character varies from culture to culture and period to period. Joyce's sense of character is radically different from George Eliot's or Kafka's and their characterization reflects that. But this is another reason why we need pluralistic readers who respond to each novel's rhetoric and who at the same time realize that their responses are shaped by the interpretive community to which they belong. Do not characters resist their narrator's omniscient – or first-person – efforts to define them? They take on lives of their own, refuse to submit to patterns, distract our attention from form and often go astray from the intended characterization to project a challenge to form and pattern. For most of us, Leopold Bloom's complexity refuses to submit to the patterning and plotting of Joyce's overstylized episodes from 'Wandering Rocks' through 'Circe'.

As characters changed, readers changed, and vice versa. We need to emphasize the gradual historical movement to the interior lives of characters, even while acknowledging exceptions such as Sterne and Richardson. Does not the gradual shift toward self-consciousness in characters as we move from the nineteenth to the twentieth century *create* and *reflect* the self-consciousness of modern readers? As Alex Gelley remarks,

> In the realist–psychological novel the function of character cannot be restricted to denoting certain types of agents for certain typical acts. Such a limitation ignores, for one thing, how character has served within this tradition to elicit the interest and participation of the reader in ways that mark a departure in narrative art.[11]

Joyce's masterworks – *Ulysses* and *Finnegans Wake* – challenge the notion of nineteenth-century fiction that the self is 'discrete, isolate and unique' by showing how the encroachment of others defines self; but finally does he not recentre, in part at least, the self-creating self of former eras, even in the encyclopedic, poly-lingual, narrative voice of the *Wake*?[12] Eighteenth-century and Victorian novels assert the possibility of a stable identity that can be retrieved from historical circumstances – the telling of the pattern in *Great Expectations* and *David Copperfield* assumes a consistency of self – whereas the modern novel shows characters in search of that self; retrospective narratives, such as *Notes from Underground*, 'The Secret Sharer', and *Heart of Darkness*, reveal a teller probing into a prior version of himself, a version now oblique if not incomprehensible to his present self.

II

Let us turn to Joyce's 'The Dead'. Because we are interested in Gabriel's behaviour, because we see it as representative of our own lives, we organize our experience of his tale in terms of psychological and moral codes. To be sure, we also see Gabriel as a victim of his social milieu as produced by historical forces beyond his control, but this is also to see him in metaphorical terms, as a representative of socio-economic forces which Joyce did not render completely. If we want – following recent theory – to consider telling as seduction, or manipulation, or the assertion of power, we must realize that these ways of considering *telling* are metaphorical. Let us acknowledge that they are substitutions for traditional interpretive metaphors of recuperating and naturalizing character. But like all metaphors, they distort and simplify; like all tellings, they reveal their tellers.

If a humanistic poetics is to flourish as an ideology of reading, it will depend in part upon retrieving the subject in the form of recentring character. Character eludes, challenges, and undermines the Derridean master term 'writerly'; for character speaks of human actions and thought and must be spoken of in those terms. Authors write in part from the human impulse to think and speak about other humans, and readers respond in part in those terms. Rhetorically, this interest depends on how we privilege human characters in our mind, and how the trope of prosopopoeia – the trope that pretends that language can render human qualities – dominates our imagination.

At the opening of 'The Dead', we watch Gabriel from an ironic distance when he behaves clumsily to Lily and we respond with a complex set of emotions – sympathy, judgement, impatience – to his failure to connect fully with other people. As he vacillates uncomfortably from self-diminishment to self-aggrandizement, as we realize that his social clumsiness relates to an emptiness within, does not the ironic distance narrow at least for many readers and particularly for rereaders, whose responses are likely to be even less visual? Can we look at this paralytically self-conscious man from a steep and icy peak? Do we maintain the same distance as we would to Milton's epic figures or even his pastoral elegist? If not, why not? What factors determine our distance, judgement, sympathy? We respond to rhetorical codes in the text; certainly when Gabriel suddenly shifts to Elizabethan language to distance his feelings of sexual awkwardness – 'how vain it would be to try to lead her wither he had purposed' – most readers respond to this ostentatious linguistic code. But do we not also respond to factors that are part of our own unique sense-making and our inability to recapture the historical past and rhetorical codes?

Notice how Gabriel's own narrative of failure begins with Lily's retort: 'He was still discomposed by the girl's bitter and sudden retort. ... He *would* only make himself ridiculous by quoting poetry to them which they could not understand. They *would* think that he was airing his superior education. He would fail with them just as he had failed with the girl in the pantry. He had taken up a wrong tone. His whole speech was a mistake from first to last an utter failure.'[13] His sense of superior education, debilitating self-consciousness, and emotional dwarfism not only reflect his creator, but speak to a characteristic paralytic self-consciousness of modernism. More than that, it reflects Joyce's fear that education isolates us from our focus as well as our doubts that it anaesthetizes us to feelings. As academics, do we not feel this? Do we not worry about our performances? When we read the paragraph and see the words 'discomposed', 'undecided', 'feared', 'make him ridiculous', can we really see Gabriel as if he were a part of a code that prepares for his later failure – or his perceptions of that failure?

> Gabriel felt humiliated by the failure of his irony and by the evocation of this figure from the dead, a boy in the gasworks. While he had been full of memories of their secret life together, full of tenderness and joy and desire, she had been comparing him in her mind with another. A shameful consciousness of his own person assailed him. He saw himself as a ludicrous figure, acting as a pennyboy for his aunts, a nervous well-meaning sentimentalist, orating to vulgarians and idealising his own clownish lusts, the pitiable fatuous fellow he had caught a glimpse of in the mirror. Instinctively he turned his back more to the light lest she might see the shame that burned upon his forehead. (*Dubliners*, 219–20)

When we look at this passage should we respond pluralistically to Gabriel's psychological drama in terms of other characters, of Joyce's doubts and fears, and of his narrator's elegizing a culture that now lacks coherence? We should see, too, Gabriel as an instance of *fin de siècle* intellectual isolation, which looks forward to that theme in *Portrait* and *Ulysses*. Should we not both respond to the implied reader's expectations and desires, and understand how Gabriel speaks to each of us as a modern reader whose own vulnerability and curiosity create a unique process of effects?

Do we not respond to characters both in terms of their mimetic function – their particularity – and in terms of their universality – what they represent? Thus the conflict – much debated among Aristotelians – between mimetic and didactic functions is reductive. A rhetoric of character would need to take account of the rhetorical function of characters – what they signify within a text and how they shape the reader's experience. It would realize that the linearity of reading makes character an evolving and dynamic concept – a verb, not a noun – that expresses simultaneously an action of an imaginary human and an action which is described by the narrator. But the action originally impresses itself on the author and urges that it be presented in language *for* the reader who in turn acts upon that creative act.

As we read we respond in multiple ways, including our awareness of how each of these aspects alternately becomes more dominant and then recedes in the face of the claims of the other. Does not the ending of 'The Dead' make this clear? For as the last protagonist in a series of stories about moral paralysis in Ireland, Gabriel's paralytic self-consciousness and inability to connect with Gretta gives him significance as a representative of the failure of will, breakdown of family, and sexual inadequacy that – along with (and perhaps as a result of) Catholicism and English imperialism – is paralyzing Ireland. But as a particularized figure who has realized his limitations as a lover and a man and feels generosity to his wife, Gabriel is interesting and significant because he has the potential for growth and transformation. Thus Gabriel's transformation at the end of 'The Dead' is a personal one – one that does not free the rest of the Dublin residents from moral and spiritual paralysis – but it is a moment of hope rendered as a performance in which the reader participates:

Generous tears filled Gabriel's eyes. He had never felt like that himself towards any woman but he knew that such a feeling must be love. The tears gathered more thickly in his eyes and in the partial darkness he imagined he saw the form of a young man standing under a dripping tree. Other forms were near. His soul had approached that region where dwell the vast hosts of the dead. He was conscious of, but could not apprehend, their wayward and flickering existence. His own identity was fading out into a grey impalpable world: the solid world itself which these dead had one time reared and lived in was dissolving and dwindling.

A few light taps upon the pane made him turn to the window. It had begun to snow again. He watched sleepily the flakes, silver and dark, falling obliquely against the lamplight. The time had come for him to set out on his journey westward. Yes, the newspapers were right: snow was general all over Ireland. It was falling on every part of the dark central plain, on the treeless hills, falling softly upon the Bog of Allen and, farther westward, softly falling into the dark mutinous Shannon waves. It was falling, too, upon every part of the lonely churchyard on the hill where Michael Furey lay buried. It lay thickly drifted on the crooked crosses and headstones, on the spears of the little gate, on the barren thorns. His soul swooned slowly as he heard the snow falling faintly through the universe and faintly falling, like the descent of their last end, upon all the living and the dead.[14]

What is performed is the suspension of rational and linear thought. While, as we know from John Huston's film of 'The Dead', the passage can be visualized, does it not enact a state of being that finally transcends the visual, a state when the soul claps hands and sings? It is Gabriel's reward – just as the vision of Rudy is Bloom's reward – for loving Gretta, for understanding that passion is itself a value ('Better pass boldly in that other world, in the full glory of some passion, than fade and wither dismally with age'). Discursively, the passage makes little sense. One cannot hear snow falling and the antecedent of 'their' is indeterminate (snowflakes? all the dead? Gretta and Michael? Gretta, Michael and himself? all the past and future dead?). Gabriel's move outside the enclosure of his ego is enabled/performed by the phonics and reversals of the passage, particularly the last sentence. The passage's meaning derives from its place in a process; it contrasts with the mimesis of the preceding pages of the story and with Gabriel's paralytic self-consciousness, rationality, and literalism.

The ending is discourse not story; yet as discourse it shows us what Gabriel needs and lacks: song, lyricism, metaphoricity, escape from time into non-rational, passionate states of being, a loosening of the bonds of self-consciousness. It is a moment of rare serenity – visual, tonal, emotional serenity – a moment which resists (perhaps resents?) the critic's rational efforts to order it because it is allegorical and asyntactical. Even while acknowledging the brilliance of Huston's visualization, do we not feel that it encroaches on our interior experience, on our private admiration of the scene – and reduces our rich, poly-auditory response to Gabriel's interior life and Joyce's rendering of it to a sequence of visual images? Isn't that often the problem when we see our intimate reading experience transformed into a film?

What is absent is as important as what is present in responding to character. The snow imagery focuses our attention on a world outside Gabriel – a natural world where generations live and die and survive their sense of self-importance; we recall that snow has the potential to become ice (death) and water (life). Obviously, as ice, it also suggests the emotional sterility of a world reduced to social gestures, empty talk, and loveless relationships – a world where a tiny pathetic 'I' cannot connect to others to form a loving, passionate, tender couple, a world that does not even give the feeling that he so desperately needs that he is part of a social mosaic. We can never be sure whether Gretta is waiting for Gabriel in the way that Molly is waiting for Bloom, because we see less of Gabriel's dignity and integrity – and we know more of Gabriel's selfishness and narrow-mindedness. Thus we do not quite sympathize with Gabriel's sense of isolation and disappointment as we do with Bloom's.

Note how the mimetic code insists itself when basic emotions of love and death are the subject. It is all very well to talk about the free play of signifiers and to claim that there is nothing outside the text, but do we not respond powerfully to descriptions of Gabriel's transformation; his realization that conscience and self-consciousness are not the full parameters of living; and that the love shared by Michael and Gretta contained passion, intensity, love and intimacy that go beyond concern with whether Gretta wears galoshes?

Yet we realize, too, that because Gabriel lacks a coherent self and radically oscillates between feelings of superiority and inferiority, he diminishes the value of the affection and respect that he does have and poignantly and pathetically thinks that Michael and Gretta's youthful love, or her memory of it, represents a threat to his present. We might therefore speak of the precedence of subjects not only to note how our aesthetic sense itself is more likely to be pushed aside and relegated to the back burner when we are engaged by issues that matter to our human feelings, but to say that each of us will be engaged most by the representation of emotions that interest us. Indeed, in speaking of the precedence of subject, should we not acknowledge that a culture's ever-changing preference and interest in certain themes and problems helped create and recreate its canon? For male academics, does not Gabriel matter in part because they (we) fear, as Joyce feared, that he is *us* – the fastidious professional learned teacher to whom books have become a surrogate for love and passion? We fear that Gabriel is us as we fear that Aschenbach, too, is a version of *us* – the man whose quest for renown, whose commitment to work and word has left him emotionally barren? Indeed, when in the late 1960s feminist academics rightly objected to the male canon and turned *their* attention to female authors, such as Mary Shelley, the Brontës, and

Woolf (and to complex, appealing, and frightening figures in Woolf – such as Lily Briscoe and Mrs Dalloway) were they not expressing interest in the character of particular kinds of women that they found compelling and frightening?

It is worth distinguishing between character and characterization. Characterization is a formal concept – the organization of words to depict a particular kind of trope, namely a trope of human action; 'character' refers both to the depicted figure within a fictive world and to qualities – traits – we use to describe fellow human beings. Character is a more unstable concept; it is at once formal, describing an ingredient of textuality, and informal, loose, and indeterminate because we use it to describe traits. We read character as we read the language of complex texts; sifting evidence for hints and clues, finding patterns from obscure associations, looking for parallels, comparing 'behaviour' or 'passages' with others, and imposing tentative explanations; in both cases we proceed inductively and deductively. Character and characterization – each belongs to both story and discourse, although it is usual to locate characterization with discourse, form, and aesthetic issues, while character is considered with 'content' or 'story' as the results of mimesis. Since we search for a determinate centre of meaning, a radial principle, from which we can organize our responses, we read characters linearly and spatially.

When Aristotle in the *Poetics* wrote of the supremacy of plot to character, he was examining a dramatic form, the tragedy: 'Tragedy is essentially an imitation not of persons, but of action and life, of happiness and misery. . . . Character gives us qualities, but it is in our actions – what we do – that we are happy or the reverse. . . . It is the action in it, i.e. its fable or plot, that is the end and purpose of the tragedy; and the end is everywhere the chief thing.' Of the *Poetics*, as of the US Constitution, I favour an evolving meaning rather than an effort to find the *original* meaning. It is the human urges to tell and to listen that are at the basis of our reading experience. It is worth noting that while Aristotle thought of characters as referring to figures within the imaginary world and defined by plot, we now think of the character of the speaker both as a shaping force of narrative and as a self-revealing figure whose uniqueness is revealed by the teller. Do we not see that in both Aristotelian and reader-response criticism – and, specifically, in the work of Wayne Booth and Stanley Fish – the reader is described as if he were a human character created by the process of reading? And do not most readers read to recreate the human presence of the author within a text; do we not recreate in our response at least a metaphorical relation between Joyce and his work; or Erica Jong and *Fear of Flying*, and her subsequent novels; or Woody Allen and *Hannah and Her Sisters* and *Annie Hall*? Thus the concept of character necessarily informs discussions of reader, author, and narrator. Rhetorically, this interest depends on how we privilege human characters in our mind, and how the trope of prosopopoeia – the trope that pretends that language can render human qualities – dominates our imagination.

Aristotelians argue that we perceive and respond to character conceptually and hypothetically within a fictive system conditioned and mediated by language rather than in terms of the reality of past associations and prejudices. Yet those associations and prejudices are there. When I show my own novel-in-progress to readers, their first impulse is to see themselves or others they know in my fictive characters, to even feel threatened by any resemblance to them, to want to wander around in my imaginary world and rearrange my fictive furniture according to their view of themselves.

Characterization is the formal pattern by which characters are realized; since characters exist within the imagined world, they are not conscious of the formal patterns in which we readers construe them. Yet because characters challenge form and assert their individuality, taking on in their imagined ontology lives of their own, character is the most difficult issue to discuss. It belongs to the humanistic part of the provocative and (for some) oxymoronic term, humanistic formalism, that I have been using to define my theoretical approach.[15] Characters in the novels are means by which we learn about true and false, integrity and dishonour, motives and obsessions. In recognizing pluralistic responses, we must allow for subjectivity. For do not readers respond to characters both in terms of the system of the imagined world in which they live, as a function of authorial choices that precede their existence, as a production of the era in which the text was produced, *and* as a function of the audience which reads the text? Should we not see characterization in terms of both its thematic and its mimetic functions, even as we recognise that each reader's sense-making is a function of the textuality of each reader's prior reading?

Let us look at the author's role in trying to shape and control the responses of readers. Characterization depends on the author's conscious and unconscious decisions; it is a structure of effects perceived by the reader in her/his process of reading. Authors' impressions of major characters are more cognitive than visual. Thus in poems like 'Mrs Alfred Uruguay' and 'Anecdote of the Prince of Peacocks', Stevens is cognitively shaping the visual images into parables or what he might call tropes of the 'capable imagination'. Yet even in such a complex, seemingly non-mimetic poem as 'Mrs Alfred Uruguay', do we not wish to ground both the elegant woman's journeying up the mountain of the real, and the fleeing, visionary horseman rushing to the 'ultimate elegance: the imagined land'? Do we not ask who is the Prince of Peacocks and how he has been changed by meeting Berserk on his night journey? And in my deliberately ambiguous prior sentence, does my reader not seek the antecedent of *his* and perhaps wish I would say 'their night journey'?

Of course, while we respond to character partly in mimetic terms and partly in metaphorical terms, we also respond to characterization in aesthetic terms, aware of the author's artistry, of his or her selection and arrangement of perceptions into a coherent artistic form. It is obvious that within our fictions, character does not exist without characterization. The relation between character (human voices and actions) and characterization (the formal and linguistic embodiment of character) is dynamic, ever-changing, inextricable and messy. Paradoxically, character is always presented by another character – in the form of a narrator who self-dramatizingly reveals his values and pysche through speech, or by an author who creates the narrator as a formal presence enclosed for all time within the formal pattern of the text. Moreover, character depends on other characters: the system of imagined characters in which we judge and respond to him or her. It also depends on the character of the implied reader addressed by the narrator to decode the characters in the text and the character of the present reader – us – whom the storyteller could not possibly imagine.

Characters must be understood in terms of the historical situation which gave rise to them, the historical situation within the imagined world, as well as the historical situation of the contemporary audience, and we must acknowledge that this latter situation is different for each reader. Prior to the kind of relatively easy economical travel we now enjoy, part of the power of nineteenth-century texts was to render a world elsewhere: Hardy's Wessex, Dickens's London, Dostoevsky's Leningrad. But awareness of the socio-economic implications of people living together in a cityscape does not mean that we need reduce examination of all motives to economic powerlessness of the dispossessed or the will to power on the part of the privileged classes or gender. While I welcome the recent refocus on mimesis of anterior reality, do we not need to go beyond seeing historical causes in Marxist terms? The recent quest for historical explanations has stressed socio-economic aspects in the code of dialectical materialism, but characters can reflect other kinds of historical focus, cultural values and personal needs. Thus, Lyndall Gordon has shown how Mrs Ramsay in *To the Lighthouse* is a personal expression of Woolf's mother and a 'performance of Victorian womanhood'.[16]

What Bakhtin says of the family role speaks to our utopian desire to return to family – in the form of idealized parent–child relations; a tender, passionate relationship with a lover; a sense of being appreciated and loved by the community – and enacts, I suspect, the tendency of novel-readers to want to know about basic family relations rather than politics, psyches rather than ideologies.

The family of the family novel is, of course, no longer the family of the idyll. It has been torn out of its narrow feudal locale, out of its unchanging natural surroundings – the native mountains, fields, rivers, forest – that had nourished it in the idyll. At best the idyllic unity of place is limited to the ancestral family *town* house, to the immovable part (the real estate) of the capitalist property. But this unity of place in the family novel, is by no means a necessity. What is more, there is a break-off in the course of a character's life from a well-defined and limited spatial locale, a period of wandering in the life of the heroes, before they acquire family and material possessions. Such then are the distinctive features of the classic family novel. What is important here is precisely the stable family and material goods belonging to the heroes, how they overcome the element of chance (random meetings with random people, random situations and occurrences) in which they had initially found themselves, how they create fundamental, that is, *family* connections with people, how they limit their world to a well-defined place and a well-defined narrow circle of relatives, that is, to the family circle. It often happens that in the beginning the hero is homeless, without relatives, without means of support; he wanders through an alien world among alien people; random misfortunes and successes happen to him; he encounters random people who turn out to be – for unknown reasons at this early point in the novel – his enemies or his benefactors (all this is later decoded along family or kinship lines). The novel's movement takes the main hero (or heroes) out of the great but alien world of random occurrence to the small but secure and stable little world of the family, where nothing is foreign, or accidental or incomprehensible, where authentically human relationships are reestablished, where the ancient matrices are re-established on a family base: love, marriage, childbearing, a peaceful old age for the in-laws, shared meals around the family table. This narrow and reduced idyllic little world is the red thread running throughout the novel, as well as its resolving chord. Such is the schema for the classic family novel, which opened with Fielding's *Tom Jones* (with certain adjustments, the same schema underlies Smollett's *Peregrine Pickle*). But there is another schema as well (whose foundations were laid by Richardson): an alien force intrudes into the cozy little world of the family, threatening it with destruction. Dickens' variations on the classic scheme (Fielding and Smollett) make his novels the highest achievement of the European family novel.[17]

Is it possible that our political unconsciousness includes a desire to find refuge in comprehensible family and community structures? Is not our desire to *know* more personal than political – do we not wish to know ourselves, control our destiny, appreciate the human uniqueness of those about whom we care? Do we dare say that many of us have within our *social unconsciousness* a desire to eschew conceptual, global politics and return to the more primitive and comprehensible structure of family and to a comprehensible community? Wasn't that part of the appeal of the familial and homey rhetoric of the Gorbachev/Reagan dialogue? How many of us secretly share Gabriel's, Stephen's, and Bloom's impatience with political shibboleths, particularly when those shibboleths are disguises for empty places within the speaker, as in the case of Ms Ivors, Mr Deasy, and the Citizen?

Characterization is a presentation of the trope of personification within the structural context of an imagined ontology, an ontology that is ever-changing through time. It is presented by a teller whose rage for order and understanding compels him to undertake the story, to see if the acts of memory and repetition will discover meaning for us. (In that sense, we as readers are in the position of analyst and the teller is the analysand.) The presentation of the narrative includes the plotting of the story to give the characters' actions – including the narrator's telling – shape and significance.

When we use the term 'character', our emphasis is upon a fully developed person functioning in diverse social and family situations, although the degree of externalization varies from text to text and from period to period. According to some humanistic perspectives, the character must have universal significance; according to Marxism, it must typify social and economic conditions. Yet it is safer to see that our interest in character derives from its signifying function – its metaphorical relation to a world outside a text. Does not the reader's desire to reach that world evoked by the text propel him forward, but does not his desire to escape from his confining world into an innocent world beyond time have in it the trace of a death wish?

A grammar of characterization must allow for differences in functions. It must differentiate among diverse representational or mimetic functional (thematic) and rhetorical (aesthetic) functions of character.[18] Let me suggest a division into three types – cartoon, caricature, and character – moving from the least to the most mimetic form of characterization. While fully-developed characters change more than cartoons or caricatures, all characters are realized in partially mimetic, partially aesthetic dimensions by the action of plot presented by language. Cartoons are characters that are illuminating distortions for a thematic or didactic purpose. Cartoons have *functions* in terms of themes. In 'The Dead' such figures are Mr Brown or Freddy Malins. Caricatures are parodies of behavioural patterns; they are halfway between *function* and *mimesis*; they have a strong basis in anterior reality but function to bring out thematic points. In 'The Dead' the Irish nationalist Miss Ivors and perhaps Michael Fury play such roles.

As we progress through a novel, most personifications combine aspects of cartoon, caricature, and fully-realized character – but the ratio is radically different. As we move along the continuum from cartoons to caricatures to characters, we perceive less by types or cultural modes and more by nominalistic, specific detail. Fully-developed characters are understood both in terms of what they typify and as individuals within psychological, sociological, and historical dimensions; their individualizing qualities are what engage our attention and separate them from others and from the basic plot.

The imagined world of 'The Dead' or *Ulysses* urges us to the familiar and the human. By contrast Stevens deliberately disarms our expectations of a short lyric which will reveal the psyche of the speaker and asks us for a different kind of transaction when he begins 'The Well Dressed Man with the Beard': 'After the final no there comes a yes / And on that yes the future world depends. / No was the night. Yes is this present sun', and concludes his short lyric, 'It can never be satisfied, the mind, never.'[19] Yet even in the abstract world of Stevens's poetry we refocus on character as essential to our exploration of aesthetic and moral values. We try to locate the identity of the speaker and the subject. Do we not realize that beneath his masques and evasions (Who is the man with the beard? Stevens the poet? Or the *ideal* poet?) Stevens is qualifying our understanding of 'Mrs Alfred Uruguay' where he has written of the elegant lady, 'Her no and no made yes impossible'; there he has urged us to see that her quest is inextricably related in a proleptic way to the horseman's and that there is a possibility she will also descend in imaginative frenzy, and that the horseman may well have first fully and futilely ascended toward the real. Thus, even in Stevens's remote poem, reading about people enables us to know others because the present of the text displaces our presence; we learn the familiar, the preconceived, the limits of ourselves, and become someone else.

Yet because each of us reads differently we always recuperate this someone else, this other, in terms of the self we are. Reading is a dialogue between this real self and another self that leaves the real self behind and ventures forth only to find herself or himself; or as Joyce says in his 'Scylla and Charybdis' chapter of *Ulysses* of Shakespeare and implicitly of all great artists who read the text of the world:

> He found in the world without as actual what was in his world within as possible. Maeterlinck says: *If Socrates leave his house today he will find the sage seated on his doorstep. If Judas go forth tonight it is to Judas his steps will tend.*[20]

The character who tropes this way of reading the world is Leopold Bloom; for Bloom ventures forth to find compensation for his wife's adultery only to rediscover his love for his wife and affirm his own dignity and integrity. Some fully-developed characters evolve and change, while others, like Tristram Shandy, are basically revealed in their essential nature by the narrative. While characters differ in whether they are more idiosyncratic or representational, readers differ in how they respond to them, depending on their perspectives and needs.

Given the still pervasive influence of Freud, I suspect that most readers respond in terms of the human psyche more than they do in terms of the action. Rightly or wrongly, we recuperate or domesticate what we read in terms of what we understand. And we understand psychoanalytically via the mediation of language. In his prefaces to the New York edition of his novels, James, the father of both the modern novel and the modern theory of the novel, privileged character over plot. In his essay on Trollope he wrote: 'Character, in any sense in which we can get at it, is action and action is plot, and any plot which hangs together, even if it pretends to interest us only in the fashion of a Chinese puzzle, plays upon our emotion, our suspense, by means of personal references. We care what happens to people only in proportion as we know what people are.'[21] Isn't he saying with Iser that the illusion-making capacity of a text depends on its human interest?

Martin Price compellingly argues that the characters are a function of the imagined ontology in which we find them:

> Character may be said to exist within a novel as persons in a society, but the 'society' of the novel is one with intensive and purposive structure. We read the novel immersed in its complexity, it is true, but with confidence in its resolution and its ultimate significance. . . . In that sense one can say that characters exist for the sake of novels rather than novels for the sake of character.
>
> If characters exist for the sake of novels, they exist only as much as and in the way that the novel needs them.[22]

But how do we read novels like *Finnegans Wake* where character is a trace or shadow, never quite emerging from the obscurity of disrupted syntax and barely readable language, and giving us a sense of an imagined world lacking coherence and purposefulness? To an extent, we call novels obscure when we cannot get a handle on characters, when verbal patterns undermine our sense-making. Of course, we often perceive that characters in novels are unruly and refuse to submit to Aristotelian rules about probability and necessity in their behaviour. Often in *Ulysses* and especially *Finnegans Wake*, for example, resolution is an expectation that is defeated not only for characters but readers; our desire, our demand, for order and significance is frustrated; the plot may fail to provide a fulfilling pattern; language may withhold the possibilities we desire; the iterations of plot may become more obsessive than revealing. But all these phenomena are part of the way that a reader of capable imagination experiences the odyssey of reading. Or resolution may come in surprising ways – including irresolution, or patterns that characters see as resolutions, but that author and reader see as irresolution. Such an ending is the boy's epiphany at the end of 'Araby' as he looks back on his youthful quest and believes that he had been 'a creature driven and derided by vanity'.

The concept of characterization challenges the Derridean master-term 'writerly' because it wants us to conceive the *telling* of tales about humans. Let us make several observations about characterization:

1. The author creates a narrator who perceives and presents in terms of the codes and values of the imagined world he discovers for us and his own quirks and values. The narrator chooses among infinite possibilities of categorizing and defining: visual appearance, clothing, choice of possessions, dietary habits, anything that individualizes or typifies his physical habits.

2. How a character speaks reveals his inner being, his state of mind, his way of being in the world. The characters' speech acts differ from one another and the narrator's. Yet we also know that telling reveals more than the speaker means it to, and will create an ironic tension between what the speaker says and what she or he reveals. Because for most readers mimesis of character is privileged, dialogue plays an important role in our illusion-making. Paradoxically, the less the dialogue, the more we pay attention to it. Thus in *Ulysses*, much of the rather limited dialogue – as when Bloom speaks eloquently about love to the Citizen – becomes privileged and significant and resists textual irony.

3. The author has his narrator penetrate the minds of characters in the form of interior monologues; in this situation we have a sense not only of the mind that is being refracted, but of the mind through which it is refracted. That mind, as in the work of Henry James, often emerges as a shaping force or a force that we hear and to which we respond. But narrators are also

characters. When a narrator speaks of humans, he does so in terms that do not merely create the tale of characters through his speech act, but dramatizes himself as character. Marlow is an excellent example of this, but so are the various frame narrators that present him. Both dialogue and the narrator's penetration of characters stress character in terms of a grammar of manners and motives; our response is shaped according to the specific grammar revealed by each text.

4. The author has the narrator perform or enact a state of mind less in terms of external events and more in terms of emotional responses, visions, dreams, or transformation of a feeling and unconscious responses. Rhetorical in affect, these passages have relatively minor mimetic components, while often having thematic functions that resist didacticism. An example would be the last passage of 'The Dead' or Bloom's vision of Rudy. 'Circe' and *Finnegans Wake* are performances of feelings as well as unconscious and dream responses more than a rendering of the external world.

5. The author's rendering of character in terms of genre, even if the rendering plays upon and at times reverses the expectations of genres. As with all generic perspectives, it is the combination of expectation, similarity, and difference from the generic model that makes the generic perspective interesting. *Tristram Shandy* takes its ironic meaning from prior and subsequent fictional and non-fictional discussions about the growth of a character. *The Rape of the Lock* depends on mock epic, and so does *Ulysses*. From the outset when the ventriloquistic voice of *Ulysses* shows Stephen as Telemachus in search of the father to the final chapter in which we hear the lusty modern-day Penelope speak, Joyce is continually playing upon our experiences with the epic genre.

6. Related to genre, with its nominal focus on form, is the author's rendering of characters in terms of, and as variations of, preconceived roles, archetypes, or cultural models – what Eliot has called mythic method. Isn't this the major thrust of Frye's proto-structuralist study, *Anatomy of Criticism*? Thus, Seley's Herakles, Bloom as Ulysses, Hamlet or Moses, are both a fulfilment of expectations and a rewriting of them. And *Finnegans Wake* perceives all 'characters' in terms of recurring male and female archetypes.

7. Characters can be rendered in terms of biographical evidence (which, when we know it, changes the reader's response). For example, knowing Ellmann's biography, do we not respond to

Stephen as a version of Joyce as well as a *character* created by
Joyce? Can we draw absolute lines between the text and the
author–creator as a life being represented within his text? Do
not characters often have a metaphorical relationship to their
creator? Isn't the fastidious, sensitive, middle-aged Gabriel – the
teacher and book-reviewer defined by a mediocre Irish culture –
an expressive metaphor for a figure Joyce feared becoming?

8. Presentation of character in terms of a physical setting that
reveals his or her way-of-being in the world. (Thus in *Death in
Venice* setting is character: i.e. the rationality and austerity of the
Apollonian Munich and the lack of discipline and lewdness of
Dionysian Venice.) Place embodies both a geographical (and
historical) entity and a system of values. As in *Dubliners*, place
can become not merely an environment but an actualization of
the characters' moral condition. Can we separate the Dubliners
from their historically-determined setting? Indeed, in works
such as *Bleak House* and *The Secret Agent*, a cityscape of London
can become the antagonist, a kind of impersonal personification
with which each character struggles. When characters are
rendered in terms of social and economic contexts, setting
becomes not only a cause, but by implication also an effect on
how life is lived, and has been lived in that place. Hardy's
Wessex or Faulkner's Yoknapatawpha County become constituted by the quality of life that has been lived there; in those
novels the historical past 'writes' or has written its text or place
on the lives of its inhabitants.

The rendering of all characters draws simultaneously upon
several of the above methods, but always has mimetic, thematic,
and rhetorical aspects; indeed, our response to this 'rendering'
itself is a dynamic and ever-changing part of the challenge and
excitement of the process of reading. Gabriel is transformed as a
character because he is transformed as a characterization, more
and more happens in less time (to himself and Gretta and finally to
himself); dialogue and social gesture become less prominent as the
focus detaches him from a social setting and moves to his private
interior world. His public role gradually disappears, to be replaced
by a focus on the poignance of lost illusions, disappointment, self-
diminishment, and self-knowledge. At the end, a voice separated
from Gabriel emerges to place Gabriel in a larger context – one that
includes not only knowledge of the prior stories, of *Dubliners*, but
knowledge of Christian and pagan contexts; yet finally the centre

of consciousness returns to Gabriel's perspective to show how, to recall our Benjamin quote, he rescues meaning from the sanction of death in the form of love.

III

It is clear that a dialogical or pluralistic aesthetic will see characters in diverse ways; at the same time, we see characters as determinate parts of a thematic pattern and as tentative, indeterminate signifiers whose meaning is never fully realized. At times creators lack control over our response; for what is necessary and probable, or what is nominalistic or representative – even what we consider a caricature rather than a fully-developed character – varies from period to period and reader to reader. We find ourselves displacing characters in all sorts of odd ways, thinking of our responses to their behaviour while we read the author's judgements, and even superimposing our experience on theirs. As readers we 'hybridize' texts – respond to them in multiple ways depending on our interpretive communities – as much as authors do when presenting them. Characters are part of the text's code and teach us how to read them. But since we as readers respond in terms of the interpretive communities to which we belong, it should be a goal of ours to be as open-minded and pluralistic as possible lest we limit the possibilities of reading experience by blind adherence to a few points of view.

Let us state a paradox: as readers, we become both empathetic and ironic characters in the authors' novels or narrative poems even as the authors to whom we respond become *imaginary* readers of our 'novels' – our imagined worlds created by our readings of theirs; finally, because our novel reading changes us, authors affect not only our 'readings of novels', but our readings of experience. Does not the word 'novel' remind us that we are always reading for the first time, if by reading we mean that imaginative activity by which we leave ourselves to find ourselves by entering the world of another? Is that not the essence of reading? As readers we not only take on the identities of characters, but we become part of the author's characterization. The author seeks to speak and define herself/himself while writing to a human audience – as narratee, as a representative audience in the author's mind, as her/his living coherent self. Are we not the most important character, the *other* that the writer seeks, the *self* that would confirm herself/himself?

In an era of moral confusion when stable relations and values are not sustained by extrinsic social structures we are odyssean readers who read to return home – or to the ideological *home* of our interpretative families. That is a way of saying that human actions, too, are open to interpretation depending on which interpretive community one belongs to and what one's needs are at a given time. Just as the interpretation of human character is a function of the author's anterior reality – the economic situation, locations, locutions, and laws – so do these factors in the anterior world of the reader shape his response. While our criticism, including mine, is always disguised autobiography, do not most of us privilege the discovery of mimetic codes in the great texts of Joyce? Do we not – men and women, young and old – recuperate our moments of fulfilled or half-fulfilled putative or disappointed passion because that is where for most of us the mimetic stakes are highest? How can we fail to sympathize with, rather than patronize, Gabriel's irrational certainty that Gretta's nostalgia for Michael – or a fiction of Michael that she has carried about for so many years – consigns his love to a subsidiary position in her eyes? In the major poems of Stevens, we find mimesis in the tension between dreamscape and imagination, between imagination and real. When I read 'Anecdote of the Prince of Peacocks' with my students and they speak of seeing in the poem the experiences of 'insomnia', 'stress', 'nightmares', 'narcissistic sexuality', are they not closer to the experience of the poem than those who speak of homophonic relations between 'feel' and 'fall'? Should we not attend to resolving signification – partial, incomplete – from the dance of signifiers to suggest ways of seeing the speaker's detumescence *and* explosion into lyrical innocence?

> I knew from this
> That the blue ground
> Was full of blocks
> And blocking steel.
> I knew the dread
> Of the bushy plain,
> And the beauty of the moonlight
> Falling there,
> Falling
> As sleep falls
> In the innocent air.

IV

The battle between those who want to talk about the novel as representation and those who wish to reduce it to a linguistic game has been fought and on the whole – to their surprise – those in the former camp have won. The traditional humanists have been reinforced not only by feminists such as Gubar, Gilbert, Showalter, but even by Marxists and New Historicists.

It is interesting that discussion of reader has replaced that of character as if to reintroduce the human by way of the backdoor. For example, Jonathan Culler writes, 'In place of the novel as mimesis we have the novel as a structure which plays with different modes of ordering and enables the reader to understand how he makes sense of the world.'[23] In reader-response criticism, the reader is conceived less as a representative human being than as a unique entity whose responses – no matter how idiosyncratic – are described in terms of attitudes and feelings. His *materiality* is taken for granted. And I applaud this. But the very objections that deconstructionists made to talking of characters within novels could be made to their own discussions of readers and what they do in their sense-making. What Culler writes of critics such as Stanley Fish is true of virtually every story of reading: 'Their stories follow an innocent reader confident in traditional assumptions about structure and meaning, who encounters the deviousness of texts, falls into traps, is frustrated and dismayed, but emerges wiser for the loss of illusions.' As I have argued elsewhere,[24] Hillis Miller has a great deal of difficulty describing what happens to readers in *purely* rhetorical terms. And *critics'* behaviour is humanistically described in terms once reserved for authors and characters – as if their actions were what literature was about: '[Wolfgang Iser's] account of reading is eminently sensible, designed to do justice to the creative, participating activity of readers.'[25] Ironically, these critics naturalize or 'domesticate' responses to texts in human terms in much the way they object to older ways of reading that do the same for characters and actions.

Is it not clear at this point that discussion of character has important implications for defining a humanistic alternative to rigid Marxism? Need we believe that novels enact a political unconscious? Isn't the novel – particularly the English novel – about the desire for love and community outside politics? Within the English novel – the novel of Dickens, Lawrence, Conrad, Joyce and Woolf – isn't the materiality of social and economic forces – and its political philosophy – the alien outsider that authors cannot avoid but must wilfully contain, turn around, and keep at bay? A humanistic poetics sees the value of responding in Marxist terms by those whose readings – whose own plot – demand such narratives, but it also stresses the richness of pluralism that responds to the plenitude and variety of fiction and of its characters.

Can we not say with Ricoeur that 'In the same way that a text is detached from its author, an action is detached from its agent and develops consequences of its own'?[26] Can we explore reading as a mode of perception that is crucial to a theory of character? Texts, with some exceptions, refer back to a speaker and refer to a world which they implicitly claim to express, describe, and represent. Have we fully explored the speech act as a mimetic reading model – a model not only of what we tell but how we tell ourselves what we read? As Bakhtin notes, 'The text as such never appears as a dead thing; beginning with any text – and sometimes passing through a lengthy series of mediating lines – we always arrive, in the final analysis, at the human voice, which is to say we come up against a human being.'[27] Because speech is directed to a particular 'you', its locutionary, illocutionary and perlocutionary aspects need a somewhat different model than does writing. Moreover, writing, like speech, assumes an audience from which it (and its creator) expects a response. While the audience whom the author had in mind is different from the contemporary savvy reader – conditioned by the interpretive communities of which he is part – it is well to remember that the potential audience is whoever knows how to read.

Our interest as readers depends in part on the temporal movement of characters' lives that mime our lives, the way that the plot plays upon our expectations for meaning, the way we can seal off the turmoil of our world and participate in a not-I world without risk – for do we not share Gabriel's fear of insignificance and rejection? We read to have our humanity validated – to be able to move beyond our self-conscious place in time and to be able to have an emotional life (tears, laughter, anxiety, fulfilment) without *risk*. We read to be in a world elsewhere.

Each of us responds differently to characters and plots. To some the tendency of novels to establish unity and meaning is itself an appeal of reading, while for others tentativeness and disorder and awareness of the impossibility of significance is a favoured plot.

When we call the first humanistic formalism, the second deconstruction, we realize that we are describing the plotting of readers
as much as the plotting of texts. Paradoxically, within the space/
time of our reading, we move always back and forth, from metonymic reading to metaphoric reading. We read metonymically to
satisfy our curiosity in incidents and details. Our metonymic
reading is horizontal and temporal because it resists total patterns
and looks for variations of patterns. As our reading proceeds, as
we immerse ourselves in the coded details of text, including the
details of human character, does not the metaphoric reading – the
reading that insists on our plotting and patterning – become more
dominant? As we notice the iteration of patterns and their meaning, we read metaphorically. We read metaphorically for the
fulfilment of our desire for coherence; we weave the contiguity
of metonymic reading into a metaphorical meaning, and our
metaphoric reading finally has a spatial and vertical dimension, a
stable *parable* of metonymic reading that traces an interpretation of
the world on our minds. And do we not recall our reading in terms
of that metaphorical structure?

The idea of reading as transaction between reader and text
makes both elements active participants in the process of understanding; but the idea of reading as transaction has implications for
our study of character. Let me quote Iser who writes of reading as a
transaction in ways I endorse:

> A literary text must therefore be conceived in such a way that it
> will engage the reader's imagination in the task of working
> things out for himself, for reading is only a pleasure when it is
> active and creative. In this process of creativity, the text may
> either not go far enough, or may go too far, so we may say that
> boredom and overstrain form the boundaries beyond which the
> reader will leave the field of play.[28]

Can we not substitute in the above passage 'literary character' for
'literary text'? It is because of interest in human actions and words
that we read; in other words, we are 'buyers' or consumers in the
fictional transaction because of our interest in character. We might
think of characters as models for texts, and think of our meeting
literary characters – as we do texts – midway between the author's
creation and our reading. As Ricoeur notes, 'To understand a text
is to follow its movement from sense to reference, from what it

says to what it talks about.'[29] But humans are not merely texts; they are us. We read to learn about us, and to learn about how we can respond to us. Reading texts thus has continuity with reading lives. Interpreting character outside texts – in life – takes similar skills to interpreting texts; when we interpret language – what is said – we do it in terms of motives and needs of the speaker or writer.

Because of our human interest in other humans, the reader does much of his creative work as a reader of fictional characters, including the narrative voice. The stories characters tell themselves often compete for our attention with those of the narrators; their telling proposes multiple perspectives, including possible alternatives to the telling of the narrator/author; like detectives – readers of experience – we must sort out the *real* reality from its various versions of reality and we can never quite do it because each of us reads differently. Indeed, we as literary teachers should and need to argue for the view that reading is a window into the human mind, and that learning how to read and interpret imaginative literature is basic to training more perceptive and perspicacious social scientists, lawyers, doctors, politicians, consumers, and voters – as well as helping us to be more sensitive parents, children, spouses, lovers, colleagues, friends, and teachers.

Notes

1. Martin Price, 'The Other Self: Thoughts About Character in the Novel', *Imagined Worlds*, ed. Maynard Mack and Ian Gregor (London: Methuen, 1968), p. 287.
2. Margery Sabin, *The Dialect of the Tribe: Speech and Community in Modern Fiction* (New York: Oxford University Press, 1987).
3. Edward Pechter, 'The New Historicism and Its Discontents', *PMLA* 102:3, pp. 292–313.
4. Wolfgang Iser, *The Implied Reader* (Baltimore: Johns Hopkins University Press, 1974), p. 285.
5. Ibid., p. 286.
6. Ibid., pp. 288–9.
7. Peter Brooks, *Reading for the Plot: Design and Intention in Narrative* (New York: Knopf, 1984), p. 3.
8. Walter Benjamin, *Illuminations*, trans. Harry Zohn (New York: Schocken Books, 1969), p. 91.

9. Paul Ricoeur, 'The Model of a Text: Meaningful Action Considered as Text', *Social Research: Fiftieth Anniversary* 51:1 (Spring 1984), p. 217.
10. Hans Meyerhoff, *Time and Literature* (Berkeley and Los Angeles: University of California Press, 1985), p. 152.
11. Alex Gelley, *Narrative Crossings* (Baltimore: Johns Hopkins University Press, 1987), p. 60.
12. W. J. Harvey, *Character and the Novel* (Ithaca: Cornell University Press, 1965), p. 119.
13. Robert Scholes and A. Walton Litz (eds), *Dubliners: Text, Criticism, and Notes* (New York: Viking, 1969).
14. Scholes and Litz, *Dubliners*, pp. 223–4.
15. See my *The Humanistic Heritage: Critical Theories of the English Novel From James to Hillis Miller* (London: Macmillan; Philadelphia: University of Pennsylvania Press, 1986), and *Reading Joyce's 'Ulysses'* (London: Macmillan; New York: St. Martin's Press, 1987).
16. Lyndall Gordon, *Virginia Woolf* (New York: Norton, 1984), p. 11.
17. Mikhail Bakhtin, *The Dialogic Imagination*, ed. Michael Holquist; trans. Caryl Emerson and Michael Holquist (Austin: University of Texas Press, 1981), pp. 231–32.
18. See James Phelan's excellent, 'Character, Progression, and the Mimetic–Didactic Distinction', *Modern Philology* 89:3 (February 1987), pp. 282–99.
19. 'The Well Dressed Man With a Beard', *Wallace Stevens: The Palm at the End of the Mind*, ed. Holly Stevens (New York: Vintage Books, 1972), p. 190.
20. James Joyce, *Ulysses: The Corrected Text* (New York: Vintage Books, 1986), ix. 1041–5.
21. Henry James, quoted in *Theory of Fiction: Henry James*, ed. James E. Miller (Lincoln: University of Nebraska Press, 1972), p. 200.
22. Price, pp. 288–9.
23. Jonathan Culler, *Structuralist Poetics* (Ithaca: Cornell University Press, 1975), p. 278.
24. See my *The Humanistic Heritage*.
25. Jonathan Culler, *On Deconstruction* (Ithaca: Cornell University Press, 1982), p. 75.
26. Ricoeur, 197.
27. Bakhtin, *The Dialogic Imagination*, pp. 252–3.
28. Iser, *The Implied Reader*, p. 275.
29. Ricoeur, p. 219.

4

The Narrative of
Paul de Man: Texts, Issues,
Significance

I.   NARRATIVE AS INSIGHT

Narrative is both the representation of external events and the telling of those events. My interest in narrative derives from my belief that we make sense of our life by ordering it and giving it shape. The stories we tell ourselves provide continuity among the concatenation of diverse episodes in our lives, even if our stories inevitably distort and falsify. Each of us is continually writing and rewriting the text of our life, revising our memories and hopes, proposing plans, filtering disappointments through our defences and rationalizations, making adjustments in the way we present ourselves to ourselves and others. To the degree that we are self-conscious, we live in our narratives – our discourse – about our actions, thoughts, and feelings. While there is always a gulf between imagined worlds and real ones, does not the continuity between reading lives and reading texts depend on understanding reading as a means of sharpening our perceptions, cultivating discriminations, and deepening our insights about ourselves? For reading is a process of cognition that depends on actively organizing the phenomena of language both in the moment of perception and in the fuller understanding that develops as our reading continues as well as in our retrospective view of our completed reading.[1]

I would like to examine the text of Paul de Man's life and work – to understand the progressive narrative that he has left us, even while acknowledging that every day might bring new data to modify our reading. What I shall call the 'de Man narrative' teaches us not merely about de Man but about the nature of the narratives we humans inevitably tell ourselves. The issues raised by the revelations about de Man's past strike to the very heart of debates about the direction of literary studies. They raise questions about the relationship between texts and anterior reality, about the necessity of understanding the author's pysche and historical circumstances, about the relationship between style and substance within a text, about the role of silence in narratives, about the very process of looking for aberrations in texts while neglecting major motifs. The 'de Man narrative' actually includes several narratives: the diachronic organization of episodes of his life, the evolution of his writings from his earlier (by which I mean his wartime work) to the later writing (by which I mean his postwar work), the specific narrative of his development into an academic mandarin and the narrative of suppression and silence which is a supplement to the narrative of development, and, finally, the narrative of academic response to the revelations about his past. My own narrative includes: a) a narrative of de Man's career, itself composed of two phases: his anti-Semitic and pro-Nazi writings and his later writings which we now must read as coloured by his suppression of the first phase; b) the narrative of academic response to the revelation of his past – what might be called a narrative of the sociology of response; and c) the narrative of my own reaction to both the original revelation and to what I am calling the sociology or, perhaps I should say, epidemiology of response.

Who is Paul de Man and why does he matter? He is the central figure in a movement that argues that there is nothing outside a literary text and that literary texts are simply linguistic tropes which have no meaning beyond themselves. Following Jacques Derrida, he proposed a theory of literary study known as deconstruction, which challenges the referentiality of literature and disdains hermeneutics – the quest to understand complex texts – and favours instead the structure of language, what he calls rhetoric – the study of tropes and figures – and semiology, the study of how words mean rather than what they mean. For him history and literature are not human, because both '[pertain] strictly to the order of language; it is not natural, for the same reason; it is not phenomenal, in the sense that no cognition, no knowledge about man, can be derived from a history which as such is purely a linguistic complication' (RT, 92).[2]

How did such a theory gain credibility? For one thing, deriving its impulse from structural linguistics, it claimed to have scientific rigour; deriving its impulse from philosophers such as Nietzsche and Derrida, it seemed to have sophistication. Under the name of deconstruction, it seemed to be questioning accepted distinctions.

Its claims that language does not mean absolutely and that we cannot evoke *exactly* an anterior reality – be it author, historical context, or intended theme – had plausibility. When I say 'The Holocaust', it means something different to each of us; so does 'Little Rock' or 'apple'. There is an indeterminate aspect to language. Furthermore, not only context determines how a word is received; so does the reader's experience and mood. 'Eve ate the apple' is different if it is said in church or synagogue by the priest or rabbi than if a man tells his wife what happened to the apple that he gave their daughter Eve. Her response is different if she had promised the only apple in the house to their son, who may or may not be named Adam. Thus language is indeterminate, metaphorical to some degree, and never fully represents anterior reality. No history or narrative does full justice to the past; our stories necessarily select and distort – and become more interesting because they do so.

As we use a narrative approach to the de Man story, we shall see the folly of ignoring historical contexts, authors, and the power of language to affect action. If the de Man narrative makes us more aware that writing cannot be divorced from its historical contexts, it will be helpful in refocusing literary study away from overemphasis upon complex tropes – what de Man calls rhetoric – which ignores author, theme, and context. In other words, the combination of putative compensation, atonement, and disguise in de Man's deconstructive phase paradoxically underlines how texts do refer to prior reality. The de Man narrative creates a necessary and probable plot which enacts both the hubris and arrogance of cultism and how language always has moral implications; had de Man lived to experience the peripeteia or tragic reversal, the narrative would have followed the pattern of classical tragedy.

As a teacher of narratives, I can find no better narrative to enact my theoretical position – the position that I have been calling humanistic formalism – than the narrative of the career of Paul de Man. Like Conrad's Jim, we shall see that his subsequent behaviour, when given a second chance, not only reflects but in some ways repeats his prior history; for him, as for Jim, we recall what George Eliot wrote of Bulstrode, another character who cannot escape his consciousness of the past: 'A man's past is not simply a dead history, an outworn preparation of the present; it is not a repented error shaken loose from life: It is a still quivering part of himself.'

The de Man narrative enables us to see the essential moral dimension of story and to see the impossibility of understanding one aspect of a narrative without rereading all the available episodes. What we have is a linear text – with gaps, fissures, and omissions – that needs to be understood as we understand all narratives, that is, in terms of expectation, fulfilment, transformation, displacement, iterations, evasions, and mysteries. I want to discover if by rereading the de Man saga as a continuous narrative with a beginning, middle, and end, we can discover the essential principles by which that narrative can be teleologically organized into a necessary and probable process to generate a particular structure of effects. Such a narrative needs to take account of the various kinds of narratives de Man would tell, including those about himself that obsessively evaded the most crucial aspects of *his story*. It may even be that we should propose the following: given a genre in which the object of mimesis is a character wilfully avoiding self-revelation and suppressing his self, how would the necessary and probable plot structure be organized to teach us the terrible price of evasion in moral terms? The episodes of our plot must select and arrange the fundamental premise of our mimesis: de Man's evasion of a heinous early career of propagandizing for a regime that was responsible for genocide. If we discover the necessary and probable plot, it shall also remind us of the fundamental formal narratological principle that no phase of narrative can be regarded as discrete (notably de Man's subsequent critical career) and that, contrary to some of de Man's pronouncements, narratives do not completely transcend their temporal structures – although readers may *urge* narratives to do so in the interest of creating their own allegories of reading.

The most problematic aspect of the de Man narrative is to read the later work – episodes – with the earlier work – episodes – in mind. In our necessary and probable telling of the de Man narrative, is it not essential to focus on the narrative in terms of a linear process with iteration and modification of patterns; prolepsis, analepsis; the relation between story and discourse; fulfilment, postponement, displacement, modification? In the face of later knowledge, derived from the subsequent episodes of a narrative, our readings of earlier passages change. Just as the first three sections of *Ulysses* look radically different when we reread them after reading the subsequent Bloom chapters, so does de Man's major work look different when examined in the light of his wartime essays. As de Man during the war used his texts for polemical purposes, so he does in the later work. If he originally sought to be a cultural critic placing himself on a rock and observing with the most sweeping generalizations the stream of history as it flowed by, he later sought a refuge in arcane discussions of often-neglected texts. But, as we shall see, often within his critical essays, these elucidations are preceded by his recurring bent for totalizing generalizations.

De Man's own later work seeks to elide narrative. De Man not only represses the narrative of his own life as well as the historical circumstances in which it took place, but, in his postwar phase, writes critical essays that are virtually devoid of discussion of authorial development, chronological relationships among the works of a canon, the historical circumstances in which works were written, and the dialogue between the creative imagination and the anterior mind. As he puts it,

> It is necessary ... to read beyond some of the more categorical assertions and balance them against other much more tentative utterances that seem to come close, at times to being contra-dictory to these assertions. ... The insight seems instead to have gained from a negative movement that animates the critic's thought, an unstated principle that leads his language away from its asserted stand, perverting and dissolving his stated commitment to the point where it becomes emptied of sub-stance, as if the very possibility of assertion had been put into question. ('The Rhetoric of Blindness: Jacques Derrida's Reading of Rousseau', in *BI*, 102–3)

Such a passage as the foregoing is typical of his penchant for substituting what he calls allegories of reading for narratives of reading that might speak to the movement of a work. Whether we consider narrative as a form of representation or as a manner of speaking that stresses the continuity and contiguity of events, de Man's work is puzzlingly deficient in narrative. If one has not read the primary works he discusses, one would never guess their basic 'story' or plot structure; if he is discussing, as he often is, a critical work, he feels no obligation to render accurately the *movement* of the argument.

Yet following de Man's own method, we should stress the ostentatiously absent subject to see what he is up to. The evasion of narrative is part of the effort to write about literature without stressing the human element. As Hayden White puts it,

> Far from being a problem, then, narrative might be considered a solution to a problem of general human concern, namely, the problem of how to translate *knowing* into *telling*, the problem of fashioning human experience into a form assimilable to structures of meaning that are generally human rather than culture-specific.... [F]ar from being one code among many that a culture may utilize for endowing experience with meaning, narrative is a metacode, a human universal on the basis of which transcultural messages about the nature of a shared reality can be transmitted.[3]

For to omit narrative is to de-emphasize the kind of ordering on which we depend to convey meaning. As White remarks, 'the absence of narrative capacity or a refusal of narrative indicates an absence or refusal of meaning itself' (White, 2). De Man would have us believe that we can have narrative without reference to anteriority, as if our very concepts of narrative were not anterior to the text – including the concept of a teleologically ordered plot that represents something to which we respond by means of the power of shared codes of language and experience. In a passage that characteristically finds in other critics the critical goals he seeks, he praises Poulet for a 'critical narration' that 'has no reference to anything outside the work and is constructed from the entirety of the writer's texts surveyed as in a panoramic view. It is articulated, however, around a number of centers without which it could not have taken shape. The plot of this critical narrative falls into an almost uniform pattern, which does not prevent individual or group variations but defines, in its uniformity, a literary consciousness as distinct from other forms of consciousness' (*BI*, 90–91).

II.   THE NARRATIVE OF MY RESPONSE

While in London I picked up the 2 December 1987 *International Herald Tribune* to read that Paul de Man had written 100 or more articles for an anti-Semitic newspaper.[4] My first response: here was de Man teaching us that language is polysemous and arguing for the free play of signifiers and telling us that language cannot signify a reality beyond itself, when – if the translation could be trusted – he had written in his twenties: 'It shows the strength of our Western intellectuals that they could protect from Jewish influence a sphere as representative of the culture at large as literature. Despite the lingering Semitism in all our civilisation, literature showed that its essential nature was healthy' (see *WJ*, 45, 286–92). Not only was the above article originally published in a 'special supplement on Jews', but as the original piece in the *International Herald Tribune* accurately reported: 'Next to the essay is a caricature of Jews with horns and claws who, wearing prayer shawls, pray that "Jehovah will confound the gentiles."' My original questions: How could this brilliant scholar, many of whose colleagues and admirers were Jewish, live every day in silence with the burden of having written these words? Wasn't his public posture similar to that of Waldheim, the moral dwarf who was president of Austria? If the articles that he had written for the collaborationist Belgian newspaper *Le Soir* had been made public, would de Man have even been admitted to the United States after the war? Did he unconsciously invent a theory of language to justify his own moral crimes to himself?

The article included words from ex-president of Yale Giametti's obituary which eulogized him as a 'tremendous light for human life and learning' after whom 'nothing for us will ever be the same'. But, as justifications for a man who was regarded by his followers as a seminal intellectual figure of the twentieth century, the defences in the original *Herald Tribune* article were as pathetic as they were unintentionally ironic; some defended him as having been a young man, influenced perhaps by an uncle, Hendriki de Man, who was a minister in the collaborationist Belgian Government. Could not Eichmann or Waldheim have made the same claim that they had been influenced by others? Had the Nuremberg trial admitted as defence evidence the formal argument known as 'an uncle's influence'? (While one can snidely remark, 'How many of us number uncles among our greatest influences?' the real issue is that morality must transcend issues of influence – hereditary or environmental.)

More than a year after these revelations, and after reading de Man's wartime writings, and rereading his later work, I am still struggling with my own response. We can now recite the bare outline of the scandal. After the Nazi occupation of Belgium, when he was in his early twenties, de Man wrote for the collaborationist newspaper *Le Soir* as a book reviewer and culture commentator. Later, without ever revealing his Nazi past, he came to America and, after teaching at Sarah Lawrence, wrote his dissertation at Harvard, taking his degree in 1960. Had he revealed his past, it is doubtful that he would have been admitted to the United States – since he was not a rocket scientist. He became a prominent professor of comparative literature, and taught at Cornell and at Johns Hopkins before becoming a major figure at Yale until his death in 1983. He was held in great esteem by students and colleagues; yet he was unusually diffident about discussions of his past. To many he seemed distant and iconoclastic about American culture; in his writing and lectures he identifies himself as belonging to a European tradition. Since the original revelations about his political past, it was revealed that he left a wife and bad debts in Europe and married a second wife in America – apparently before divorcing his first wife; she was a student at Sarah Lawrence, where he taught before he earned his Ph.D.

Believing as I do that the very mindlessness and crassness – linguistic and moral – of some of de Man's prewar texts have inexorably shaped the crudity of the ensuing critical and intellectual discussion of those texts, I write with a good deal of hesitation. If I seem to overuse the interrogative mode in what follows, it is to raise questions that I believe each of us needs to consider as well as to leave intellectual space for responses. For is this not an issue that requires what Bakhtin might have called dialogic criticism rather than what I believe is the monologic perspectives of some of de Man's early texts and – notwithstanding their elaborate arguments – of his academic defence attorneys?

Here was a man – de Man, to use the very pun once favoured by those involved in his beatification – who taught that all readings were 'allegories of reading' because they reduced and distorted the complex rhetorical events in a text. And yet some of his early wartime work perniciously and wilfully simplified and allegorized the phenomena of European history into a Manichean narrative in which the Jews played the villains.

I do not claim to be a strong partisan of deconstruction, but I have been challenged by and learned from de Man's writings, as any professor of literature has unless he has had his head in the sand or simply chanted an 'Everlasting No' to the theoretical developments of the past few decades. (Those who are sceptical about the impact of deconstruction should be wary of finding solace from those traditional critics who have been proclaiming the Death of Deconstruction, for often what those traditionalists have meant is, 'I do not have the time nor interest to read literary theory that challenges my most central assumptions about literature.') De Man, like the New Critics whom he at times patronized, insisted that the text be examined carefully and attentively without pre-ordained ideologies which are magnets for the data that fulfil *a priori* notions of organic and unified texts; he taught us that texts disseminate their language polysemously and often generate meanings quite different from those intended by their authors.

What had always troubled me about the major figures in the deconstruction movement was their obliviousness to the texture of history. Several years ago, after speaking for a few hours to one of the major deconstructors, I remember asking myself whether *The New York Times* was delivered in New Haven and whether the network news penetrated through the invisible shield of post-structural assumptions about the meaninglessness of language. While deconstruction claims that finding the rhetorical patterns undermined authoritative readings and the hegemony of traditional thematic readings, the result at times has been an abdication of responsibility to render the text in the spirit in which it was written and a privileging of idiosyncrasy for its own sake. Accuracy of interpretation takes a back seat to what was 'interesting', without regard to intention or the anterior reality which a text is representing.

III.   NARRATIVE AS BLINDNESS: THE SOCIOLOGY OF RESPONSE

Let me turn for a moment to what I call the Narrative – really the sociology – of Response. At the December 1987 MLA convention in San Francisco, some of de Man's zealous followers relied facilely upon history, the metaphysics of presence, and positivistic cause and effect – all until recently disdained by them – to muster an extenuating argument for de Man's early writing; in a sense we had the spectacle of deconstructionists deconstructing themselves in the interest of maintaining their position. Thus, in San Francisco, I was assured by a number of my friends with stock in de Man's reputation that he (or she) had heard that de Man had confided in

Harold Bloom and/or Geoffrey Hartman and/or Derrida about his past – as if Bloom's or Hartman's or Derrida's Jewishness made de Man innocent by association.

But, one might archly ask, who – Jews or human beings – has conferred confessor status on either Bloom or Hartman or Derrida? Even if de Man had confided in them, and it now seems doubtful that he did, do such exercises in transference – and/or the kind of countertransference that we shall see enacted in the Hillis Miller and Derrida defences to be discussed below – have any bearing on the issue? Certainly the 1955 private letter to the Harvard Society of Fellows which Derrida cites as evidence that de Man came to terms with his past shows little awareness on de Man's part of the enormity of his moral crime. At the December 1987 MLA, I was also told in hush-hush terms that it was rumoured that de Man was a double agent and really part of the Resistance. It was whispered that if we were patient, the untold rest of the story would exonerate de Man. Well, as the years have passed, nothing, to my knowledge, has appeared to support these optative claims. Do not such reassurances and excuses that de Man was really this or meant that as well as obsessive efforts to recreate a determinate past call into question the insistence of de Man and his followers that nothing lies outside the text and that language is polysemous?

IV.   ALLEGORIES OF READING DE MAN

Let us examine the most heinous of de Man's texts and the attempt by his followers to create an explanatory *midrash*.[5] In his 4 March 1941 *Le Soir* article entitled 'Les Juifs dans la litterature actuelle', de Man had written his insights on Jews and history in the kind of Germanic master style – a style which depends fully on the assumption that it can evoke the presence of history and culture in sweeping, elegant sentences – that Thomas Mann had parodied in *Death in Venice* when making fun of Aschenbach. Indeed, what is striking is how often in 1940–42 the young de Man writes in the most arrogant tone as if he were surveying history from a steep iconoclastic peak without regard for the human lives caught up in the maelstrom of mindless Nazi violence.

For Hillis Miller, the issue is not de Man's moral apostasy but the way the press has reported the issue. The reasons for the hostility of the press, according to Miller, are: 'a suspicion of any new and difficult mode of thought, especially (in the United States) when imported from the continent; a general hostility to critical theory ... [and] a widespread concern to identify the last remnants of the Nazi regime and to purify ourselves of them, to cut ourselves off from that period of history and to deny that anything like that could happen again' (*TLS*, 17–23 June 1988, 676, 684). The arguments of de Man's defenders enact the point that the here and now of the 1988 discussion includes the very extension of the frontiers of permissible discourse that took place in the early 1940s. Did not the mere act of discussing racist and genocidal proposals in the incendiary climate of the early 1940s help give such proposals a life of their own? If we speak of the 'violence of the reaction', as Miller does in his *TLS* piece, are we not confusing the original heinous rhetoric of de Man with the understandable shock of the response? But then, has not Miller told us that the Holocaust is 'a fantastic example ... of ... some mistaken effect of language'?[6]

Hillis Miller's present linguistic theories apparently deflect him from understanding what happens when one confuses language and events. For in the same piece he asks of a glib, and of course deeply regrettable hyperbolic comment, 'Let's turn Libya into a parking lot': 'Is that so different from the Holocaust?' But, unlike the foolish loose talk about Libya, the Holocaust was an historical event resulting in part from the gradual change in what were the acceptable limits of civilized discourse. Are we not more rigorous in assigning the guilt and blame for loose talk that results in violent action? The regrettable expression 'I am going to kill you' becomes a crime when someone is dead or injured. For Miller, as he wrote in *The Ethics of Reading*, 'the study of literature ... remains within the study of language'; yet his defence, like Derrida's far more eloquent and impassioned one in *Critical Inquiry*, rests on a facile and disturbing use of the very historical data that deconstruction has been banishing from its critical domain.

In Derrida's *Critical Inquiry* piece, he translates the passage I cited from the *International Herald Tribune*, including the even more damning ensuing sentences with which the piece concludes:

The observation is, moreover, comforting for Western intellectuals. That they have been able to safeguard themselves from Jewish influence in a domain as representative of culture as literature proves their vitality. If our civilization had let itself be invaded by a foreign force, then we would have to give up much hope for its future. By keeping, in spite of semitic interference in all aspects of European life, an intact originality and character, it has shown that its basic nature is healthy. What is more, one sees that a solution of the Jewish problem that would aim at the creation of a Jewish colony isolated from Europe would not entail, for the literary life of the West, deplorable consequences. The latter would lose, in all, a few personalities of mediocre value and would continue, as in the past, to develop according to its great evolutive laws. (de Man, 'The Jews in Present-Day Literature', quoted in Derrida, *Critical Inquiry* 14:3 [Spring 1988], 623)

We should, I think, be sceptical of Derrida's effort to present strong misreadings of such passages as the following from the first paragraph of 'The Jews in Present Day Literature':

Vulgar antisemitism readily takes pleasure in considering post-war cultural phenomena (after the war '14–18) as degenerate and decadent because they are *enjuivés*. Literature has not escaped this lapidary judgement. It has sufficed to discover a few Jewish writers behind Latinized pseudonyms for all of contemporary production to be considered polluted and harmful. This conception entails rather dangerous consequences. First of all, it condemns *a priori* a whole literature that in no way deserves this fate. What is more, from the moment one agrees that the literature of our day has some merit, it would be a rather unflattering appreciation of Western writers to being mere imitators of a Jewish culture that is foreign to them.

The Jews themselves have contributed to spreading this myth. Often, they have glorified themselves as the leaders of literary movements that characterize our age. But the error has, in fact, a deeper cause. At the origin of the thesis of a Jewish takeover is the very widespread belief according to which the modern novel and modern poetry are nothing but a kind of monstrous outgrowth of the world war. Since the Jews have, in fact, played an important role in the phony and disordered existence of Europe since 1920, a novel born in the atmosphere would deserve, up to a certain point, the qualification of *enjuivé*. (Ibid., 624)

Both as a Jew and a friend of de Man's who is heavily invested for professional reasons in de Man's reputation, Derrida, by means of an elaborate deconstructive reading of the first two paragraphs and subsequent paragraphs, tries to extenuate de Man's conclusion that Jews should be deported and isolated in order that a master culture might continue to evolve. When Derrida tries to claim that de Man is arguing against 'vulgar anti-Semitism', he misses the point that it is de Man's rhetoric that deconstructs such an argument. The very speaking of 'a solution of a Jewish problem' and 'the creation of a Jewish colony' necessarily – by its outrageousness and insensitivity – becomes the *dominant* strand of the argument. Does not the use of the masterphrase 'solution of the Jewish problem' call attention to itself as if it were a rhetorical magnet that rendered subsequent qualification null and void? History renders the user of such a phrase as 'a solution of the Jewish problem' in the early 1940s with an awesome burden of guilt, just as the person whose bullet strikes its human target must bear a greater responsibility than the person who shoots and misses. Do we not teach our students that if the length of a piece does not permit the elaborate presentation of evidence, the author must be extremely careful about the claims made by generalization? Does not the younger de Man reveal his intellectual irresponsibility by revelling in his categorizing sensibility without regard to evidence or argument: 'Jewish writers have always remained in the second rank and, to speak only of France, [they] are not among the most important figures, they are especially not those who have had any guiding influence on the literary genres' (Derrida, 622)? Finally, in these meditations on Jews in present-day literature, is not one struck by the relentless mediocrity and pretentiousness of de Man's mind and by his inability or failure to use evidence to make substantive distinctions?

In his piece, Derrida ignores context to make a case that de Man's words are something other than the worst kind of anti-Semitism. Derrida claims that we should regard de Man as 'the nonconforming smuggler' who really is saying something quite different from what we are reading (Derrida, 625). But, one must facetiously note, for 1941 readers not aware of the secret code – non-Derridean readers – 'The Jews in Present-Day Literature' would have been evidence that the unspeakable could be discussed by intellectuals in a gentle, 'civilized', discourse; for confused 1941 Belgian readers, would his work not have provided an example of how the most outrageous sentiments could be domesticated within intellectual discourse?[7] The more de Man spoke in this way, the more he became in thrall to that way of speaking; the more readers then and now consume such drivel from minds they respect, the more drivel becomes a possible way of arguing. Indeed, within the context of the noble gesture of defending their friend, are not Derrida and Miller such readers and have they not become inadvertent thralls to such discourse?

Responses to de Man's apostasy include the most bizarre appropriation of language. Thus in *Critical Inquiry*, Derrida writes:

> To judge, to condemn the work or the man on the basis of what was a brief episode, to call for closing, that is to say, at least figuratively, for censuring or burning his books is to reproduce the exterminating gesture which one accuses de Man of not having armed himself against sooner with the necessary vigilance. (Ibid., 651)

Notice the rhetorical zeugma by which judging de Man's work (or even a part of it) or condemning some of his past behaviour becomes equated with book-burning as if *Kristallnacht* was simply a trope rather than a horrendous event. Indeed, does not the term 'exterminating gesture' define what the Nazis were doing to the Jews at the very time when de Man was writing, from the crude and gross Darwinistic perspective that typified National Socialism's theory of racial evolution? But let me quote from a 1942 de Man piece:

> What is proper to our time is the consideration of this national personality as a valuable condition, as a precious possession, which has to be maintained at the cost of all sacrifices. This conception is miles apart from sentimental patriotism. Rather, it concerns a sober faith, a practical means to defend Western culture against a decomposition from the inside or an over-whelming onrush by neighboring cultural norms. (translation of a review of 'Art as Mirror of the Essence of Nations: Considerations of "Geist der Nationen" by A. E. Brinckman', *Het Vlaamsche Land*, 29–30 March 1942, p. 3; WJ, 303)

What Derrida has done is confuse gesture and action by reducing everything to rhetoricity; but those whose families disappeared in the Holocaust, or Cambodians whose families were decimated by Pol Pot, cannot resolve historical events on some imaginary linguistic plane. *Historical effects*, such as the Holocaust, warn us that 'exterminating gestures' are far more than rhetorical; such gestures become a version of how metonymy becomes metaphor becomes fact and how words become grotesque prolepses for gas chambers and death camps. Isn't this especially and egregiously true in totalitarian cultures like the Nazi one in which words are more and more used instrumentally to create an alternative reality rather than to reflect an anterior reality? In totalitarian societies the figurative possibilities of language are paradoxically vastly reduced except in the areas of discourse where it is the instrumental agent of the ruling authority. We recall such phrases as 'inferior race', 'world dominating Zionist clique', and 'tribal area land set aside for colored development'.

However well-meaning, Geoffrey Hartman's notion that such passages as those I have cited from 'The Jews in Present-Day Literature' are 'polished' rather than 'not vulgar anti-Semitic writing, not by the terrible standards of the day', is another example of how the discourses about de Man's texts are controlled by the moral assumptions about the man behind those texts. While touched by Hartman's friendship and loyalty, should we not see that the passages that I have quoted from 'The Jews in Present-Day Literature' have within them the very *origins* and *presence* – to use terms that de Man and his followers dismiss – of the Final Solution?

In the early forties when Belgium was under Nazi rule and when Belgians knew about the war against the Jews – due to the constant flow of information and troops between Germany and Belgium – was not 'Jewish Colony' already a terrifying metaphor for death camps or at least for dehumanizing prison camps and ghettoes where people were deprived of human dignity? It does not matter, as Hartman and others have claimed, whether de Man took this position under the guise of Flemish nationalism. We are asked by Hartman to believe that de Man is so caught up in history that he *justifiably* loses sight of moral responsibility: 'To judge from his articles, de Man felt he was living in a revolutionary epoch, in which politics and a sense of collective action were an essential part of intellectual regeneration' (*The New Republic*, 7 March 1988, 28). If the de Man narrative teaches us that context and circumstances create greater demands not lesser ones – as we should have learned from foes of apartheid like Gordimer, Serote, and Mattera, as well as from Sakharov and others confined to the Gulag, it may be a fable that has applicability beyond parochial academic debates. The more the pressure of politics and historical circumstances, the greater the need of integrity in writing. It is interesting that de Man is now being defended in the very historical terms that his work denied. Yet was it not the essence of his project to claim that linguistic events take precedence over historical events that shaped them, and to claim that literature had little to do with life in action and everything to do with language that existed as a separate self-reflexive textuality?

In light of Derrida's tortured defence, it is ironic that Christopher Norris, arguing in the deconstructive manner of quoting from an apostolic tradition, summons the authority of Derrida's reading of de Man to extenuate the bare facts of de Man's apostasy.[8] It seems to me that Norris's abstruse discussion has not only missed crucial points, but has troped the very historical apostasy that de Man's work illustrates and the very acceptance of discipleship to which students and followers of de Man subscribe. Indeed, he urges us to forgive de Man his discipleship to his anti-Semitic collaborationist uncle, Hendrik de Man, and offers the most insipid of historical justifications: 'It is fair to conjecture that [de Man] thought the only prospect of survival for the Belgian people, languages and culture lay in making terms (at least temporarily) with the fact of German occupation, and hoping that National Socialism might indeed be "re-interpreted" in a more favorable light' (Norris, 7). Norris's account of de Man's supposed autocritique – namely, de Man's acknowledgement that critical truths are always tinged by critical self-doubt because of textual and rhetorical complications – is based on slim reeds. Indeed, for me, rather than exonerating de Man from the charge of Nazi collaboration, Norris proves the very point he wishes to refute. One concludes, after reading quotations cited by Norris to support his view of de Man's transformation, that most of the quotations he cites do not support his contention and that if this is the best a defender of de Man can do, de Man is in real trouble.

Are not the apologists for de Man apologizing for themselves? Everyone assures each other – by recuperating the author, desperately searching for historical ground, looking for a narrative presence that de Man's self-referential work had nearly succeeded in banishing – that 'this was not the man they knew'. Apparently, history can be conjured, reinvented, and fantasized, just as de Man did himself when history was needed as a context for his early literary essays in Belgium. When it is not needed it is sent, in the words of Joyce's Buck Mulligan in *Ulysses* while speaking of other ghostly presences, 'back to the barracks'. But was there not a prior de Man, a collaborator, who revealed himself in his words and were those words – even if barely a trace – not a still quivering part of his later self, as sure as George Eliot's Bulstrode's and Conrad's Jim's pasts remained with them? Can *anyone* exorcise the ghost of his or her past?

The ahistoricism of de Man's mature work is troped by the hagiography of his followers who would ignore history – until now when they rush to find the flimsiest historical excuses. In his chapter on Rousseau's *Confessions* in *Allegories of Reading*, de Man wrote of how it is always possible to face up to any experience (to excuse any guilt) because 'the experience always exists simultaneously as fictional discourse and as empirical event and it is never possible to decide which one of the two possibilities is the right one. The indecision makes it possible to excuse the bleakest of crimes' (*AR*, p. 293).

V.   REREADING DE MAN

Let me pose provocative questions. Should we consider de Man's postwar career, including the gradual movement to deconstruction, a response to or an evasion of trauma? Is it a displacement of guilt and an act of repression of his past actions? Is it not necessary to consider the possibility that his subsequent work is a repression of the past, particularly when the very essence of his theory is a disregard for reading in terms of themes and values, a disregard accompanied by a belittling of the possibility of determinate meaning and significance? To put it baldly, by claiming that language creates its own world, separate and distinct from the real world, does he not evade the responsibility of his own prior virulently racist words and their relationship to actions that follow from them? Why had de Man – whose early work seemed focused in a cultural context, albeit reductive – retreated into a bizarre formalism where the central strategy was the isolation and discussion of rhetorical tropes and their inherent contradictions and the wilful identification of supposed gaps and fissures in construing meaning? Does not this deconstructive formalism have the same relationship to our empirical sense of what language does and how it is culturally produced by real circumstances – circumstances that always must be seen in an historical and political context – as the fantasy world of griffins and unicorns has to our daily life? Given the revelations of the early episodes of the de Man narrative, does not the self-referentiality of his later criticism, and its insistence on evading history, representation, and personality become indistinguishable from amorality? And yet the later work depends on a human voice which has as strong a presence as the voice of the early pieces; it, too, speaks at times oracularly, confidently and sophistically, even if at other times it speaks more sceptically, carefully, defensively, and arcanely than the earlier de Man.

Let us consider de Man's deconstructive project. He wishes to see language as a system of signs and signification rather than as established patterns of meaning: 'It is therefore not *a priori* certain that literature is a reliable source of anything but its own language' (*RT*, 11). He argues that hermeneutics (the quest to understand what a text meant) should give way to semiology (the study of how words mean) and rhetoric (the study of tropes and figures). He wants to replace historical, moral, and non-linguistic criteria with linguistic ones. His work stresses theory over the analyses of literary texts, and in his work he reads texts for the purpose of developing a theory: 'Literary theory can be said to come into being when the approach to literary texts is no longer based on non-linguistic, that is to say historical and aesthetic, considerations or, to put it somewhat less crudely, when the object of discussion is no longer the meaning or the value but the modalities of production and the reception of meaning and of value prior to their establishment – the implication being that its establishment is problematic enough to require an autonomous discipline of critical investigation to consider its possibility and its status' (*RT*, 7).

In the opening chapter and the title essay of the posthumous volume *The Resistance to Theory*, de Man again puts himself – as he had in Belgium in the early 1940s – against the resisters as if to reverse the wrongs of history. But in resisting the resistance isn't he resisting, in psychoanalytic terms, acceptance of the historical facts of his past? Those who resist literary theory do so, he argues, because they find it 'threatening'. And de Man is dismissive about resistance in terms that not only claim a space for theory, but make that claim in terms that have political echoes: '[T]he arguments in favor of the legitimacy of literary theory are so compelling that it seems useless to concern oneself with the conflict at all. Certainly, none of the objections to theory, presented again and again, always misinformed or based on crude misunderstandings of such terms as mimesis, fiction, reality, ideology, reference, and for that matter, relevance, can be said to be of genuine rhetorical interest' (*RT*, 12).

In Olympian terms he speaks of those who disagree with him: 'The attack [on theory] reflects the anxiety of the aggressor rather than the guilt of the accused' (*RT*, 10). But does not his guilt peek through in the intemperateness of his attack on those siding with the resistance? Given the burden of guilt he must feel for using language as an historical tool, in the service of what he believed was true – or at least advocated in the service of a poisonous regime – how do we read his insistence that language has 'considerable freedom from referential restraint ... since its use can no longer be said to be determined by considerations of truth and falsehood, good and evil, beauty and ugliness, or pleasure and pain' (RT, 10)? He goes to great pains to deny literature both its aesthetic quality and its mimetic or representational one.

It has been facetiously and bitterly remarked that the publisher should change the name of de Man's *Blindness and Insight* (1970) – a collection of essays written in the late 1960s – to *Blindness and Amnesia*. As we reread de Man in light of what we now know, we should ask why de Man is so concerned with seeing insight as a result of blindness. But we would be guilty of amnesia, too, if we didn't examine the relationship between de Man's passionate advocacy of the indeterminacy of language and his memories of his past writing, if we did not relate de Man's later ideology of reading to his earlier ideology of history. Did not de Man himself teach us to read criticism with an awareness of the critics' blind spots, and to see how their major insights often occur in spite of their intentions? How does the anti-historicism of most of de Man's work relate to the relentless and simplistic historicism of his early work in which he speaks glibly of 'national character traits of nations' and euphemistically of the Nazi conquest of Europe as 'contemporary revolutions' and of the resulting 'European unity' – obviously under Nazi auspices – as something to be desired (*WJ*, 302–3; 309–10)? Do not guilt, trauma, displacement and repression play a role in his adopting an ahistorical phenomenology in the 1960s and his insistence that the greatest insights of major critics come when they inadvertently do in practice the very opposite of the general principles they advocate?

To explain the relationship between de Man's later work and earlier work, let me cite Neil Hertz's brilliant piece, 'Freud and the Sandman':

[S]urely the awareness of the process of repetition is inseparable from the awareness of something being repeated, for there can be no such thing as sheer repetition. Of course: repetition becomes 'visible' when it is colored or tinged by something being repeated, which itself functions like vivid and heightened language, lending a kind of rhetorical consistency to what is otherwise quite literally unspeakable. Whatever it is that is repeated – an obsessive ritual, perhaps, or a bit of acting-out in relation to one's analyst – will, then, feel most compellingly uncanny when it is seen as *merely* coloring, that is, when it comes to seem most gratuitously rhetorical.[9]

Isn't de Man's evasion of history, elusive style, and insistence that language does not mean, a troping of the trauma of his prior views – or of the Holocaust – or his guilt – or of his suppression of his guilt? How hard is it to tell what de Man's later work signifies and what inner turmoil it is acting out, once we understand that language does mean?

If one believes, as de Man correctly insisted, that the performative and demonstrative, the rhetorical and the referential, can never be separated, we must be attentive to de Man's texts. Thus what de Man writes of Rousseau obliquely describes the qualities favoured when he wrote the Rousseau essay over against the dominant qualities that seemed to control his wartime work: 'Diachronic structures such as music, melody, or allegory are favored over pseudo-synchronic structures such as painting, harmony or mimesis because the latter mislead one into believing in a stability of meaning that does not exist' (*BI*, 132). His very choice of subjects is revealing. Why tortuously argue that Rousseau – that seemingly most self-revealing of artists and the author of *Confessions* – espouses a 'theory or representation' that 'is not directed toward meaning as presence and plenitude but toward meaning as void' (*BI*, 127)?

It is as if de Man were writing not about Rousseau but about the relationship between his own later work and the wartime work: 'The elegiac tone that is occasionally sounded does not express a nostalgia for an original presence but is a purely dramatic device, an effect made possible and dictated by a fiction that deprives the nostalgia of all foundation' (*BI*, 133). Does not careful analysis of de Man's Rousseau show that not only is *his* Rousseau different from Rousseau's Rousseau – construed Rousseau – but that *his* Rousseau is de Man in disguise? For de Man uses *his* Rousseau to reject construed Rousseau. And *his* Rousseau, we realize, is *later* de Man, rejecting not only construed Rousseau but early de Man. Did not de Man's early work – the wartime essays – reveal a deeply-felt belief in mimesis, historical harmony, and stability of meaning? Does de Man not use Rousseau to say all the things de Man wants to say about the mistakes of traditional criticism that assumes the metaphysics of presence, origin, and the primacy of oral communication over written communication? 'Rousseau's own texts provide the strongest evidence against his alleged doctrine', a doctrine that includes, according to de Man, Rousseau's 'assertion of the primacy of voice over the written word, his adherence to the myth of original innocence, his valorization of unmediated presence over reflection' (*BI*, 114). But were not the implicit doctrines in de Man's early writing – primacy of voice, myth of original innocence, valorization of unmediated presence – those very concepts that Rousseau is purportedly rejecting? And do not de Man's own early texts provide evidence against his later deconstruction?

In de Man's insistence that criticism says something other than it means, do we not see both a defence of his earlier writings – a necessary defence for a jury of one: himself – and his calling attention to how we must read the author of such words?

It is necessary . . . to read beyond some of the more categorical assertions and balance them against other much more tentative utterances that seem to come close, at times, to being contradictory to these assertions. The contradictions, however, never cancel each other out, nor do they enter into the synthesizing dynamics of a dialectic. No contradiction or dialectical movement could develop because a fundamental difference in the level of explicitness prevented both statements from meeting on a common level of discourse; the one always lay hidden within the other as the sun lies hidden within a shadow, or truth within error. The insight seems instead to have been gained from a negative movement that animates the critic's thought, an unstated principle that leads his language away from its asserted stand, perverting and dissolving his stated commitment to the point where it becomes emptied of substance, as if the very possibility of assertion had been put into question. (*BI*, 103)

Why would a critic compulsively repeat in various forms versions of the following sentence? '[N]ot only does the critic say something that the work does not say, but he even says something that he himself does not mean to say' (*BI*, 109). Should we not attend to both the meaning and rhetoric of his later arguments, his actual performances, and stylistic quirks to discover if de Man is telling us something more than he realizes?

To deconstruct narrative, one must undermine memory as an act of ordering the past into stories, and that is exactly what de Man seeks to do:

The power of memory does not reside in its capacity to resurrect a situation or a feeling that actually existed, but it is a constitutive act of the mind bound to its own present and oriented toward the future of its own elaboration. The past intervenes only as a purely formal element, as a reference or a leverage that can be used because it is different and distant rather than because it is familiar and near. If memory allows us to enter into contact with the past, it is not because the past acts as the source of the present, as a temporal continuity that had been forgotten and of which we are again made aware; the remembrance does not reach us carried by a temporal flux; quite to the contrary, it is a deliberate act establishing a relation between two distinct points in time between which no relationship of continuity exists. Remembrance is not a temporal act but an act that enables a consciousness 'to find access to the intemporal' and to transcend time altogether. Such transcendence leads to the rejection of all that precedes the moment of remembrance as misleading and sterile in its deceptive relationship to the present. The power of invention has entirely passed into the present subject as it shows itself capable of creating relationships that are no longer dependent on past experience. The point of departure was originally a moment of anxiety and of weakness because it felt no longer supported by anything that came before; it has now freed itself from the deceptive weight under which it was laboring and has become the creative moment par excellence, the source of Proust's poetic imagination as well as the center of the critical narrative by means of which Poulet makes us share in the adventure of this creation. This critical narrative turns around the central affirmation: 'time recovered is time transcended'. (*BI*, 92–3)

While it is one thing to acknowledge that memory of the past creates our stories or readings of our experience and that memory distorts and reshapes and transforms the original events, it is another to exorcise memory as our means of understanding ourselves or to pretend all our memories have zero truth-content. Why is de Man reading Poulet as if Poulet were trying to create a perpetual state of aesthetic ecstasy that would displace our sense of historical time?

At the start, a deceptive priority of the past over present and future was being asserted; this stage was followed by the discovery that the actual poetic power resides in a time-transcending moment: 'It is not time that is given us, but the moment. With the given moment, it is up to us to make time.' But since the moment then becomes reintegrated within time, we return in fact to a temporal activity, no longer based on memory but on the future-engendering power of the mind. (*BI*, 93–4)

We should notice the kinship with Pater's aphorism, 'To burn always with this hard, gemlike flame, to maintain this ecstasy, is success in life' (Conclusion, *Studies in the History of the Renaissance*). But in recalling Pater's effort to escape chronological time in acts of aesthetic contemplation and acts of 'exquisite passion', do we not see the continuity of de Man's attacks on history and reality with the European aesthetic movements in the nineties? In the late nineties, utilitarianism and rationality were patronized by those seeking a higher intuitive truth and an escape from the tediousness of logical behaviour and moral duty. But the *ennui* and fascination with odd formulations that we associate with the unconventional behaviour in Huysman and Wilde are in de Man restricted to provocative and idiosyncratic linguistic theories even as he, like Pater, wears the mask of institutional respectability.

Of course, de Man cannot elide narrative completely; the very linearity of syntax and the need for an argument in order that he have the vestiges of continuity and entailment prevent that. But notice his disdain for the nature of shared reality on which narrative depends: 'It can always be shown, on all levels of experience, that what other people experience as a crisis is perhaps not even a change; such observations depend to a very large extent on the standpoint of the observer' (*BI*, 6). As, we might recall, if he were excusing his own conduct in the days of Nazi occupation of Belgium, he praises Blanchot's impersonality: 'An intensely private figure, who has kept his personal affairs strictly to himself and whose pronouncements on public issues, literary or political, have been very scarce, Blanchot is primarily known as a critic. . . . Blanchot's critical reflections offer us no personal confessions or intimate experiences, nothing that would give immediate access to another person's consciousness and allow the reader to espouse its movements' (*BI*, 61, 63). Blanchot, in fact, was also a collaborator.

According to de Man, we should obliterate our values when we teach and write. Because de Man is fascinated, if not obsessed, by scenarios which allow for the replacement of prior versions of the self, he finds appealing Poulet's erasure of the reader's cogito before the text's: 'In criticism, the *moment de passage* changes from a temporal into an intersubjective act or, to be more precise, into the total replacement of one subject by another. We are, in fact, dealing with a substitutive relationship, in which the place of a self is usurped by another self' (*BI*, 95–6). In his resistant reading of Georges Poulet – one that displaces Poulet's phenomenology with the ironic scepticism of the deconstructive Picaro – de Man not only discovers another means of usurping the real self with another self, but a way of questioning the very concept of any self:

> But how are we to understand a movement which allows for a superior or 'deeper' self to take the place of an actual self, in accordance with a scheme of which the encounter between author and critic was only the symbolic prefiguration? . . . Nevertheless, this relationship exists first of all in the form of a radical questioning of the actual, given self, extending to the point of annihilation. . . . What was here being described as a relationship between two subjects designates in fact the relationship between a subject and the literary language it produces. (*BI*, 98)[10]

We need to inquire into why de Man has proposed an ideology of reading that eschews personality, representation, narrative, history, and author. Why must the origins of a writer's intellectual and psychological contexts be discarded? Why must we seek arcane explanations when, following Occam's Razor, more simple explanations would be helpful? Thus, in the de Manian mode of finding in critics he admires qualities which are more indigenous to his own work than the critic's on whom he is writing, Poulet's project is described in terms which really describe de Man's own:

> The unity of his thought exists on the ontological and on the methodological level, not with regard to history. Since he conceives of literature as an externally repeated sequence of new beginnings, no meaningful relationship can exist between the particularized narrative that traces the itinerary of a writer *ab ovo* and the collective narrative that aims to describe the cumulative movement of history. Some historical articulations can be described as if they were collective *moments de passage*, altogether similar in structure to the points of departure of an individual *cogito*. But the historical framework is kept only as a principle of classification without intrinsic significance. (*BI*, 90)

De Man's *Blindness and Insight* calls into question the concepts of representation, presence, signified self, and history, and insists that it is *better* for literature and criticism to move beyond those concepts. It seems desirable to find literature that has an 'allegorical style' which he characterizes as 'the absence of any reference to an exterior reality of which it would be the sign' (*BI*, 174); in other words, allegory always displaces narrative: 'All representational poetry is always allegorical, whether it be aware of it or not, and the allegorical power of the language undermines and obscures the specific literal meaning of a representation open to understanding' (*BI*, 185). Perhaps in the context of what we now know we can understand de Man's compulsion to reject history 'as a generative process' and to speak snidely of 'history as a temporal hierarchy that resembles a parental structure in which the past is like an ancestor begetting, in a moment of unmediated presence, a future capable of repeating in its turn the same generative process' (*BI*, 164). Do we not think of de Man's relationship to traditional criticism when he defines the relationship between modernity and history? 'Modernity and history relate to each other in a curiously contradictory way that goes beyond antithesis or opposition. If history is not to become sheer regression or paralysis, it depends on modernity for its duration and renewal; but modernity cannot assert itself without being at once swallowed up and reintegrated into a regressive historical process' (*BI*, 151).

In 'Semiology and Rhetoric?', originally written in 1973 and later used as the opening chapter of *Allegories of Reading* (1979), de Man mocks the effort to reconcile the claims of formalism with the demands of attending to mimesis:

> By an awareness of the arbitrariness of the sign (Saussure) and of literature as an autotelic statement 'focused on the way it is expressed' (Jakobsen), the entire question of meaning can be bracketed, thus freeing critical discourse from the debilitating burden of paraphrase. The demystifing power of semiology, within the context of French historical and thematic criticism, has been considerable. It demonstrated that the perception of the literary dimensions of language is largely obscured if one submits to the authority of reference. It is also revealed how tenaciously this authority continues to assert itself in a variety of disguises, ranging from the crudest ideology to the most refined forms of aesthetic and ethical judgment. It especially exploded the myth of semantic correspondence between sign and referent. . . . (*AR*, 5)

But what does it mean for de Man to turn his back on history and mimesis in the name of either a kind of critical modernism, or of impersonality, or of allegory? If in the following passage, we substitute 'deconstruction' for 'modernity' – an apt substitution since deconstruction has become a metonymy for critical modernism – we see how prophetic de Man is, for when writing of Nietzsche is he not describing his own plight? 'Considered as a principle of life, modernity becomes a principle of origination and turns at once into a generative power that is itself historical. It becomes impossible to overcome history in the name of life or to forget the past in the name of modernity, because both are linked by a temporal chain that gives them a common destiny' (*BI*, 150). For 'life' in de Man's reading of Nietzsche in the above passage, might we not substitute the 'free play of signifiers'? How prophetic, too, for him to have written, '[T]he writer's language is to some degree the product of his own action; he is both the historian and the agent of his own language. The ambivalence of writing is such that it can be considered both as an act and an interpretive process that follows after an act with which it can coincide' (*BI*, 152).

Does de Man not force texts to expel their historical contexts? Reading Nietzsche's *Second Discourse on the Origins of Inequality*, he applauds Nietzsche's insight – or assertion – that 'the most important and most original of experiences' are when we 'experience life in a nonhistorical way'. De Man glosses the foregoing passage: 'Moments of genuine humanity thus are moments at which all anteriority vanishes, annihilated by the power of an absolute forgetting' (147). Yet, although his sense of tradition is idiosyncratic and privileges those texts that undermine the imitation of exterior reality, concepts of coherent self, and organic texts, de Man is a writer for whom past writers are the subject and the catalyst.

In *Allegories of Reading*, de Man uses a variety of European texts by Rousseau, Nietzsche, Rilke, and Proust to propose a general theory of reading, a theory which calls into question such staples of traditional criticism as unity, meaning, intention, and authorially-created structures of affects. Indeed, he proposes deconstruction as a philosophy which calls into question Western concepts of self, love, man, and voice as they are perceived linguistically. As a deconstructive Picaro, a kind of hyperintellectual Andy Warhol, he attacks accepted concepts of meaning, morality, authors, and history. He reads each of his texts as if they were created by de Man for his theories and finds in them – surprise – evidence of early pre-Derridean and deconstructive readings. For de Man meaning is impossible because one can always find inconsistencies in the relationship between grammar and rhetoric; furthermore, the persuasive aspect of rhetoric always undermines the rhetoric as a system of tropes: 'Considered as persuasion, rhetoric is performative but when considered as a system of tropes, it deconstructs its own performance. Rhetoric is a *text* in that it allows for two incompatible, mutually self-destructive points of view, and therefore puts an insurmountable obstacle in the way of any reading or understanding' (*AR*, 131).

Wherever de Man begins and however brilliant his critical journey, the conclusion is always the same: language does not mean and our belief in authors, themes, values and history is an illusion: 'Allegorical narratives tell the story of the failure to read whereas tropological narratives ... tell the story of the failure to denominate. The difference is only a difference of degree and the allegory does not erase the figure. Allegories are always allegories of metaphor and as such, they are always allegories of the impossibility of reading' (*AR*, 205). It is almost as if the allegorical were a necessary but regrettable component of reading:

> Allegories are always ethical, the term ethical designating the structural interference of two distinct value systems. In this sense, ethics has nothing to do with the will (thwarted or free) of a subject, nor *a fortiori*, with a relationship between subjects. The ethical category is imperative (i.e., a category rather than a value) to the extent it is linguistic and not subjective. Morality is a version of the same language aporia that gave rise to such concepts as 'man' or 'love' or 'self', and not the cause or consequence of such concepts.... [E]thics (or, one should say, ethicity) is a discursive mode among others. (*AR*, 206)

By freeing the 'ethical' from the conduct and will of the subject or author, isn't he creating a code by which to exonerate himself? Because we judge human behaviour according to values and standards, I would argue that the ethical becomes a privileged referential category, not merely another system of structures or tropes. But de Man's basic point is that nothing is what it seems, and that there is always a hidden text that undoes any reading. Thus, as we read, we can never find positional assurance; in de Man's world there are only paradoxes and aporias. And he seems to revel in this epistemological quandary which he uncovers everywhere: 'Deconstructions of figural texts engender lucid narratives which produce, in their turn and as it were within their own texture, a darkness more redoubtable than the error they dispel' (*AR*, 217). It is as if figuring out how to escape from values, meaning and self were a kind of intellectual triumph.

What is the relation between de Man's scepticism about reading and knowing, his reduction of all texts to one homogenized text, and his own prior conduct? For de Man, the responsible agent for a text – or action – is submerged under a welter of complex, convoluted paradoxes. Reading becomes a kind of magic show or shell game where nothing is what it appears. According to de Man the activity of reading had to do with recognizing the multiple possibilities and aporias generated by the tropes: 'Rhetoric radically suspends logic and opens up vertiginous possibilities of referential aberration.... I would not hesitate to equate the rhetorical, figural potentiality of language with literature itself' (*AR*, 10). Does not de Man make the error of equating the rhetorical, figurative potential of language with *language* itself? Isn't that basic metonymic substitution at the heart of his method? If one refuses to accept de Man's first principles, if one believes that language can be at times more or less determinate and that we recuperate character and action in terms of a mimetic code, then we cannot accept his basic argument.

My questions: Why do we need to focus on the structure of figurative language to the exclusion of meaning? Does so-called 'rigor' mean the exclusion of questions of values and referentiality? Is criticism not a search for meaning and an effort to place that meaning in a cultural context or is it, as de Man argues, 'the deconstruction of literature, the reduction to the rigors of grammar of rhetorical mystification' (*AR*, 17)? De Man never takes account of the narrative integrity of a work and that is the aspect of a work that requires memory to understand it; put another way, to deny narrative is in a way to deny memory and reality. Or, as Freud puts it,

[S]atisfaction is obtained from illusions, which are recognized as such without the discrepancy between them and reality being allowed to interfere with enjoyment. The region from which these illusions arise is the life of the imagination. . . . Another procedure operates more energetically and more thoroughly, it regards reality as the sole enemy and as the source of all suffering with which it is impossible to live, so that one must break off all relations with it if one is to be in any way happy. The hermit turns his back on the world and will have no truck with it. But one can do more than that; one can try to re-create the world, to build up in its stead another world in which its most unbearable features are eliminated and replaced by others that are in conformity with one's own wishes.[11]

VI.   THE RETURN TO PHILOLOGY: DE MAN'S LATER STYLE

What we need to do, I am arguing, is to reread de Man's work in view of the historical knowledge we now have. Isn't that the very essence of the scholarly method, to reform our hypotheses in light of new data? For a man who can be so careful in his local distinctions that it is difficult to follow the conception and argument, is not the conclusion to the brilliant essay 'Intentional

Structure of the Romantic Image' another instance of the sudden
introduction of language that has politically apocalyptic overtones?
'We are only beginning to understand how this oscillation in the
status of the image is linked to the *crisis* that leaves the poetry of
today under a steady *threat* of extinction, although, on the other
hand, it remains the depository of hopes that no other activity of
the mind seems able to offer' (my italics).[12] I would tentatively
raise question about the style of de Man's postwar writings: why
does he import into his literary work – work, after all, remote from
the external world and having its own self-conscious metonymic
textuality – the language of politics, combat, and police? He seems
to have a bent for speaking in facetious terms of 'manifestoes for
critical terrorism', and 'mobilization against a common enemy'.

For example, in the second chapter of *The Resistance to Theory* – a
chapter entitled 'The Return to Philology' – he draws upon military
and political tropes to describe differences between opposing
viewpoints in recent critical discussion. Even if used ironically,
phrases such as 'troublemakers', 'critical terrorism', 'matter for
law-enforcement' and images that suggest positions 'under fire' –
indeed even the necessity to 'shoot back' – give the sense of a
beleaguered figure who has displaced political conflict into the
academic arena and who enjoys describing parochial critical differences in terms of policing and imposing authority. Surely, his
rhetoric in some ways is far more excessive than the rhetoric of
Walter Jackson Bate to whom he is responding.

For de Man, what he calls the 'Return to Philology' is a return to
a position where professors of the humanities can no longer claim
that literature teaches us how to be moral human beings. He
ironically invokes the image of an absolute humanist who is
threatened by the return to philology because he believes that his
mission is under siege: 'The professor of literature has good
reasons to feel appeased; his scientific conscience is satisfied by the
positive rigor of his linguistic and historical knowledge, while his
moral, political and (in the extensive sense) religious conscience is
assuaged by the application of this knowledge to the understanding of the world, of society and of the self' (*RT*, 22). It is as if
the humanist has replaced the Jew in his psyche; he concludes,
'[T]hose who refuse the crime of theoretical ruthlessness can no
longer hope to gain a good conscience. Neither, of course, can the
theorists – but, then, they never laid claim to it in the first place'
(*RT*, 26).

While we are told by some of de Man's defenders that his deconstruction is an 'autocritique', do we not see in de Man's syntax and diction – his rhetoricity – a need to control opposition and impose order?

We may no longer be hearing very much about relevance, but we do continue to hear a great deal about reference, about the nonverbal 'outside' to which language refers, by which it is conditioned, and upon which it acts. The stress falls not so much on the fictional status of literature – a property now perhaps somewhat too easily taken for granted – but on the interplay between these fictions and categories that are said to partake of reality, such as the self, man, and society, 'the artist, his culture, and human community,' . . . *With the internal law and order of literature well policed*, we can now confidently devote ourselves to the foreign affairs, the *external politics of literature*. Not only do we feel able to do so, but we also think we owe it to ourselves to take this step; our moral conscience would not allow us to do otherwise. (*AR*, 3; my italics)

In this dismissive and sarcastic passage – and its use of the kind of globalizing rhetoric, replete with images that evoke nation-states as presences shaping the destiny of their denizens – do we not feel traces of the passages I have cited from his earlier wartime writing? When in the opening piece of *Blindness and Insight*, a piece entitled 'Criticism and Crisis', he describes the 'polemical violence' of critical debate and 'crisis aspect of the [critical] situation', should we not realize that the trace of his political past is shadowing these phrases (*BI*, 5, 3)? And what do we now make of the following sentences from the same piece?

We can invoke the authority of the best historians to point out that what was considered a crisis in the past often turns out to be a mere ripple, that changes first experienced as upheavals tend to become absorbed in the continuity of much slower move-ments as soon as the temporal perspective broadens. . . . It can always be shown, on all levels of experience, that what other people experience as a crisis is perhaps not even a change; such observations depend, to a very large extent on the standpoint of the observer. (*BI*, 5–6)

As trained readers, must we not read such passages with grim irony in the context of the entire narrative of de Man's life *and* the text of his writings? Must we not also note how much belief he has in the most sweeping generalizations – 'It can always be shown, on all levels of experience' – that depend on complete faith in the metaphysics of presence?

Let me consider another striking stylistic point of de Man's later work: Why does he often begin an essay by proposing issues in the clearest terms – often an echo of his youthful master style, including heavy doses of irony and sarcasm – and then, without finding a middle level of discourse, move to the most difficult and tortured logic and diction which is only fully accessible to insiders and cognoscenti? It is as if his psyche needs to evoke a shadow of that traumatic past in his syntax and imagery, only to suppress and displace it as the essay continues; his texts trope his later silence and suppression by their failure to include a middle level of discourse linking the broad and even crude generalizations of the openings with the abstruse and convoluted analysis that follows as well as by a conscious or unconscious strategy of evasion and obscurity.

What I am arguing is that some of de Man's later pieces recapitulate linguistically the history of his life, including his inability to be present to the consequences of his own past. Moreover, should we not wonder aloud if displaced and repressed guilt did not play a role in de Man's desperate search for an alternative vocabulary to the organicist one that he used in his Darwinian stage – the stage when he argued for, or, rather, crassly assumed, the evolution of nations and literature in the most simplistic terms? We recall how the Nazis adapted Darwin to their own purposes. Isn't the de Man narrative in part the story of a search for the *essential* totalizing language with which to master literature and the alternative story of the search to find the names of things – anything? But isn't this double quest – Platonic and Aristotelian, conceptual and nominalistic – related to a repressed history of a person who once befouled language, once used it instrumentally to further his career, and whose younger self revelled in his wartime role of precocious cultural critic without taking responsibility for creating a poisonous atmosphere?

In both his Nazi and later deconstructive phases, de Man participated in a collective effort to separate language from the events that produce it and from what it signifies. In the case of his views on Jews, de Man's language has almost a zero truth-content, and yet its rhetoricity performs a dance upon anterior reality that becomes an important strand of the reality of his text. Do the conclusions about language come from the texts de Man examines or does he impose them from without? The rhetorical performance of his signifiers unattached to anterior reality but conjoined to a context of language became the very basis of referential meaning on which historical events were structured because he wilfully appropriated language to shape history. Language speaks as he directs it to and in his early stage – if not the later, too, at times – it speaks *lies*.

Beneath the surface of de Man's later prose is a deep despair approaching nihilism. Even the aphoristic and oracular style is a way of controlling the dark vision that, like an underground stream, always threatens to erupt above ground. At times it is as if his style struggles to control the underlying gloom of his vision, only to be overcome by sudden leaps of despair. Thus, writing on the Nietzsche essay *On Truth and Lie in an Extra-Moral Sense*, he comments:

It shows, for example, that the idea of individuation, of the human subject as a privileged viewpoint, is a mere metaphor by means of which man protects himself from his insignificance by forcing his own interpretation of the world upon the entire universe, substituting a human-centered set of meanings that is reassuring to his vanity for a set of meanings that reduces him to being a transitory accident in the cosmic order. The metaphorical substitution is aberrant but no human self could come into being without this error. Faced with the truth of its nonexistence, the self would be consumed as an insect is consumed by the flame that attracts it. (*AR*, 111)

His desire to minimize humans to a 'transitory accident' recalls the rhetoric of religious zealots who privilege the hereafter and minimize the present. Do we not understand why de Man has such a stake – a compulsion – to set aside prior definitions of human consciousness and reduce good and evil, truth and lies, to the same linguistic plane?

De Man's aphoristic style, combined with his speaking in a language that depends not merely on accepting his first principles but also on being privy to the particular jargon of his cult, gives him an ineffable presence within his work. It is as if he alone has heard the Holy Word and can deliver it to his followers. And the self-created presence resists his past, resists in the Freudian sense of defensively rejecting and denying crucial information to the restoration of a healthy and coherent self. What de Man suppresses is not only his *story* – with the pun on *history* – but all stories; for in his criticism he rarely considers what happens next in a text or why. And in suppressing story, he suppresses memory. But at what price? For when we read de Man we feel the absence of wonder, of innocence, and playfulness and we realize that the child which should be father of even the most mature man – to use a pun once favoured by his followers, *de Man* – has been displaced in some remote place and time. Finally, has not our narrative come full circle and let us see that the refugee from his past and from himself, the marginalized outsider deprived of ethical bearings, the figure of the wandering Jew beset by shame and guilt – even if unacknowledged to himself – is none other than de Man himself?

VII.   CONCLUSION

It has been claimed, by Norris and others, that de Man's later work was a criticism of his earlier work and a recognition of the need to take account of history, but I find little evidence for that view. Even if de Man made his mistakes as a young man – his silence about his life's anterior reality was *committed* as a mature adult and he had ample opportunity to speak of his past errors and to speak of his personal crises of values and the memories that haunted him. The *suppression* of information was not an event of his younger days. If autocritique is an elegant form of self-criticism, and confession a vulgar one, then this was an occasion when vulgarity was called for.

As a Jew and English teacher who has read and admired de Man's work, I *need* to conclude my narrative with an imaginative rebuke to de Man: 'You have taught us that language was polysemous, and we participate in the free play of signifiers; ah, yes, Professor de Man, but did you not, while writing as a young man in the European master style, fall into the error of believing you could evoke a metaphysics of presence? Indeed, did you not do this while globalizing about an entire people? A people who were at that very moment the victims of genocide? And what if that bit of thematizing contributed to racial hatred? What if it affected readers to support such policies promulgated by the Nazi occupying forces and their collaborators? Did you not write in the belief that such historical generalizations and conceptual formulation were the very stuff of intellectual discourse? Professor de Man, what kind of *man* could have written such articles about a people and disguised race hatred in the guise of reasonable intellectual argument? Was it the same *man* who tells us that language does not represent human life in action, that it is only itself and does not language mean in any real sense?'

Isn't what George Kennan wrote of those who repress their shameful political past – in this case, he is speaking of Stalinists not Nazis – applicable to de Man's narrative?

> What is not so often understood is that this capacity for repression of memory can be easily transferred from the individual's sense of responsibility for his own conduct to the behavior of a political collectivity into whose hands he has committed his confidence and loyalty.... [H]ere the moral responsibility is shifted to someone else.... And if it turned out that what the Party required to be done, whether by oneself or others, involved apparent injustice or cruelty – well, one might regret that it was found necessary; one might wish that it could be otherwise. But it was not one's own responsibility; and one was justified in later years – was one not? – in pushing the memory of it back into those dim precincts of forgetfulness that already veiled so many other evidences of man's savagery and nastiness, so many other evidences of the triumph (momentary and unavoidable, of course) of the best over his tragic cousin, the saint.[13]

It was Orwell, responding to the Communist Party's attempt to control thought by manipulating language, who stressed how the abuse of language precedes the abuse of power. No matter how well-meaning, it does violence to say, as some deconstructionists seem to imply, that the Holocaust was a 'problem in rhetoric'. To say this is either a bizarre misconception about the relative importance of writing versus action or a moral crime against real people who have died – a moral crime committed in the name of enlightenment and intellectual 'rigor' by those who think they are on the frontier of linguistic and literary study. This kind of reverse recuperation or naturalizing, where everything is wilfully perceived and resolved on a flat linguistic plane, is not merely ahistorical but ahumanistic. It is ahumanistic in its callous disregard that language is written and spoken by humans about humans and for humans, and that language catches our attention most when its content represents humans. It is because we want to know how others think, plan, behave – including how they use and abuse language, how their psyche responds to their acknowledged and repressed past – that we read. Should we not use our models of close reading of texts to learn how to read lives, including our own? As we profess literature, should we not suggest the continuity between reading texts and reading lives?

Notes

1. See Chapter 2.
2. I have used the following abbreviations for de Man's works: *BI* for *Blindness and Insight: Essays in the Rhetoric of Contemporary Criticism* (New York: Oxford University Press, 1971); *AR* for *Allegories of Reading: Figural Language in Rousseau, Nietzsche, Rilke and Proust* (New Haven: Yale University Press, 1979); *RT* for *The Resistance to Theory* (Minneapolis: University of Minnesota Press, 1986). The early pieces appear in *Wartime Journalism 1939–43*, eds Werner Hamacher, Neil Hertz, and Thomas Keenan (Lincoln and London: University of Nebraska Press, 1988), which I abbreviate as *WJ*.
3. Hayden White, 'The Value of Narrativity in the Representation of Reality', in *On Narrative*, ed. W. J. T. Mitchell (Chicago: University of Chicago Press, 1981), pp. 1–2.
4. It now seems de Man wrote over 290 articles and reviews for various publications between 1939 and 1943, but most of his pieces were for *Le Soir* when it was a collaborationist newspaper.
5. The recent volume, *Responses on Paul de Man's Wartime Journalism*, ed. Werner Hamacher, Neil Hertz, and Thomas Keenan (Lincoln and London: University of Nebraska, 1989), contains responses by a wide range of critics and scholars, most – but not all – of whom are, from an ideological standpoint, followers of de Man or, at the very least, sympathetic to de Man's later ideology of reading.

    Many of the essays are written by apologists who employ a bizarre logic by which the arguments of de Man's later work are supposed to cast aside the sentiments of the wartime pieces and/or engage in a rhetoric of insult that denigrates those who feel that de Man's reputation has been tarnished by these revelations. On the whole, these essays propose a wilful misreading of the possibility that there might be a connection between de Man's earlier life and his later writings. Yet, given that we always read texts in terms of patterns and we train our students to do so, isn't this rather odd? Many of the essays apologizing for de Man's behaviour deconstruct themselves, as if they could unweave by logical leaps at night the indicting evidence – often deriving, as in the pieces by Alice Yaeger Kaplan, Edouard Colinet and Ortwin de Graef, from important historical knowledge – that they weave by the light of day.

Among those contributors whose pieces address what I am identifying as the central issues are Sandor Goodheart, Alexander Gelley, and William Flesch as well as Kaplan's. For me, the effect of a complete reading of the diverse essays in *Responses* is to further implicate de Man as someone deeply engaged in defining a collaborationist culture and defending Belgian fascism as well as the values of German Nazism. Kaplan, in particular, shows how de Man's writing supported fascism and participated in the process of legitimizing anti-Semitism. The argument of several apologists that he could have done worse carries little weight. In my judgement, Paul de Man did enough to deserve severe condemnation.

6. Irene Salusinsky, *Criticism in Society* (New York, 1987), p. 222.

7. For other responses to Derrida's essay, see *Critical Inquiry* 15:4 (summer 1989). See the eloquent and convincing pieces by Marjorie Perloff and W. Wolfgang Holdheim.

8. 'Paul de Man's Past', *The London Review of Books* 10:3 (4 February 1988), pp. 7–11.

9. 'Freud and the Sandman', in *Textual Strategies*, ed. Josue Harari (New York: Cornell University Press, 1979), p. 301.

10. I have discussed my understanding of Poulet's phenomenology in Chapter 10 of my *The Humanistic Heritage: Critical Theories of the English Novel from James to Hillis Miller* (Philadelphia: University of Pennsylvania Press, 1986).

11. Sigmund Freud, *Civilization and its Discontents*, trans. James Strachey (New York, 1962).

12. *Romanticism and Consciousness*, ed. Harold Bloom (New York: Norton, 1970), p. 77.

13. George Kennan, 'The Buried Past', *The New York Review of Books* 35:16, p. 6.

5

Towards a Humanistic Poetics: Challenges and Contributions

Let us review our humanistic poetics before turning to recent critical theoretical studies. Without neglecting formal considerations such as voice, genre, narrative structure, and linguistic patterns, humanistic critics focus on the dialogue between the anterior or real world and the imaginative world of fictions as well as upon the author's creative process and how that is shaped by the historical period in which he or she wrote. They stress the mimetic quality of literature and insist that literature is by human authors, about human actions, and for human readers. They believe that readers and text meet at the seam of reading. These critics believe that a) the form of a literary text – style, structure, narrative technique – expresses its value system; b) a literary text is a creative gesture of the author and the result of historical context; c) a literary text imitates a world that precedes it; d) literary texts usually address how and why people behave – what they do, desire, fear, doubt, and need. Humanism does not mean 'life-affirming', but concern with how and why people live, think, act, feel, read, write, and speak. While acknowledging variations in the diverse responses of readers, humanistic criticism believes that there is the possibility of approaching a determinate meaning by studying an author, his period, and his canon. Thus humanistic criticism does not accept the tenets of deconstruction, that 'there is nothing outside the text' and that literary texts are 'the free play of signifiers'.

To be sure, the Arnoldian tradition of moral seriousness informs the humanistic ideology of reading, but does that mean that each reading depends on isolating themes, or validating conservative values, or upon monolithic one-dimensional readings that are indifferent to ambiguities and multiple possibilities? Not at all. The focus of humanistic criticism is how people live in all their personal and cultural diversity; this encompasses the various hypotheses (philosophical, psychological, linguistic, socio-economic, and historical) for explaining how and why people behave, including their propensity for supernatural explanations – most notably but not exclusively theological ones. An enlightened humanistic poetics need not be labelled conservative, for its emphasis on mimesis of anterior reality includes feminism, Marxism, and minority studies. Indeed, New Historicism and feminist criticism have helped reestablish the validity of representation.

Humanistic criticism acknowledges the presence, individuality, and personality of the critic, even while trying to use an empirical evidentiary test when presenting readings or arguments. While striving for an objectivity that depends upon shared perceptions among readers – an objectivity that goes beyond subjectivity – the humanistic critic eschews self-effacement and the pretence of *absolute* objectivity and situates himself or herself as self-dramatizing subject and is self-aware of his or her values and principles. A humanistic criticism is aware of man's limitations and foibles – including those of the critic – but values the uniqueness of the individual as author, subject, and reader. The humanistic critic values lucidity and direct speech and writing and avoids obscurity and obscurantism, for he/she knows that if we invent arcane language, we will insulate ourselves from affecting the culture of which we are a part. The humanistic critic feels an obligation to write and speak in language that is accessible to literate adults. She or he values rationalism and openmindedness, probing questions and exploratory answers, pluralism over polemics, the mind at play over pontificating; he or she is sceptical of authoritarianism, including citing prior theorists as if they were apostolic figures, rather than as other humans holding their own opinions.

In the current Balkanization of the profession of teaching literature, the diverse interpretive communities disagree on the evidentiary test for argument; this makes it all the more difficult to discuss our differences. We cannot discredit another person's hypothesis by experimentation as if we could test our readings like we can test cold fusion in a jar. Perhaps anxiety about our inability to establish the accuracy and truth of our work by the agreed-upon evidentiary tests is the reason for vituperative attacks against the work of others. Definitions of liberal and conservative have become muddled; to respect the integrity of the text, to believe that the act of reading and teaching should approach the conscious or unconscious purpose of the text; to believe that it is the function of literary criticism to make difficult texts accessible by examining the text for the relationship between form and content is to be labelled a conservative or an old-fashioned humanist. Yet should we not continue to value the humanistic liberal intellectual who values tolerance, openmindedness, clarity, responsiveness to and respect for the points of view of others? Should we not value a pluralism that values diversity and tolerance?

The issues that face those who believe that there is much worth retaining in traditional studies are: how to preserve the most valuable aspects of the canon in the face of legitimate claims for canon revision by those who had previously been marginalized, particularly women and blacks. How does one continue to teach the major British and American writers when half the faculty is engaged in theoretical and ethnic studies? If major writers are taught from the enriching standpoint of resistant readings – be they Marxist, New Historicist, feminist or gay – do we not still need alternative courses that respect the author's intended meaning or, better yet, dialogic courses that respect both authorial and resistant readings and the work of diverse interpretative communities? How can we talk about representation of an anterior reality without falling into naive equations about art and life? Should we necessarily accept absolute differences between the discussion of poetry and fiction, or do we recuperate meaning in similar ways?

I

Because humanistic criticism has been often maligned as a kind of disguised conservatism that blindly embraces New Criticism and is resistant to canon reformation, let us discuss John Paul Russo's fine book on I. A. Richards (*I. A. Richards: His Life and Work* [Baltimore: Johns Hopkins University Press, 1989]) – who holds an honoured place in the humanistic pantheon – by defining the principles and values of a contemporary humanistic aesthetic. If we are to understand the foundation of a humanistic poetics, we need to understand the work of I. A. Richards. Richards did much to contribute to the tradition of close reading *and* to the tradition that we read closely to know about a world beyond ourselves. Richards believed in close reading as an essential activity for improving the quality of the mind. As Russo puts it, Richards believed that 'If we could learn more about how a poem works, we would know more about how the mind works – and this was the point – how to assess and rank its possibilities in terms of growth, power, capaciousness, and control. Poetry was capable of saving us with the help of science' (91–2). In his early years, Richards believed in science and progress and believed that he could discover scientific methods of literary analysis and improve the act of reading. Poems make 'distorted references' or 'pseudo-statements' as opposed to empirically verifiable statements. In Russo's words, 'They are "distorted" because they have pulled into emotionally charged, tonally complex systems that refract appearances, twist purposes, and subsume local meanings into other, larger ones. They are "pseudo" because they only seem to make assertions in the same ways scientific references do' (239). How a poem worked was important because it enabled us to see the various ways it means. While Richards was influential in literary theory, in his most important study, *Practical Criticism* (1929), theory was subservient to practice. With its full and minute detail, its stress on figurative language and its ability to synthesize diverse strands of meaning into an organic whole, its responsiveness to tone and speaker, its mastery of rhythm and metre as an integral source of meaning, Richard's method of close reading was appropriate to the ambiguities, innovation, complexities, fragmentation, and seeming obscurity not only of modernist poetry but to the stylistic experimentation of modern fiction. Indeed Richards' method had much to do with the increased critical attention given to modern literature in the subsequent two decades – at a time before major biographies, collections of letters, standard editions, domesticated high modernism into the canon.

Richards, like Arnold and Leavis, believed in what literature can do for society; in that sense, they have links to the English utilitarian tradition of Bentham and Mill. As Russo puts it, Richards believed 'that the immensely rich and varied body of world literature must be restudied and absorbed, not by the few, but by the many, and at a far deeper level of linguistic comprehension, for its emotional and intellectual insight, its discord and harmony, its internal debate over central themes' (91). Given that Arnold was a major influence upon Richards, it is not surprising that Richards inherited a good many nineteenth-century beliefs about how the world was ordered and how each of us could affect it; although an atheist, he believed in the possibility of man's improvement – but for him man's improvement depended on his capacity for rational behaviour and his questing intelligence; he believed that each of us had the potential for growth and that mankind could progress if he used his intelligence. He believed that men share what Wallace Stevens called a rage for order, and that we respond to patterns and meaning in literature in our search for coherence in life.

As M. H. Abrams noticed in 'The Mirror and the Lamp' in *Coleridge on Imagination*, Richards knowingly brings a Benthamite and associationist perspective to Coleridge's idealism. Indeed, in considering Richards' influence in proposing a formal criticism which broke radically with narrow philological studies, textual scholarship and editing, belletristic impressionism, and naive kinds of autobiographical criticism which algebraically equate the characters of a literary work with the author's life, we must not forget that he understood that each critic expressed a sense of his own values and that any pretence of objectivity was necessarily an overstatement: 'The critic cannot possibly avoid using some ideas about value. His whole preoccupation is an application and exercise of his ideas on the subject, and an avoidance of moral preoccupations on his part can only be either an abdication or a rejection under the title of "morality" of what he considers to be mistaken or dishonest ideas and methods' (*Principles of Literary Criticism* [1925], 35).

It may be that no one work of Richards compares to the most profound and complex studies of Kenneth Burke or has been absorbed into the way we think and teach to the degree of, say, Booth's *The Rhetoric of Fiction*, and that Richards never achieved the mastery of a period or a canon in the manner of M. H. Abrams – who was once his student at Cambridge. But there can be no doubt that *Principles of Literary Criticism* and, even more profoundly *Practical Criticism* – based on his teaching in 1925, 1927, 1928 – were seminal works in the creation of the humanistic ideology that dominated literary criticism until the mid-1970s. Unlike deconstructionists like de Man, Richards never separated hermeneutics – what things mean – from what de Man calls rhetoric – the study of tropes and figures: indeed he understood rhetoric in the Aristotelian sense of how words persuade, i.e. what they do. He provided a methodology and a vocabulary for converting Arnold's idealism about the function of literature and criticism into practice. While Arnold could only quote lines to show what he meant by 'poetic truth and poetic beauty' or 'the accent of high seriousness',

Richards developed a methodology which provided empirical evidence to support his hypotheses.

Although his associationist psychology has been substantially discredited and few now take seriously his programme for an 850-word basic English, his influence has been immense. Richards was a crucial influence on Empson, F. R. Leavis (who, characteristically, subsequently found much to disparage in Richards), and the American New Critics. As Russo notes, while 'Empson developed the linguistic, technical, and methodological lines of Richards' thought, F. R. Leavis pursued its educational, social, and moral themes and expanded a few key ideas into an original reinterpretation of literary history' (534). Because Richards focuses on what language *does* as well as what it *is*, he also influenced the Chicago Aristotelians – although Russo fails to mention that important strain of influence. Thus Wayne Booth quotes him in epigraphs to Part One and Part Three of *The Company We Keep: An Ethics of Reading*.

It is ironic that Russo's splendid biography enables us to see Richards' work in the very personal, social, and historical context that Richards' method eschewed in his paradigmatic text, *Practical Criticism*. Perhaps we should rethink the need to understand authors and the historical context which produced them. Indeed, as Russo shows us, perhaps we need consider the entire concept of the biographical fallacy and consider how much more we learn when we know about the author as well as the period in which he wrote. Do we not need to understand the authorial presence to which we respond in a text as metaphor for the actual author?

Just as we have come to understand de Man's formalism by using the historical and biographical contextualism that he – in his postwar years – rejected, Russo's contextual work helps us to understand Richards' formalism. But in strong contrast to de Man, Richards' life and work have a moral consistency and intellectual continuity that bespeaks the integrity of his mind: 'Sincerity – the feeling that comes from speaking the truth, the deepening sense of inner coherence and stability – held', as Russo puts it, 'as high a place in Richards' life as in his criticism. . . . [I]n the oldest tradition of humanism, his theory directed readers outside themselves and to the text: to the "sense", "feeling", and "intention" of writers who set the standard of sincerity' (356).

Russo has written a learned and elegant study, one that takes into account major strands of twentieth-century criticism. He understands the ambiguities in Richards' work. He has read widely in the history of criticism and theory, although he is not as fully conversant with the history of Anglo-American fiction criticism as he might be. For example, with the possible exception of Booth's *The Rhetoric of Fiction* (1961), the most important work of postwar fiction criticism in terms of how it shaped the reading, teaching, and professional critical community was Dorothy Van Ghent's *The English Novel: Form and Function* (1953). Russo fails to mention either. Van Ghent's central tenet that a novel is 'the idea embodied in the cosmology', recalls a crucial statement in Richards' *Principles of Literary Criticism:* 'To make the work "embody," accord with, and represent the precise experience upon which its value depends is the [artist's] major preoccupation, in difficult cases an overmastering preoccupation' (*Principles of Literary Criticism*, 26). Following Richards, Van Ghent believed that aesthetic experience was not so different from other kinds of experience. Like Richards, she advanced claims for studying how the content was dependent on technique, while insisting that the quality of an author's vision was a legitimate aesthetic standard.

On the whole, Russo's readable and often elegant study justifies its vast length. But at times one wishes for a shorter, more succinct version that did less with Richards' later years and left out digressions referring to how other critics regard and even *might regard* Richards. Thus he places Richards' work synchronically in the context of current critical debate, as when he tests Richards' concepts of belief and sincerity with 'an Adornian critique' (352): 'Any reappraisal of Richards on belief and authenticity should take into account Theodor Adorno's Hegelian–Marxist critique of inwardness and authenticity' (351). Maybe – but whether such digressions are necessary or useful is debatable. But we should, I think, express our gratitude for Russo's splendid biography, which helps us to appreciate Richards' generous spirit, energy, immense learning, and probing intellectual curiosity.

II

For the past three decades, a major voice in critical theory has been that of Wayne C. Booth, the most influential of the Chicago Neo-Aristotelians – a group whose leaders included both his mentor, R. S. Crane, and Richard McKeon. While I have discussed Booth's achievement in *The Humanistic Heritage: Critical Theories of the English Novel from James to Hillis Miller* (University of Pennsylvania Press, 1986), it is worth reviewing the scope of his work if only for a few sentences. What he has done in a series of important books – most notably, *The Rhetoric of Fiction* (1961), *A Rhetoric of Irony* (1974) and *Critical Understanding: The Power and Limits of Pluralism* (1979) – is provide a theoretical model which allows for considering how literary texts shape an audience. Booth insists that an author affects the reader as the author intends, and communicates human emotions and values to an audience; the reader in turn responds to the implied author or felt presence within the text. Booth believes that each book teaches us how to read it and that we must eschew universal standards for a pluralistic credo which enables us to respond to each text according to its aesthetic and moral assumptions. He is perceived as a defender of the legitimacy of what we now call authorial readings, readings that try to discover what formal and representational principles are created by the author. Authorial readers believe that the text was created for a particular purpose at a particular time; the reader, by responding to the plot, genre, language, voice and characters, can appoach the realized intention of the author. As Booth puts it in *The Rhetoric of Fiction:* 'Nothing is real for the reader until the author makes it so, and it is for the reader that the author chooses to make [a] scene as powerful as possible' (*RF*, 108). In that book, he teaches us how authors build 'aesthetic form . . . out of patterned emotions as well as out of other materials', and, by example, teaches us how to locate and define the implied author in individual works (*RF*, 248). By contrast, resistant readers respond in terms of their own perspectives and create their own texts.

Booth has always stressed the study of what works are made to *do* rather than the study of what work has been made to *be*. In *The Company we Keep: An Ethics of Reading*, he adds the codicil that we as readers change and we should acknowledge – while reading and in our retrospective response – who we are and why we read as we do. Booth regrets the current unwillingness to talk about the ethical effects of our reading experiences. What he proposes is not a one-dimensional ethic which condemns books as 'good' or 'bad' but a critical pluralism in which we can speak about what happens to each of us while we read and about why we prefer one text to another. He argues for the importance of considering the values of a reading experience: 'Ethical criticism attempts to describe the encounters of a story-teller's ethos with that of the reader or listener' (8). The *donnée* of the book is an incident at Chicago when the late Paul Moses – a young assistant professor and a black man – objected to being expected to teach *Huckleberry Finn* because it was to him racist. Booth argues that, contrary to formalist critical ethos, we should consider what books do to readers: 'Paul Moses's reading of *Huckleberry Finn*, an overt ethical appraisal, is one legitimate form of literary criticism' (4).

Booth is an articulate spokesman for a humanistic poetics that emphasizes how human readers respond to human subjects presented by human authors within an imagined world that represents – even if only as an illuminating distortion – anterior reality. He speaks of the experience of actual readers responding to actual texts, and his commonsense approach speaks, I believe, to the empirical experience of real readers: 'In short, the ideal of purging oneself of responses to persons, the ideal of refusing to play the human roles offered us by literature, is never realized by any actual reader who reads a compelling fiction for the sake of reading it (rather than for the sake of obtaining material for an essay, dissertation or book)' (255–6). He argues, I believe correctly, that we respond to literary characterizations not as tropes but as representations of something anterior to the text: 'When we lose our capacity to succumb, when we reach a point at which no other characters can manage to enter our imaginative or emotional or intellectual territory and *take over*, at least for the time being, then we are dead on our feet' (257). In our response to imagined worlds, do we not privilege our recognition of kinship with realized characters and our interest in their problems?

Booth uses the metaphor of friendship – the metaphor of *people meeting* as they share stories – to describe the interrelationship between readers and books during the process of reading: 'Perhaps most obviously, this metaphor spontaneously revives a kind of talk, once almost universal, about the types of friendship or companionship a book provides *as* it is read' (170). He is concerned not only with the affect of narratives on audiences but on the tellers themselves: 'Any story told with genuine engagement will affect its teller fully as much as it affects listeners' (42). According to Booth, 'our reading friends vary' according to seven criteria: 'the sheer *quantity* of invitations they offer us'; the degree of *responsibility* they grant to us; the *degree* of intimacy in the friendship; the *intensity* of engagement; the *coherence*, or consistency of the proffered world'; the *distance* between their world and ours'; and 'the kind or *range of kinds*, of activities suggested, invited, or demanded' (179–80). 'In our living friends,' he asserts, 'we find these same variables' (180). Even those sceptical about seeing books as self-created texts or as seeing them as historical or cultural productions, which is often the same, may be uncomfortable with the ways that Booth anthropomorphizes books as if they were people and thinks of them as if they were human company.

One of the best-kept secrets in the American classroom is that, notwithstanding the past decade's theoretical explosion and the now waning influence of deconstruction and the current high tide of various forms of Marxism – sometimes in the guise of so-called New Historicism, which is often most interesting in its non-Marxist version – Booth's less rigorous Aristotelianism (particularly that in *The Rhetoric of Fiction*) influenced a generation of teachers. No matter what we think of as our critical orientation, most of us have in our intellectual fabric a strong strand of Booth. The work of such diverse figures as James Phelan, Peter Rabinowitz, and Elizabeth Langland testifies to the importance of the Aristotelian tradition Booth represents. Still central to Booth's approach are the questions 'Who is speaking to whom?' and 'For what purpose and on what occasion?' And according to Booth's compelling argument, what speakers talk about is plots, and plots have an ethical dimension: 'Most of the great stories show characters of a moral quality roughly equal to that of the implied reader . . .; the plots are built out of the characters' efforts to face moral choices. In tracing those efforts, we readers stretch our own capacities for thinking about how life should be lived, as we join those most elevated judges, the implied authors' (187).

As an Aristotelian, Booth regards ethics, rhetoric, and politics as inextricably related. The followers of Derrida and de Man have sought to define rhetoric as the study of tropes and semiology as the study of how language means, and to separate both from hermeneutics, what language means. But for Booth rhetoric – as the art of persuasion *and* as the study of how language means – cannot be separated from hermeneutics or ethics: 'If "virtue" covers every kind of genuine strength or power, and if a person's ethos is the total range of his or her virtues, then ethical criticism will be any effort to show how the virtues of narratives relate to the virtues of selves and societies, or how the ethos of any story affects or is affected by the ethos – the collection of virtues – of any given reader' (11). Booth believes that criticism is necessarily ethical and that not only feminists, blacks concerned with racism, and Marxists, but 'even those critics who work hard to purge themselves of all but the most abstract formal interests turn out to have an ethical program in mind – a belief that a given way of reading, or a given kind of genuine literature, is what will do us the most good' (5). Of course, we all approach texts with preconceived ideologies of reading and of what we should be teaching. Every question we ask in our classrooms is an ethical and political question, deriving from our hierarchy of what is essential and what needs to be known. Are not our syllabi and reading lists political and ethical statements?

Authoritative, learned, and elegant – qualities due to the scope of his reading, the keenness of his logic, and the confidence in his position – Booth talks about what texts do to us and for us. Indeed, Booth writes as if he were engaging us – his *company* – in conversation. He is affirmative and shares with us both his joy in reading and ethical responses to texts. Because he addresses us as if we were colleagues and friends, and because he has reprinted some sections that he once gave as talks, he often enacts the very metaphor of keeping company with friends which he advocates. As in *The Rhetoric of Fiction*, at times he recalls the host of *Tom Jones* inviting us to partake of what we wish from his smorgasbord.

Even if Booth is occasionally anecdotal and chatty and often eschews what some call rigour and the pretence of objectivity, he nevertheless engages the reader in a sustained conversational tone and reasoned argument about essential issues of our reading experience. His voice is that of a traditional humanist inquiring about why and how we read; he is committed to reading as an essential activity and passionate in his enthusiasm for books that he admires. Sometimes he can be engagingly ingenuous as when he tells us why he has changed his mind about Lawrence:

> [R]eading him, I find myself conversing with a peculiarly in-sistent, intent, passionate, and wide-ranging friend, one who will respond in some interesting way to every important ques-tion I can think of. . . . His quest to make a larger self that would really respect the Other – including the *others* who represent Him or It – is to me one of the most impressive efforts at religious fiction of this century, at least in English. . . . What I am impressed by is Lawrence's capacity to dramatize rival positions

... oppositions that become emotionally and psychologically plausible and engaging because of the author's vigorous penetration of the souls of those whose stories he tells. (451, 453, 455)

No matter how disarming its tone, and no matter how familiar Booth is with Lawrence, such criticism is somewhat subjective. Yet perhaps at times because of Booth's magisterial intelligence we give him permission to generalize without full evidence. Thus within one paragraph three sentences begin with the following sweeping – and not fully argued – assertions: 'Many thinkers have seen Western individualism. ... Indeed, many of the classics of our literature. ... Many of our most powerful moral heroes in literature' (240–41). But notwithstanding that quibble, Booth's book is a splendid contribution to the current revival of humanistic approaches to literature that is accelerating because of the de Man scandal.

III

In his *Intellectuals in Power: A Genealogy of Critical Humanism* (New York: Columbia University Press, 1986), Paul Bové's subject is the rise of criticism in literary studies and the importance it plays not only in canon formation but in shaping literary and intellectual values. He understands the history of criticism in terms of intellectual, historical, and, especially, political contexts. Discussing an odd configuration, including Foucault, Said, Richards, Auerbach and the Orientalist Matthew Hodson, his purpose is 'to place the leading figures of our profession within a partial genealogy of their discursive and nondiscursive practice and, second, to attempt to show how positioned, indeed, how responsive to their historical position, those we have come to think of as greater critics, like Auerbach and Richards, might be' (x). Following the model of the New Historicism, which is less concerned with positivistic cause and effect than with a constellation of intersecting and interacting aspects, his method is to involve Nietzsche's genealogy as his historical model: 'As historical research it highlights and disentangles a skein of documentary and cultural traces of how the present was formed' (10). But Bové also finds in Nietzsche an alternative model to the humanistic intellectuals who, in his view, disregard issues of history and power: 'Throughout Nietzsche's writings, the critical intellectual appears in the figure of a genealogist. This figure is represented dramatically as always concerned with the material configurations of power, with the possibility and legitimacy of certain tropes and interpretations, and with the concrete human efforts of such power structures' (10).

Bové's perspective is Marxist and the history of criticism is seen as part of a dialectical process: 'My aim all along is to help the profession confront the materiality of its practices and institutions, to recognize how it operates, and to call into question the secular humanistic rhetoric that makes a self-understanding of the profession materially difficult to achieve' (xiii). Under the guise of examining critical history, this book is a diatribe against the influence of 'leading intellectuals', sometimes called 'mandarin humanists'. He buys into the current fashionable Marxist view that universities are constructed to bully students and that 'leading' professors are the means by which that is accomplished: 'At the heart of the project [of creating a sane and balanced world], however, lies the arrogant figure of the leading intellectual whose authority, interacting with that of the institutions and discourses in which he practices, legitimates the disciplinary extension of humanism in an essentially antidemocratic process of subjugating people within categories of social being constituted by the discursive and nondiscursive practices of humanism' (52). Foucault is a Bové hero because he is 'an historian, a philosopher, a genealogist, a theoretician of power' (210) and because, more than Derrida, Foucault takes account of historical and institutional priorities: 'People who take Foucault seriously do so, not because they believe he has said the final word on social reality, but because he has said a few words on the relationship between truth, intellectuals, and human misery' (236).

While this is often a brilliant, provocative, and learned book, it is far too idiosyncratic to take its place with such major books as Lentricchia's *After the New Criticism* or Culler's *On Deconstruction* as central to understanding the current critical mindscape. For me, in its mode of argument, its subject-matter, its style, and its assumption of what is important, this book enacts what I call the Theoretical Fallacy; that is, it weaves a web of abstract speculation out of a wide range of diverse material in the current fashion of intertextuality. But that web exists at such a remote distance and at such an abstract level that it does not lead to increased understanding of literary or critical works. Thus Bové's book does not sufficiently emphasize how the critics he discusses address central conceptual problems in literary study, such as the precise dialogue between readers and texts, or how texts reflect anterior reality.

To take issue with Bové's central premise, I believe that 'leading' intellectuals are valuable in literary studies: if such a figure establishes a paradigm for literary study – like Leavis, or the Chicago School, or Derrida or Foucault – does not this paradigm become an intellectually provocative occasion for someone to come along and question the assumptions of the paradigm? Moreover, it is less the humanistic critic who thinks of the individual critic and scholar in 'sublime or heroic terms' than the followers of current cult figures whose political pronouncements acquire a legitimacy because of their authority within literary studies. The great humanists – Richards, Auerbach, Crane, Abrams – have tended to consider the critic as a rather humble middleman mediating between literary work and world and between reader and literary work.

Bové brilliantly examines Auerbach's intellectual heritage, specifically his relationship to the intellectual and cultural politics of the Weimar period. Yet finally his real interest is not in what Auerbach teaches us about reading, but in his purported influence: 'Given the mandarins' use of certain notions of sublimity, tradition, and synthesis as weapons in a (failed) battle to regain power and authority, and given, as a result of his partial inscription in that battle, Auerbach's function as a link between German and American humanistic intellectuals, American critics' own needs, interests, and powers come into sharper focus when their responses to Auerbach are themselves reconsidered in light of these German aspects of Auerbach's genealogy' (128). But does he understand the nuances of Auerbach's *literary* insights in *Mimesis*? Does he sufficiently see the Hegelian dialectic working itself through the dialogue between the classical (Homeric) and Biblical mode? Does he show the drama of how Auerbach acknowledges Woolf's work not merely as a continuation of the great nineteenth-century realists – Stendhal and Balzac – but as a central instance of the modernist agon in which he finds himself as he writes in exile in Turkey?[1]

Although Bové objects to the 'unitary narration' of humanism, I would submit that his own homogenizing sensibility disregards commitment to evidence and to cause and effect. For Bové, it is self-evident that 'the major interrelations between state, corporation, and ruling class, on the one hand, and university intellectuals, on the other, is important to understanding the critical mindscape' (308). While obviously the universities are shaped by political reality and values, and we certainly should worry about government support of weapons research, are our most influential critical figures – Todorov, Derrida, feminists such as Kristeva and Showalter, Marxists such as Eagleton – really sustaining the values of political status quo? Of which country and which system? Writing of the work of I. A. Richards, Bové remarks, 'Quite literally, then, practical criticism is a pedagogy and theory intended for the maintenance and management of the status quo' (155). But is it really bad that we seek to understand poems as complex models of reality or that such reading skills might be useful to perceiving reality? If our minds have a rage for order, then it follows that we shall discover unity and order in the world, even if we understand that the unity and order may be putative and that reality always has instability and ambiguity.

My understanding of the history of Anglo-American criticism is far different from Bové's. Except for Bové's discussion of I. A. Richards, on whom he is interesting if not always persuasive, Bové does not give a compelling presentation of the history of criticism as it pertains to English studies. For English literature, particularly the English novel, has its own tradition that stresses manners and morals rather than historical cause and effect. And that tradition, as I have argued in my *The Humanistic Heritage: Critical Theories of the English Novel from James to Hillis Miller*, creates its own critical traditions that stress a grammar of motives, voice, tone, and close analysis of ironic passages. Bové never mentions the Chicago Critics – McKeon, Sacks, Crane, and, most notably, Booth; yet they have been as influential in novel criticism as the New Critics in poetry. And aren't James's prefaces and Forster's *Aspects of the Novel* important in defining the tradition of Anglo-American criticism? And what about Van Ghent's seminal *The English Novel: Form and Function*, which as much as any other work shaped the canon and approach to the English novel? Should he not mention the role of D. H. Lawrence and Richard Chase in shaping the American canon? Is Said really as influential as, say, Frye was in the 1960s, when at some leading departments, Frye was taken as seriously as Derrida is now? Shouldn't we address why Frye – with his insistence on non-referential poetics – was such a major figure of the 1960s? Why did Kermode's *The Sense of an Ending* – with its insistence that fictions matter in our lives – become a kind of sacred text in the late 1960s? What were the reasons that phenomenology gave way to structuralism and structuralism to post-structuralism? Nor am I sure that Auerbach's *Mimesis* played the central role in English studies that Bové claims, after it entered through the back door of Romance studies and comparative literature. Until the recent impact of Marxism and some strands of feminism, English departments continued to prefer discussing novels as dramatic poems to discussing them in terms of Auerbach's historical contexts.

In the face of a fundamental change in literary studies, it is significant if not urgent that we examine our intellectual heritage. Within his discussion of critics, Bové idiosyncratically recapitulates his view of their work by providing his own Marxist reading – his *unitary narrative* – of their achievement, and makes a few feints at considering alternative evidence. On every page the air is redolent with such abstruse vocabulary as 'the structure of desire' (82), 'recontextualization' (83) and 'privatistic modernist ascesis' (90). In the 'Nestor' episode of *Ulysses* Stephen defines God as 'a shout in the street', and at times this book, for all its discursive eloquence, is a learned version of a shout from the barricade. Although Bové is a learned man, I am afraid this book will only have influence on True Believers in Bové's Marxist teleology.

IV

The question for many of us trained in traditional humanistic criticism is whether the theoretical explosion is yielding powerful readings and new perspectives. Among the more exciting results of this explosion is the effort to define the nature of the imagined world of fictional texts. This is a project which not only engages traditional humanistic criticism – criticism that takes seriously plot, character, authors, and the process and object of mimesis – but also encourages this criticism to take seriously the issues raised by deconstruction about how language means and, specifically, whether it represents an anterior world or merely defers significa- tion. Other recent contributions to this dialogue between tradi- tional concerns and recent theory, as well as between real and imagined worlds, are Adena Rosmarin's *The Power of Genre* (Minneapolis: University of Minnesota Press, 1986) and A. D. Nuttall's *The New Mimesis: Shakespeare and the Representation of Reality* (New York: Methuen, 1983).

Alexander Gelley's *Narrative Crossings: Theory and Pragmatics of Prose Fiction* (Baltimore: Johns Hopkins University Press, 1987) is a provocative, sophisticated, and insightful study of the relationship between the imagined worlds of fiction and reality: '[F]ictionality and its near cousin representation seem to me notions that are both inescapable and, finally, irreducible. . . . The fictive is not a quality or a generic category of texts, in spite of certain classifications that have become standardized (e.g., fiction/nonfiction). . . . But what is most pertinent with respect to a theory of fictionality is not whether the objects described refer to empirically verifiable "real" models, but rather how the mode of transmission, the representational practice, is able to project a meaning that derives from and yet transcends phenomenal reality and sensory experience' (x–xi). While it is true that fictionality and representation are terms which define each other and that we need attend to the mode of transmission, can we not create categories that speak to the different degrees of fictionality and representation in such diverse works as, on the one hand, Kafka's 'The Hunter Gracchus' and, on the other hand, George Moore's *Esther Waters* or Zola's novels?

Gelley convincingly shows how theoretical discourse can place in a fresh framework such humanistic concerns as the function of description, the relation between character and characterization, and how language presents a world. Thus he insists that 'scene' is an important concept in shaping the reader: 'In relation to the narrative scene, the reader becomes an unstable subject, seeking to survey and master what is being shown, but continually thwarted by the frame or "spectacle" that provides his means of access' (171). After early chapters entitled 'Premises for a Theory of Description', 'Metonymy, Schematism, and the Space of Literature', 'Character and Person: On the Presentation of Self in the Novel', Gelley's focus moves more to specific works, although the discussions of such works as *The Confidence-Man*, Hawthorne's 'Wakefield', Rousseau's *La Nouvelle Héloïse*, Goethe's *Wilhelm Meisters Wanderjahre*, and Flaubert's 'Un Coeur Simple' are cast in terms of theoretical concerns. Gelley is particularly compelling on Flaubert. Since I have a preference for stories of reading which answer Aristotelian issues of character and plot, and which entertain – even if sceptically – the hypothesis of an organic reading, sometimes I find slightly disappointing the focus on texts for the purpose of developing theoretical issues.

Gelley has read widely and deeply in both traditional and recent criticism, and his deft, logical, and lucid chapters reveal that learning. He combines his wide reading of theoretical issues with a strong historical sense: 'What distinguished the post-Renaissance novel from other literary forms was its fusion of extraliterary language practices (legal, commercial, religious, courtly) with literary modes (pastoral, epic, didactic, confessional, satiric)' (79). Thus, within a few pages he can quote Lacan, de Man, Matthiessen, and Van Ghent; indeed, at times, as in the chapter 'Premises for a Theory of Description', his own ideas get lost underneath the welter of other critics' views. Very much in the 'advanced' school of criticism which assumes that philosophical discourse needs to inform literary discussion, on occasion Gelley follows in the recent tradition of avoiding Occam's Razor that the best explanation is the simplest. If the book has a shortcoming, it is that often elaborate and careful, if not slow-moving, arguments yield fairly conventional conclusions – conclusions which I consider to be tenets of humanistic poetics: 'The presentation of self in the novel is to be sought not in terms of a priori notion of the ego but by way of what I have termed the structures of sociality that operate in literary works' (67). Finally, Gelley is a troubled, conscientious, and brilliant humanist who provides tentative answers to basic questions about the relation between formal ingredients in the novel and its mimetic content.

V

Jay Clayton's *Romantic Vision and the Novel* (Cambridge: Cambridge University Press, 1987) is a significant scholarly study that places several major English novels in the context of the Romantic tradition. Clayton is both a powerful reader of complex texts and shows the necessity of seeing canonical works in the context of literary and intellectual history. Influenced by the realization that the New Criticism could be adapted to fiction, and by seminal studies in the 1950s and 1960s by Van Ghent, Watt, and Booth – as well as by the marketplace appeal of novel courses on campuses – the study and the teaching of the novel gradually diverged from that of traditional historical periods, such as Romantic or Victorian, and became a field in itself. Yet when I first came to Cornell in 1968 and responded to inquiries about my field with the answer, 'the novel', I was regarded as something of a curiosity by scholars of an older generation who thought that a field was 'eighteenth century' or 'Romantic' or 'Victorian'.

In recent years the concept of intertextuality has called the entire concept of genre into question, although work like Adena Rosmarin's *The Power of Genre* and the living tradition of Chicago critics have kept genre in focus. Jay Clayton wants to retain respect for generic differences, while stressing the interweaving of strands from fiction with other genres. His discussion on the cross-fertilization of genres builds upon the prior work of M. H. Abrams, and, more locally, Robert Kiely and Margaret Doody, but Clayton has made an important contribution. In a chapter entitled 'Pure Poetry/Impure Fiction', he discusses how generic expectations shape our response to works in terms which will be convincing not only to Aristotelians but to those who belong to all interpretive communities.

In his 1963 essay, 'English Romanticism: The Spirit of the Age', Abrams defined Romanticism in ways that are applicable to a wide range of novels: 'Whatever the form, the Romantic Bard is one "who present, past, and future sees"; so that in dealing with current affairs his procedure is often panoramic, his stage cosmic, his agents quasi-mythological, and his logic of events apocalyptic. Typically this mode of Romantic vision fuses history, politics, philosophy, and religion into one grand design by asserting Providence – or some form of natural teleology – to operate in the seeming chaos of human history so as to effect from present evil a greater good' (*Romanticism and Consciousness*, ed. Harold Bloom, 103). Like William Thickstun in his recent *Visionary Closure in the Modern Novel*, Clayton focuses on the parallel between Romantic visionary experience and powerful character transformation in the novel: 'The novel bears testimony to the violence of transcendence in more than just the fate of its protagonists. Structurally, as well, it records the shock that a visionary experience gives to everything around it. . . . Visionary experience, then, alters a novel in at least three of its aspects: representation, sequence, and character' (2–3). In a splendid introductory chapter, 'Transcendence and the Novel', Clayton meticulously defines the grounds of his argument: 'In order to understand transcendence in the novel we need to define more precisely what constitutes a genuine visionary experience. The Romantic visionary moment is related, on one side, to the ancient tradition of mysticism and, on the other side, to the modern epiphany' (4). In a group of compelling readings of major English novels beginning with *Clarissa* and concluding with *Women in Love*, he shows how moments of transcendence affect narrative: '[T]ranscendence alters a novel in at least three of its aspects – sequence, representation, and character – and in each case the alteration possesses a liminal structure. . . . Narrative itself is a simple matter – simple in the sense of elemental, basic, an irreducible part of all other forms of discourse' (9).

Clayton outlines the two major ways transcendence affects narrative: 'On the one hand, visionary experience can interrupt a narrative, rising like Wordsworth's "Imagination" in Book 6 of *The Prelude* to block the progress of events. We might call this moment a visionary disruption, for it severs the connection between events, disrupts the bond between cause and effect. On the other hand, visionary experience can call into question all linear order, positing in its place a timeless unity. Instead of halting or interrupting the narrative sequence, it challenges the very concept of order, questioning the necessity not only of a narrative sequence but also of a finite beginning or end' (15). But Shelley goes further than Wordsworth: 'Shelley tries to circumvent the entire problem by denying that there is any necessary conflict between visionary experience and ordinary life. To believe that transcendence shuts one off from reality, isolating the visionary within the bounds of one's own self, is to Shelley, a pernicious error. . . . If Wordsworth's visionary power comes as a disruption of narrative, then perhaps the more radical breakthrough Shelley seeks can come as a disruption of the visionary power. In short, Shelley deconstructs a Wordsworthian moment of vision. He first interrupts his own narrative, then calls into question the structure of this interruption' (18, 22).

Clayton provides excellent readings of *Clarissa*, *Mansfield Park*, *Wuthering Heights*, *Little Dorritt*, *Adam Bede* and *Women in Love* – readings which focus on a dialogue between what he calls lyrical and narrative modes. He has special insights in every chapter. Because Lawrence is the best paradigm for his argument about the possibility of characters experiencing 'apocalyptic change', it is not surprising that his chapter on *Women in Love* is particularly astute. Explaining that Romantic readers considered literature's affects – whether called 'pity' and 'fear' or 'pathetic' and 'sublime' – separate from 'the specific ethical argument (or plot) of the piece' (57), he convincingly discusses the intellectual backgrounds of 'why Romantic readers were prepared to separate the transcendent scenes in *Clarissa* from the larger ethical design of the narrative' (58). Clayton argues that Jane Austen addressed issues raised by romanticism even while challenging 'the Romantic theory of poetry that values a literature "purified" of ethical concerns' (58); she favours narrative while avoiding lyrical moments. Following Hillis Miller in *Fiction and Repetition*, Clayton focuses on the role of repetition in narrative, but, as what I call a 'modified' Aristotelian, he does so with a full appreciation of the concept of plot – by which he means the organizational teleology of narrative.

Every page of Clayton's study is informed by a rich sense of literary history, a keen awareness of the novels, and a full sense of prior scholarship. His work reflects the range and depth of his reading. Well-written and carefully argued, it is informed by a sense of the relationship between formal questions and issues of content. Thus he writes of Austen that 'examination of the formal strategies that the novelist employed may suggest the outlines of the ideology she was attempting to counter' (61). He is continually aware of the anterior reality that is the object of a novel's mimesis and the process by which that reality is transformed into an imagined ontology with its own formal coherence and necessity. He understands, too, that authors express issues relevant to their lives in their novels and that awareness of the complex relationship between life and art helps us understand artistic works. 'The part of [Austen's] autobiography which Fanny Price dramatizes is the author's deep concern with both the attractions and the dangers of a Romantic vision' (61). Finally, he writes with a sense of literary and intellectual history not as a monolithic pattern but as a working hypothesis, a discursive formation, that enables us to see the constellations of diverse texts. Clayton's study gives ballast to the tradition of humanistic formalism, the tradition I discussed in *The Humanistic Heritage: Critical Theories of the English Novel from James to Hillis Miller*, in part because it creates a dialogue between texts and theoretical issues, even while showing that traditional criticism is open to learning from recent theory. Rather than a monologic reader who sees everything in terms of an *a priori* pattern, he belongs to several interpretive communities, depending on the work under discussion. Thus he can use Lacan's idea of language as alienating to create a context for *Wuthering Heights*: 'In *Wuthering Heights* Emily Brontë is even more aware of the seductive falsifications of what Lacan would call the Imaginary but we must recognize as the conditions that make representation possible in any text' (19); and he employs Freudian concepts of 'repetition-compulsion' to discuss *Adam Bede*.

Let me conclude by mentioning a few problems and omissions in this readable, erudite, and valuable study. While interesting and provocative, Clayton's readings do not always depend on his conceptual framework. It would have been better in places had he related the novel on which he focuses to the whole canon; thus in the *Women in Love* chapter, he only once mentions *The Rainbow*, which seems at least as appropriate to his argument about transcendent moments as *Women in Love*. At times, perhaps Clayton could have been more attentive to the subtleties of tone in the books he discusses – particularly playfulness, irony, and, as in *Women in Love*, moments when omniscient narrators speak in multiple voices. Clayton does not always distinguish between the character transformation that is the essence of the plot of the traditional English novel of manners and morals and what he calls 'transcendence'. Are there not degrees of transcendence? Indeed, can one think of *any* character transformation without some degree of visionary experience, even if it is offstage and/or defined as a logical decision? Clayton has limited himself to canonical figures. Among neglected figures, Disraeli not only wrote novels within the romantic framework that Clayton presents, but actually wrote a novel (*Venetia*) about Byron and Shelley. Nor does the subject limit itself to English fiction, as he might have acknowledged in a coda.

Finally, shouldn't Clayton have considered the work of Hardy, Conrad, Joyce, and Woolf in a book on Romantic vision and the novel? And what about the visionary aspect of Joyce's imagination in *A Portrait of the Artist*, *Ulysses* and *Finnegans Wake*? Since Clayton might have discussed his theory of epiphany as well as the kind of transcendent moments which punctuate the major novels of Woolf, and in particular the endings of *Mrs Dalloway* and *To the Lighthouse*, he should have been clear about his principle of inclusion and exclusion; indeed, in his introduction, he mentions how Mrs Ramsay achieves a moment of visionary stasis at the end of the first part of *To the Lighthouse*. (While Thickstun's focus is more structural than Clayton's, he continues the exploration of the visionary tradition in the modern novel, and has chapters on *The Rainbow*, *Ulysses*, *To the Lighthouse*, as well as *The Sound and the Fury* and *Howards End*.) Moreover, since Hardy is a major influence on Lawrence, especially the version of Lawrence that Clayton emphasizes, Clayton might have stressed how Hardy is as much a visionary and mythologizer as a realist and that his novels are populated by transcendent moments in the lives of his major characters (Jude, Clym, Gabriel, Henchard come to mind). In the characters of Kurtz in *Heart of Darkness* and Stein in *Lord Jim*, doesn't Conrad explore the problems of those who *believe* that they are experiencing moments of transcendence? Indeed, what if an ironic narrator renders transcendence as solipsism as Conrad does with Kurtz? But my minor reservations notwithstanding, I celebrate Clayton's outstanding critical performance.

VI

The challenge of traditional humanistic criticism is to define an aesthetic that takes seriously the challenge of deconstruction to traditional ideas of the unity of texts and the signification of language. This aesthetic must include a theoretical position that retains the anterior reality that precedes a text, demonstrates how language signifies that reality, and understands that human authors create texts about human beings for human readers. In her learned, sophisticated study of James, Lawrence, Joyce, and Beckett, *The Dialect of the Tribe: Speech and Community in Modern Fiction* (New York: Oxford University Press, 1987), Margery Sabin tries to create a dialogue between traditional humanism and more recent theory and practice, especially deconstruction, which believes meaning is a kind of mirage that recedes in proportion as it is approached.

Lucidly and readably presented, her argument is that in the English tradition, at least, language means:

> For James, Lawrence, Joyce, and Beckett, however, the speech forms of language now given up so impassively by critical theory escape systematic rejection because they are associated with such personal and even dangerously uncontrollable forces of life, and with forms of knowing and acting not readily contained in any system. I will argue that this association is itself handed down through identifiable habits and tendencies in the English tradition, where French-style intellectual disdain for the familiar and the illogical never entirely cancels out responsiveness to quite diverse signs in language of human energy, resourcefulness, and sheer physical vitality. Without ascribing to the

expectation that language works primarily as an instrument for absolute self-manifestation or thoroughly rational knowledge, this English tradition endorses the constitutive force of language as it serves desires for self-assertion and the forging of relationships: between past and present, self and world, and even between the depths and surfaces of the individual personality. (5)

She carefully contrasts the English with the French intellectual and literary tradition to support her argument that the English modern tradition is different, in part because it values idiomatic language.

If I understand her correctly, Sabin's purpose is to rescue speech and voice from the Derridean master term 'writing':

At the same time, and no less importantly, [James, Lawrence and Joyce] stealthily take certain things with them out of situations willingly and even willfully left behind. And for them, too, the drama is centered intensely in language. They were all, in their separate ways, masters of that dramatic, expressive, idiomatic English so variously 'kept,' in Frost's words, by writers and readers in English since Shakespeare. . . . (4–5)

For her, as for me, authors exist as the creative figures behind a work and as a presence within a work:

[In *Sea and Sardinia*] Lawrence's eruption of temper in Sorgono, however, becomes more comic than despairing through the deliberately melodramatic emphases of the style. The self-abuse so disturbing in *Kangaroo* is entirely absent. In this writing, black rage becomes itself colorful. Lawrence presents his own cursing self as a rather amusing spectacle. (153)

Sabin locates language within voice and shows that voice – both in external dialogue and interior monologue – is character. She focuses on speech – especially conversation – within novels, but includes the telling of the narrative voice as it renders the thoughts of others in her concept of conversation. By doing so, she reminds us that novels are not about writing but about human relationships in a social setting. In the tradition of Anglo-American humanistic formalism, she argues that speech reveals character, that language is a gesture of characterization, and that we must know who is speaking to whom and for what occasion. Because language is psychic and moral gesture, the idiosyncracies of their particular speech acts, as Sabin notes, distinguish characters: 'For it is precisely through their colloquial verve that figures like Mulligan (in speech) and Bloom (in thought) impress us with their force of personality' (29). It is because readers are drawn to dramatizations of fellow humans that in fiction characterization – whether of narrators who as they speak are always self-dramatizing characters or of characters within the plot – takes precedence, or seems to, over other ingredients. Isn't this why we read novels? As we read we find ourselves displacing characters in all sorts of odd ways; resisting authors' interpretations, we not only provide our own responses to characters' behaviour, but superimpose our experience upon theirs.

Novels are dialogues between ways of telling as well as ways of seeing, and that includes the diverse languages spoken by a single narrator. Thus Sabin shows how Lawrence and Joyce use idiomatic language to criticize other styles: '[I]diomatic language carries enough value in these writers to support more than satiric dramas of conflict and attraction between the high-toned and the idiomatic characters and between the values that different modes of speech convey, sometimes even within the personality of a single individual' (37). It is worth noting that what she is talking about – dialogues between various styles – is what Bakhtin has called heteroglossia. Since we have learned from Bakhtin, whose work she unfortunately ignores, about the dialogic nature of styles, it would have been useful for her to compare and contrast her views with Bakhtin; she also might have taken more seriously the speech-act theories of Austen and Searle and their followers.

After an introduction that might have more clearly defined her method and approach, the book has two fine general chapters entitled 'The Life of English Idiom, the Laws of French Cliché,' and 'The Community of Intelligence and the Avant-Garde'. She then presents thoughtful and insightful readings of *The Golden Bowl*, *Women in Love*, *Ulysses* and Beckett's trilogy: *The Unnamable*, *Malone Dies* and *Molloy*. Perhaps at times her readings are not sufficiently linked to the two opening chapters. Her approach is most successful for Beckett whose novels, she compellingly argues, partake of both English and French literary and cultural traditions.

Sabin is least successful in her efforts to redefine our sense of the

Anglo-American humanistic tradition. For the humanistic critic with whom she comes to terms is F. R. Leavis, whose influence in this country has always been rather marginal; unfortunately she ignores the Aristotelian tradition of McKeon, Booth, and Crane, the formalist tradition of Van Ghent and Schorer, the influence in America of Auerbach, and the work of Frye and Kermode. Since Leavis has rarely been taken too seriously in America, and now is read with declining frequency, one feels at times that Sabin is tilting at windmills. Because her own understanding of the humanistic critical tradition in fiction is somewhat limited, can she quite meet the claims of the book-jacket that 'she lucidly analyzes the biases of both the Anglo-American critical tradition and the challenge to that tradition in French literary theory and practice'?

Two of the seven chapters are devoted exclusively to Lawrence: Chapter Four, entitled 'Constructing Character: Speech and Will in *Women in Love*', argues convincingly that novel 'affirm[s] the value of language as medium especially in the form of social speech' (37). Chapter Five, titled 'Near and Far Things in Lawrence's Writing of the Twenties', includes excellent discussions of *Kangaroo*, *Sea and Sardinia*, as well as a persuasive section on *St. Mawr*. In Lawrence's prose of the twenties, Sabin contends:

> Whether or not he is literally by himself, even when he gives volleys of speech to other characters, Lawrence most often seems to be alone, wandering the world – somewhere, nowhere – while speaking to a distant reader or arguing with himself. . . . At the same time, the striking solitude of utterance makes the energy and quirky sociability all the more striking when they appear. (140)

In this chapter, as in the entire book, notwithstanding splendid insights on every page, Sabin perhaps could be more rigorous in her analysis of specific speeches by individual voices. The paradox of this study is that Sabin is herself a closet Leavisite, particularly in the Lawrence chapters. When she uses terms like 'maturity' and 'common social reality', moves without self-consciousness between author and work, and argues how an examination of social speech in *Women in Love* shows the 'interplay between deliberate will and spontaneous impulse', does she not recall Leavis's writing on Lawrence (113)? To conclude: Sabin is a sensitive, thoughtful critic, but because she is somewhat adrift from her theoretical and methodological moorings, her own often brilliant study may not be able to take as prominent a place in the current critical debate as it otherwise might.

In the past decade we have had many excellent specialized studies of Lawrence. But, in my judgement, Lawrence now needs a substantial synthesizing critical study that takes account of what we now know of his historical and personal background and his relation to other writers and thinkers. Yet what we need is a major study by a powerful critic, who would create a dialogue between texts and theory, between newer theory and traditional approaches, even while sifting through the vast research on Lawrence with intelligence and verve.

Among questions that should be asked: How and why did Lawrence's form develop and evolve? How did his concept of character and characterization change? How does his 'carbon' theory of the psyche as outlined in the famous letter to Garnett reflect developments in the English and European cultural and intellectual milieu? What are the appropriate theoretical questions to ask about Lawrence's language? Do we need an aesthetic and narratology for Lawrence that is different from the other writers of the modern British period? How does Lawrence's language signify in the intense and strained passages, such as the opening and closing chapters of *The Rainbow* and the famous 'Ever and Again' passage of the chapter 'Anna Victrix'? How can we discuss the symbolic speech acts of such works as *The Man Who Died* and *St Mawr*? How does Lawrence's use of idiomatic and colloquial speech undermine such post-structuralist master terms as 'writerly'? How does Lawrence use his letters as a threshing ground to test his ideas and fictional voices? (Of *The Rainbow* he wrote: 'Now you will find [Frieda] and me in the novel, I think, and the work is of both of us' [#718, *Letters*].) What are the reasons that his political fiction founders? Is Lawrence less a primitive and more of an intellectual – albeit a quirky one – than we thought?

VII

Let us turn to three books which speak to our human need for alternative places, whether imaginary or real: Peter Ruppert's *Reader in a Strange Land: The Activity of Reading Literary Utopias* (Athens: University of Georgia Press, 1986), Michael Seidel's *Exile and the Narrative Imagination* (New Haven: Yale University Press, 1986), and Iain Finlayson's *The Sixth Continent: A Literary History of Romney Marsh* (New York: Atheneum, 1986). Exile is a condition in which one is involuntarily removed or voluntarily removes oneself from one's roots, whereas utopias speak to our desire for a perfected world. The impulses for voluntary exile and for utopias are not dissimilar; they each depend on our hope that a better place may exist than the one we inhabit and that we may vacate the pressures and responsibilities of our world and remove ourselves to a better one. What Ruppert says of utopias is relevant to exile: 'Implicit in all utopian dreams is the urge to escape, the desire to get away from the turmoil of history and the anxiety that comes from an awareness of time and change' (3).

Seidel and Ruppert show how the mainstream of Anglo-American criticism is trying to come to terms with recent ideologies of reading, including deconstruction and reader-response criticism. Oblivious to recent theory, Finlayson assumes that readers are interested in the way that a group of writers lived at a specific place at a specific time. All three books assume that literature to some degree represents anterior reality and that it negotiates between real and imaginary experience. Seidel's focus is upon what happens within the world of texts, although he certainly is aware of the anterior world in which the author lived; Ruppert's stress is upon what happens to the reader. Ruppert and Seidel understand that readers and authors meet on the boundaries of their own separate spaces, and that readers chart an imaginary new space as they decode a text and apply their own sense-making. Thus, for Seidel and Ruppert, readers are cartographers who construct maps produced by a transaction between text and reader.

Michael Seidel has written an important study of how the experience of literary exile shapes imaginative literature. His focus is 'on literary representations of exile, especially representations in which exile or expatriation is foregrounded as a narrative action' (xii). He concentrates 'on exile as an enabling fiction, or at least a fiction enabling me to address the larger strategies of narrative representation' (ibid.). Seidel is often a compelling reader who combines erudition with perspicacity, as when he writes of *Ulysses*: 'The exilic Bloom is generated by the very mythology the narrative establishes for him, "Leopold Bloom of no fixed abode" whose exodus from one land of bondage to another is part of his defense in the phantasmagoria of "Circe", "my client's native place, the land of the Pharaoh"'' (75). Seidel also writes with great sensitivity about 'Strether's American mission' in *The Ambassadors*.

Seidel's book raises questions about the metaphoricity or disfiguration of interpretive language. Interpretations are never purely literal or demonstrative, for do they not distort and reshape literary texts just as texts reshape and distort anterior reality? Or, as Stevens's 'The Man with the Blue Guitar' puts it, 'Things as they are / Are changed up on the blue guitar.' When Seidel offers methodological and theoretical conceptual statements that seek to generalize individual acts of interpretations, he often writes with such a high degree of metaphoricity that the disfiguration of the imagined world of the novels he describes is too great for my tastes. To be sure, as de Man has taught us, all readings are allegorical; but there are degrees of allegoricity. Thus at times, such as in the following passage, I feel relatively certain that Seidel could be more precise and lucid: 'Narrative is a kind of speaking metaphor, a crossover, and its scene is set by the projection of activity in a mimetic and illusionistic space, a "conception" of what *might be* on the other side' (2).

Had Seidel emphasized clarity and precision, this perceptive and often brilliant study would have been better. Thus, the organizing principle of his two parts has not been made clear by the following explanation: 'The first set of chapters concerns the exilic adventure as an allegory of narrative properties; the second set, an elaboration of that allegory in terms of narrative and cultural "otherness"'' (xiii). Part One, entitled 'Exilic Boundaries', includes chapters on Defoe (*Robinson Crusoe*), Conrad (*Heart of Darkness* and *Lord Jim*), and Joyce (*A Portrait of the Artist* and *Ulysses*). Part Two, entitled 'Exilic Crossings', includes Sterne (*A Sentimental Journey*), James (*The Ambassadors* and *The American Scene*), and Nabokov (*Ada* and *Pale Fire*). While the Nabokov chapter is rich in insight, I am less enthusiastic about the Conrad chapter where Seidel's perspective of exile does not really add to existing readings and where his conceptual explanations seem unduly remote from the works he is describing: 'The dilemma in Conrad's fiction, at least before the severe irony of his skepticism obliterates even the sentimental romance of communal obligation, is that the narrative capacity to describe the effects of isolation is effaced by the mysterious, silent powers of the *isolato*' (44). In the following passage, how does Seidel differentiate between imagined worlds inhabited by Jim and the reader's world created by a transaction between the text and the reader? 'One of the problems in *Lord Jim* for Conrad's young hero involves the nature of the language used to represent him in a world for which he becomes increasingly unfit. Conrad centers the issue on the symbolic word *sovereignty*, a word of historical import for the exilic and imperial fiction' (51).

In its focus on how texts reflect the imaginative pressure of events that take place in the author's life and the world which produced him or her, it might appear that Seidel writes in the Columbia tradition of Trilling and Stephen Marcus. Yet this book is less in the Columbia tradition of grounded, cultural criticism than it first appears. Certainly Trilling would have blanched at Seidel's reliance on post-structuralist jargon. What does such fashionably pretentious language as the following really tell us? 'The narrative imagination inhabits exilic domain where absence is presence, or, to put it the other way around, where presence is absence' (198–9).

Insightful and persuasive, Ruppert writes from a deep conviction that utopian literature is important: 'Overall, my barely submerged chief concern in this study is to defend utopian literature and to demonstrate its continuing relevance' (xiii). Ruppert's focus is divided between genres and what utopias do to readers: 'Utopian literature is inherently dialogic in nature and is best understood as an invitation to the reader to enter into a dialectical thought process concerning the nature of social possibility. But since readers, as a rule, constitute such a heterogeneous group, reflecting many conflicting interests, tastes, and priorities, utopian literature has a varied history in which different readers, or different groups of readers, have appropriated it and imbued it with different meanings' (26). Perhaps in Ruppert's work, two books co-exist without being completely joined; one on reader-response criticism and one on utopia as genre. To be sure, he does explain that because utopias depend upon, on the one hand, creating a parallel between reading and, on the other hand, discovering an alternative space which calls the reader to re-evaluate his own space, they are models of a dialectical or transactive interaction between text and reader in which one affects the other.

What I sometimes miss in Ruppert's argument is 'for example'; yet he is splendid on More's *Utopia*. 'Rather than constituting a flawed text that is inconsistent and paradoxical, More's *Utopia* can thus be read as an effort to stimulate and provoke the reader through numerous inversions and contradictions' (96). Writing in the tradition of textuality in which the critic takes other critics as seriously as the primary work, Ruppert spends too much time responding to prior critics and scholars rather than to the literature itself. But this is an interesting and useful study.

He claims that it is Eco and Iser who most influenced him, for they see reading 'as a dialectical partnership between reader and text in which neither textual structure nor reader's performance has priority. For these theorists, reader and text are bonded together in mutual dependence: the structural components of the text control the reader, and the activity of the reader completes textual structures' (59). In practice if not theory, he often proceeds most effectively on Aristotelian assumptions: 'Like other literary texts, utopias are structured to produce certain effects in the process of reading them, to move their readers in certain ways' (xi). I wish his theoretical orientation addressed the issues that divide Aristotelian criticism, with its focus on the structure of effects made by the author, from reader-response criticism with its focus on the reader's sense-making.

Finlayson's title plays upon a remark by an early nineteenth-century resident of Romney Marsh: 'The World, according to the best geographers, is divided into Europe, Asia, Africa, America, and Romney Marsh.' Romney Marsh enabled writers to combine home with a retreat from life in the form of voluntary exile and utopian dreams. Finlayson discusses in his readable study the lives and works of a number of writers, including Stephen Crane, Conrad, James and Ford. Occasionally quoting other critics but offering few insights into literary works, his anecdotal book is more for the casual reader than for the serious student of literature. The latter will learn very little that will supplement his knowledge of authors he teaches, but may enjoy the chapters on those he knows less about. Thus I found the chapters on Aiken, Coward, and Wells more informative than those on Conrad or James.

VIII

As the high tide of deconstruction recedes, the study of Conrad is beginning to return to such crucial subjects as the relationship between his life and work, the evolution of his career, the historical context in which he wrote, the psychic and moral choices faced by Conrad's literary characters within the formal hypothesis of an imagined world, and the values he espoused. Indeed, the tradition of what I have been calling humanistic formalism has begun to reassert itself in literary studies, especially when it combines the powerful close reading that has always been its strength with sophisticated tools of narratology that are among the benefits of the theoretical explosion. Isn't the New Historicism, with its focus on the complex anterior reality that produces texts – even as it shows that this reality is partially produced by texts – contributing to the refocusing on both the traditional subjects and means of representation? No doubt the narrative of Paul de Man's career has contributed to the demise of an ahistorical approach that ignores or trivializes author, anterior reality, and historical context. As we have seen discussion of the de Man narrative demands – from both his apologists and those outraged by his wartime writings and his subsequent silence – attention to the continuity of his life and thought as well as knowledge of political and historical circumstances in Belgium in the wartime years.

It is only by ignoring the historical and personal contexts that produced his work and the evolution of Conrad's artistic career that critics reductively conclude that Conrad is a metaphysician of darkness or a nihilist. For Conrad challenges the accepted shibboleths of late Victorian and Edwardian England and speaks eloquently – that is, enacts through his complex fictions – the pretensions of imperialism as well as the emptiness of religious pieties and the various forms of Social Darwinism that draw upon those pieties to produce what he regarded as unwarranted belief in an upwardly evolving teleology. The three critical books I shall discuss – Anthony Winner's *Culture and Irony: Studies in Joseph Conrad's Major Novels* (Charlottesville: University Press of Virginia, 1988), Kenneth Graham's *Indirections of the Novel: James, Conrad, and Forster* (Cambridge: Cambridge University Press, 1988), and John Lester's *Conrad and Religion* (New York: St. Martin's Press, 1988) – stress Conrad's response to the disruptions in the dominant historical and cultural assumptions of the nineteenth century. Thus Anthony Winner sees Conrad as a figure defending a set of values derived from Victorian culture: '[Conrad's] faith is a version, combining both practical prowess and ideal meaning, of the Victorian spirit Conrad cherishes in his adopted land. . . . All Conrad's stories tell of threats and challenges that imperil belief, of flaws within and horrors without. But Conrad assumes that his readers will react to his equivocal tales and ironic strategies through the reflexes of their culture's truth: that, like [Marlow's correspondent in *Lord Jim*], they will take the high ground of the idea' (1).

Along with the studies under review, such recent work as Aaron Fogel's *Coercion to Speak* (enriched by Fogel's savvy reading of Bakhtin) and Stephen Ressler's *Joseph Conrad: Consciousness and Integrity* address the moral dilemmas that are at the heart of Conrad's universe. Throughout his writing career Conrad was pursuing not only a quest to define social, political, and moral values on which a viable social community could depend but also an agonizing personal quest to make sense of his own life and to find the appropriate form and language to render his vision. Typically, he wrote in an 1898 letter to William E. Henley: 'Were I to write and talk till Doomsday you would never really know what it all means to me . . . because you never had just the same experience.' No serious reader of Conrad can doubt that he engaged in a lifelong quest to use his fiction to define a viable set of values both for himself and for his imagined audience. Nor can one doubt that he despaired at such a project. Did he not write in an 1895 letter to Edward Noble that 'No man's light is good to any of his fellows. . . . All formulas, dogmas, and principles of other people's making . . . are only a web of illusions. . . . Another man's truth is only a dismal lie to me'? It is this deep-seated scepticism – often combined with harrowing self-doubt about his ability to find the appropriate means to express both his values and doubts – that is the source of much of Conrad's irony.

For, as Winner rightly understands, Conrad's searing irony undercuts his desire to establish cultural norms: 'What makes an account of the principles and sentiments of Conrad's irony so difficult is the competition between the romantic irony of cultural faith and a quite different ironic perspective. The self-conscious illusionism of the former explains much, but an explanation along its lines is often balked by the satiric, even cruel irony that mocks the present condition of the culture' (10–11). Winner's understanding of how *forms* of irony work enables him to address the complexities of Conrad's imagination. After an introduction focusing on *Heart of Darkness*, Winner has excellent chapters on *Lord Jim*, *Nostromo*, *The Secret Agent*, and, most notably, *Under Western Eyes*, where I admire his discussion of the character of Razumov and the narrator's complex irony.

Speaking of fictional characters in terms of their moral and psychological lives, and locating Conrad's irony and values, he is writing in the humanistic tradition of Albert Guerard, Ian Watt, and Thomas Moser; while his focus on the relationship between culture and irony modifies the Conrad we know, one cannot say that a new Conrad emerges. But should we not welcome a solid discussion of thematic issues in the face of countless and repetitious discussions of the free play of signifiers?

Although not as theoretically sophisticated as Winner, Kenneth Graham in his *Indirections of the Novel* also stresses the continuity between the Victorian and modern novel, and speaks in traditional positivistic terms of influence and historical cause and effect: 'Different though [James, Conrad, and Lawrence] are from one another, they are linked by this historically crucial development they each represented in the technique of fiction: the deployment of a radically new openness, obliquity, and contradictoriness of narrative forms, both in the large-scale movements of narration and in the smallest details of descriptive language, scene, and dialogue' (1). While I found his readings of James and Forster more convincing than his analyses of Conrad, Graham does convincingly argue that his three novelists 'are all moralists in a nineteenth-century sense, with a sardonic high seriousness that only in Conrad's case is lightened by wit, and they have an Arnoldian commitment to the critical social struggle between culture and anarchy' (2). Except for failing to see the importance of the omniscient narrator's establishing the very norms which he discusses above, his readings – stressing as they do the narrative process – are perceptive and plausible, if occasionally impressionistic and not strikingly original. Graham follows the Leavisite procedure – common for decades even among the better English critics of prose fiction – of highlighting what Graham calls 'cruces, . . . pressure points'; while such a procedure commendably stresses close reading, it tends to arrest the temporal process of reading and to impose stasis on the paradigmatic passages which crystallize a novel.

John Lester also places Conrad's works in the context of a dialogue between his moral and spiritual crises and the *Zeitgeist*: 'Conrad's use of a religious lexis in his writings indicates the spiritual nature of society's malaise. The inadequacies of established beliefs had left a gap in man's existence which he endeavoured to fill with his own concerns. This had happened in Conrad's own life with the sense of vocation he brought to his two professions once that early Catholic faith of his childhood had faded' (168). Drawing upon Conrad's comments on religious issues and stressing the narrative context rather than the mythic or archetypal implications of Conrad's religious language, Lester makes some valuable points: 'Christianity [is] mirrored by Islam in the early works and made grotesquely manifest in more direct ways later on, whilst Buddhism promises only annihilation – all exemplifying Conrad's mistrust of formulas' (170). But if Lester is going to talk about authorial presence in literary works, he had better be more precise and more attuned to the psyche of the author at the time he is writing the work under discussion. Thus, writing on *Victory* (1915), he argues: 'Heyst's prevailing mood is akin to that of Conrad while he was writing his excessively morbid letters to Cunninghame Graham in the late 1890s and that *Victory* represents a fictional refutation of that mood' (166). While not without insight, this is a minor book that does not present new readings and could have made its major points in a substantial essay.

IX

If there is a trend that humanistic critics should welcome, it is the returning emphasis in literary studies to the anterior reality which gives rise to imagined worlds and how the process of mimesis renders those worlds. The dialogue between anterior reality and texts – what Alex Gelley has recently called 'narrative crossings' – is crucial because it enables us not merely to see what texts are about but how they are created. Since so much of modern British literature is *about* the artist's creation of the text – *Ulysses*, *Sons and Lovers*, *A Portrait of the Artist*, *To the Lighthouse*, *Mrs Dalloway* – and the exploration of the process of negotiating between real and fictional worlds, it is particularly appropriate that modern British literature should not lose its historical or biographical moorings.

The common thread of recent books by S. P. Rosenbaum (*Victorian Bloomsbury: The Early Literary History of the Bloomsbury Group*, Vol. 1 [New York: St. Martin's Press, 1987]) and Janis M. Paul (*The Victorian Heritage of Virginia Woolf: The External World in her Novels* [Norman, Oklahoma: Pilgrim Books, 1987]) is that

Bloomsbury is a natural outgrowth of late Victorianism. As S. P. Rosenbaum puts it:

> Bloomsbury's writing combines two broadly different clusters of value, one of which is usually sacrificed to the other in much modern literature. The terms for these kinds of value are necessarily vague, but one of them could be identified as rational. It can be recognised by a profound belief in truth, analysis, pluralism, toleration, criticism, individualism, egalitarianism and secularism. The other cluster of values is harder to label, but it has to do with the visionary. It is to be discovered in an equally profound faith in intuition, imagination, synthesis, ideality, love, art, beauty, mysticism and reverence. (18–19)

While Bloomsbury was both a fragment of the English upper-middle class, a philosophical position, *and* a self-proclaimed avant-garde movement, these books proceed in terms of traditional motions of historical evolution. How one integrates historical argument into literary discussion is a complex matter. Can we create from the texts of longer works a grammar of historical cause and effect? Do we say that at the very heart of the transitory imagined world is a realistic hard spot? To be sure, what is called the new historicism raises legitimate questions about positivistic cause and effect that often assumes that because A precedes B, A causes B, and stresses the history of power, particularly as it impacts on women, minorities, and the poor. And it has reminded us that history not only gives shape to literature, but vice versa.

Rosenbaum, the distinguished editor of *The Bloomsbury Group: A Collection of Memoirs, Commentary and Criticism*, is writing a two-volume 'Early History of the Bloomsbury Group' of which the erudite and readable book under review is the first volume. He has put together a prodigious history that is invaluable for understanding contexts and backgrounds. Rosenbaum is a traditional literary historian – that is, someone who believes that literary events reflect the culture in which texts are written and that telling a narrative of that culture is sufficient in itself. He believes in what he calls the causal relations of historical conditions and creative processes: '[A]ny history of Bloomsbury must realise the centrality of writing in their achievements, just as any literary history must refer, implicitly at least, to the temporal order of its texts' (2).

Rosenbaum's strength is his deep immersion in diverse strands of cultural history and his ability to integrate them:

> The importance of Cambridge philosophy for Bloomsbury's writing is to be found not so much in their topics as in their assumptions – assumptions about the nature of consciousness and its relation to external nature, about the irreducible otherness of people that makes isolation unavoidable and love possible, about the human and non-human realities of time and death, and about the supreme goods of truth, love and beauty. The philosophy also underlies Bloomsbury's criticisms of capitalism, imperialism and war, of materialistic realism in painting and literature, and of sexual inequality, discrimination and repression. (12)

He divides twelve chapters into four parts – entitled respectively 'Origins', 'Cambridge: Literary Education', 'Cambridge: Philosophical Education', and 'Cambridge Writings'. While specialist readers may not change their overview of Bloomsbury, the density and range of Rosenbaum's details do give us a fuller understanding of the Bloomsbury world than we now have. For example, he carefully demonstrates how the group was influenced by the Cambridge discussion group 'Apostles' and shows the importance of both the idealistic and utilitarian influences on Bloomsbury thought.

Sometimes Rosenbaum does not get beyond surface detail to ask probing questions. Those interested in the rise of English studies will find fascinating Part II, 'Cambridge: Literary Education', especially the chapter 'Modern Reading'. But here I wished Rosenbaum had more of a categorizing sensibility and was not content to tell us who read what, but rather what their reading signified. Why did Bloomsbury read non-fiction prose more than we do? Exactly how is Pater a strong presence in Woolf's aesthetic theory?

What Rosenbaum does not do is relate Bloomsbury sufficiently to simultaneous movements in Europe. Nor does he focus on *how* the historical background shapes art or *how* art shapes culture. He relies on traditional assumptions of influences when he makes such statements as '[Henry] James's analyses of moral and aesthetic impressions made the connection between his art and Moore's philosophy inevitable for Bloomsbury at Cambridge and afterwards' (149). To borrow Sir Isaiah Berlin's terms, Rosenbaum is very much in the tradition of the linear fox rather than the integrative hedgehog. Beginning with his introduction, Rosenbaum's own narrative is slow-moving and assumes that we are as interested in the minutiae of Bloomsbury as he is. Finishing this book, one may wonder whether it would not be a good idea to later issue a one-volume paperback of 300 pages which included a concrete version of both volumes. While applauding the absence of vatic super-readers who turn history into speculation and tropes, one misses the synthesizing power of the most compelling intellectual histories and culture, such as Walter Houghton's monumental *The Victorian Frame of Mind* – a book that for all its positivism has not outlived its usefulness – and Carl Schorske's *Fin de Siècle Vienna*.

Janis Paul's able and straightforward, if theoretically naive, study argues that Woolf is more a Victorian than we once thought.

> Woolf's problematic relation to all the values of her Victorian past shaped the contours of her literary accomplishment. Her Modernism grew out of her conscious rebellion against the values of her youth: her choice of fiction as her primary genre was a rebellion against the Victorian factualism of the biography, history, criticism, and philosophy her father had written and expected her to write. Her fascination with individuality and consciousness asserted the importance of a part of human character that had been devalued and ignored in her childhood. (29)

Although understanding that Woolf's traditional and Victorian roots enables us to understand her modernism, Paul's work does not have the necessary intellectual density – the kind that Rosenbaum has – to give us a sense of Woolf's uniqueness. Thus, as far as it goes, Part One, entitled 'The Background: Victorianism, Externality, and Communication', and comprising two background chapters, is relatively valuable. Chapter Two, entitled 'The Critical Background', does not really define how the novel's generic history informs Woolf's imagination. If the first chapter is biographical background with a thin veneer of cultural history, then the second chapter is literary history without a sense of its complexity and density.

Although competent, thoughtful and respectful the texts in ways I endorse, Paul's discussions in Part Two of the first five novels

– *The Voyage Out, Night and Day, Jacob's Room, Mrs Dalloway, To the Lighthouse* – rarely probe new ground. Yet Paul's very theoretical ingenuousness enables her to see how the *personal* shapes Woolf's fiction and how Leslie and Julia Stephen – as Bell and Poole have shown – are strongly determining factors in Woolf's fiction. At times Paul's analyses not only lack a forward thrust but raise more questions than they answer. I am dubious that 'time and place seem nonexistent and evident' in *To the Lighthouse* (152). Paul's discussion of *To the Lighthouse* should have done much more with how Part Two, 'Time Passes', functions to create and discover an historical perspective that has become obsolete. Unfortunately, Paul's analyses are less related to her major argument about Woolf's heritage than they should be. For example, in discussing *Mrs Dalloway*, she does not mine the possibilities of her historical argument, and gives us a rather conventional discussion. To speak of Woolf's 'summary endings' and to argue that they are 'more closed than open' seems to me to misrepresent the *indeterminacy* of Woolf's endings. Thus, despite some promising ideas and some valuable local observations, Paul's relatively unsophisticated study does not make a substantial contribution. What is lacking throughout is not only a full sense of the fabric of the Victorian life but a sophisticated sense of both the aesthetics of the novel and of current theoretical debate.

X 'WHO'S AFRAID OF *FINNEGANS WAKE?*'

riverrun, past Eve and Adam's, from swerve of shore to bend of bay, brings us by a commodius vicus of recirculation back to Howth Castle and Environs. (*Finnegans Wake*, 3)

Finn, again! Take. Bussoftlhee, mememormee! Till thousends-thee. Lps. The keys to. Given! A way a lone a last a loved a long the (*Finnegans Wake*, 628)

If the goal of literary criticism is to open up a text, to make it possible to read it better and enjoy it more, to suggest a mode of reading for other readers, to give readers a tentative map as they experience the process of reading – a map each reader can correct for himself as he reads – then John Bishop's *Joyce's Book of the Dark: 'Finnegans Wake'* (Madison: University of Wisconsin Press, 1986) is a brilliant book. Bishop's study reflects an extraordinary knowledge of the text of the *Wake*; it is erudite and lucid, and will survive changes in literary fashion. This book succeeds because Bishop is both a powerful reader of complex texts and a pluralist who comfortably negotiates between diverse interpretive communities.

Armed with Campbell and Robinson's *A Skeleton Key to Finnegans Wake* (1944) and with such subsequent studies as those by Glasheen, McHugh, Tindall, and Norris, how many of us have plunged into the *Wake* a number of times with the best of intentions only to have our odyssey of reading frustrated because, despite great pleasure in our immersion in the local wonders of the text, we do not get from its syntactical disorder and from its polyglot, punning, neologistic language enough of a coherent sense of a plot, character, and setting? Yet, despite our frustration, many of us continue to return with ever-increasing pleasure to the fun of the *Wake*, particularly Joyce's hilarious sense of humour. Let us ask the crucial questions: How can we discuss a text when our sense-making is blunted, deflected, puzzled, and confused on every page? Should we acknowledge when and why this occurs? Customarily, as we read, we move from immersion in the text to reflection upon the meaning of a passage to understanding to cognition in terms of what we know, but can we do this when reading *Finnegans Wake*? How do we read in the absence of a coherent story? Are we often deflected from immersion in our reading experience because of the lack of a story? Can we isolate our pleasure in rhetoric from our quest for meaning and significance? Do we 'read' *Finnegans Wake*, or do we need some other term to define what we do? Does *Finnegans Wake* make us hyper-self-conscious readers of Joyce's dreamscape and thus blunt the pleasure that we seek in learning about how people act in particular circumstances, even while providing us with other pleasures as we smile at wordplay and try to solve riddles? How does *Finnegans Wake* interact with other texts in our mind? To read *Finnegans Wake*, need we accept master codes about 'writing' or 'polysemous signifiers' or can we discover aesthetic, mimetic, and rhetorical codes – perhaps more local, but generated by the text – that enable us to respond in terms of the text's values and ideas?

We must acknowledge that the *Wake* does resist what we know as reading and invites us to see it as a disruption of narrative expectations if not as a complex linguistic, indecipherable puzzle. For we cannot even look to the title character, Finnegan, as a figure to help us make sense of the plot, although the title is based on the legend of a drunken man who has fallen off a ladder and apparently dies, only to arise at his wake. As Bishop writes, 'Momentarily, we might construe the hero of *Finnegans Wake* as "Finnegan" (3.19), though for reasons gradually to become clear, this is no more his real name than "Headmound" is' (66). At the risk of being accused of lack of sophistication, I am troubled by the problem of locating coherent characterization in *Finnegans Wake*. In my judgement, a principal reason that we read is to find representations of experience that is recognizably human; most of us read because of our interest in what we say, do, think, act and in how humans take part in recognizable structures of experience.

Bishop rightfully stresses important continuities between *Finnegans Wake* and Joyce's prior work, and argues that Joyce continually uses his work to rewrite – recreate – himself. For example, he shows how in *Finnegans Wake* 52.34–53.6 Joyce echoes *Portrait*, and 'allows us, at Joyce's insistence, to compare the presentment of character in the earlier novel with "the representation of noconsciousness" afforded by the 'blink pitches" of his scotographic "book of the dark." The relevant passage in *A Portrait* shows Stephen Dedalus looking soulfully at Dublin and meditating on the "Viking thingmote," the public assembly-place around which the "the seventh city of Christendom" historically aggregated' (57). Such echoes recall how Joyce in *Ulysses* uses his own prior work – earlier chapters of *Ulysses* as well as *Portrait* and *Dubliners* – as one of his systems of allusion, just as surely as he uses *The Odyssey* and Shakespeare. It seems to me that one way of understanding *Finnegans Wake* is to see it in terms of his prior novels and to understand H. C. Earwicker and Anna Livia Plurabelle as developments of Bloom and Molly. Thus many difficult passages can be better understood by reference to *Ulysses*, *Portrait*, and *Dubliners*.

Bishop focuses on the assumption that we should take very seriously Joyce's words that he 'wanted to write this book about the night' (*JJ*, 695), and that he wanted to convey, as Joyce put it, 'A nocturnal state, lunar. . . . what goes on in a dream, during a dream' (quoted in Bishop, 4, 8). In Chapter One, 'Reading the Evening World', Bishop shows us how he believes we should read *Finnegans Wake*:

> If one operates on the premise that *Finnegans Wake* reconstructs the night, the first preconception to abandon wholesale is that it

ought to read anything at all like narrative or make sense as a continuous linear whole: nobody's 'nightlife' makes sense as a continuous linear narrative whole (150.33, 407.20). . . . Impossible as it may be to fathom as an obscure totality, even at the level of a page, particles of immanent sense will stand out from the dark foil against which they are set, in turn to suggest connections with others, and still others, until – not necessarily in linear order – out of a web of items drawn together by association, a knot of *coherent* nonsense will begin to emerge; and upon this coherent nonsense, as upon the shards of a recollected dream, some interpretation will have to be practiced in order to discover an underlying sense. (27)

Even though *Finnegans Wake* lacks the traditional narrative, character and action which we expect of novels, Bishop weaves an intricate tapestry of meaning from the text, and by doing so, rescues it from the deconstructionists who have played upon it for their own purposes. Bishop has been reading the book seriously, without sacrificing its sense of fun; with infectious enthusiasm he makes us want to join him. *Finnegans Wake* lives for Bishop in all its linguistic play:

As soon as any aspect of the book begins to make sense – the idea of 'raisin,' for example – networking depths of new associations and bottomless complications, all welling up out of the dark experience of the night, web out everywhere in all directions. . . . This is why a good reading of the *Wake*, a circular book without an end, can have no real ending. . . . There's 'lovesoftfun at' *Finnegans Wake* (607.16), a book that one might easily read for a lifetime. More people should join in its fun. (384, 385)

How many of us have thought ironically amidst frustrations with *Finnegans Wake* that Joyce had written the *wake* for the novel? Yet as Bishop tells us, '[Joyce] said that his work was "basically simple" – *if*, rather than reading it linearly and literally, we interpret it as we might interpret a dream, by eliciting from the absurd murk a network of overlapping and associatively interpenetrating structures' (274). Thus, Bishop argues, 'Rather than moving linearly through a text "imitative of the dream-state," drawing on the compromised instruments of orthodox rationalism, it might better make sense to proceed much as we might in interpreting a dream'

(39). Appropriately, Bishop begins his study with 'An Introduction: On Obscurity' in which he explains why *Finnegans Wake* must be obscure: 'Had Joyce made *Finnegans Wake* less obscure than it is, he would have annihilated everything about his material that is most essential, most engaging, funniest, and most profound – rather in the same way that an intrusive sweep of "floodlights" would destroy any nightscape (134.18). The obscurity of *Finnegans Wake* is its essence and its glory' (10).

On the model of interpreting dreams, Bishop examines the 'nocturnal life' by examining hints, echoes, gestures, silence, prefigurations, and fulfilments of other passages. Despite his denials, is Bishop not something of a Freudian who bases much of his analyses on Freud's *The Interpretation of Dreams*? 'As its spelling implies, the Joycean "UNGUMPTIOUS" has a lot of "gumption" and humor in it, and is both distinct from and yet related to the "Unconscious" in more orthodox forms. As its appearance in the text also suggests, and as many Joyceans have compellingly demonstrated, there can be no question that psychoanalysis had an impact, a deep one, on *Finnegans Wake*' (15). While Freud has recently been appropriated and distorted by deconstruction, the fundamental importance of the psychoanalytic movement was to probe deeply into the human psyche to discover motives and values. More important than what it taught us about how to discuss character – although we should not diminish that contribution – was what it taught us about language and psychic gesture and how every word-choice and pause mattered. The psychoanalyst becomes a 'reader' of experience and thus helps the subject become a reader of complex texts, most notably the text of his own experience. The psychoanalyst explains the text of experience to the audience (the analysand) or, in some versions, helps the subject explain it to himself.

As he says of Joyce – and might say of psychoanalysts, Biblical scholars, and literary theorists, Bishop likes 'to detect precisely in the trivial . . . the richest of revelations' (23–4): 'By tunneling into this "mountain," Joyce not simply mined open the twentieth-century's analytical fascination with sleep, dreams, and the Unconscious, but developed as well a modernist eschatology[:]. . . . an "eschatology" because it sends knowledge and thought to their limits and uttermost ends' (24). In writing *Finnegans Wake*, Joyce read 'experience' the way he wants us to read his text. Yet since reading for unacknowledged, embedded meaning is part of a

Western tradition that includes Biblical exegesis and psycho-analysis, reading *Finnegans Wake* is only – from one point of view – an intensification of what we do when we read any text.

If at first Bishop seems to focus less on action and plot than upon language, we shall see that the mimetic impulse forms a subtext to his study:

> Although it is currently one trend to see *Finnegans Wake* as a work 'about language' – and it surely is – Joyce himself, when-ever he was asked to clarify the book, problematically said that it was 'about the night.' This minor discrepancy as to what the book is 'about' is extremely important, as the following pages intend to show; for while a book 'about language' need say nothing at all 'about the night,' and in fact usually will not, a book 'about the night' would of necessity have to undertake an intricate and wondrously obscure inquiry into the nature of language. (19)

Yet Bishop is prepared to pursue Joyce's obscure 'inquiry', exploring the etymologies of words in erudite and excruciating detail, as when he discusses 'earwigs' which live in 'Earwicker's ears at any moment in the *Wake* . . . even while he lies as deeply dead to the world as a corpse in the Book of the Dead' (297):

> Because the name of the 'earwig' (< OE *earwiga*, 'ear-worm') maintains an odd semantic constancy in a number of European languages (the Fr. *perce-oreille* ['ear-piercer'], the Ger. *Ohrwurm* ['ear-worm'], the Da. *ørentvist* ['ear-twist'], and the Russ. *ukhovy-ortka* ['ear-borer'] all paralleling the Eng. 'earwig,' and all intimating that some darkly fundamental relation links this creature with the human ear), most books on insects find themselves in the position of having to do much what Joyce does in the second chapter of the *Wake*. . . . (296)

Indeed, from the outset of Bishop's wonderful graphs and charts, such as Figure 9:4, 'The "Otological Life" of "H. C. Earwicker," ' can be dazzlingly brilliant without sacrificing the humour of the *Wake*.

Some of us may find it dismaying when Bishop speaks of the experience of reading *Finnegans Wake* in terms of etymological explanations, particularly because such explanations are often so complex that most readers of Bishop's book will forget them by the time they reread *Finnegans Wake*. Indeed, notwithstanding post-structuralism, do most of us read etymologically or want to? While Bishop is always developing wonderful patterns and resonances, he also makes important contributions when discussing Joyce's sources, such as Vico and the Egyptian Book of the Dead.

Bishop, without saying so, wants to see *Finnegans Wake* in terms of a dialogue between, on the one hand, a polysemous text which disseminates its linguistic seeds to the readers who respond – often playfully – to multiple suggestions, and, on the other, a traditional narrative which requires that its language be gathered into explanatory codes, including those which have mimetic grounding, plot, and character. Do not Bishop's own learning and his account of Joyce's learning – including Greek, Irish, Egyptian sources – make it a trivialization of Joyce's art to reduce *Finnegans Wake* to a book about language? Paradoxically, Bishop cannot avoid using representational standards to make his point that as a book *Finnegans Wake* must be seen not merely as different in degree, but different in kind: 'Perhaps only a minute ago our rubbled hero could have identified his head and feet with as much proud precision as any wakeful rationalist, and in several languages too. Now he hasn't the vaguest awareness of their location, of their relation either to each other or to himself, or quite fully of their existence' (28). Even if 'our hero' is oblivious – as we are when sleeping – to his own body, he is described by Bishop in terms that are recognizably mimetic and that speak to our urgent need to understand what we read in human terms. Thus Bishop explains the protagonist's sleeping in terms of traditional point of view: 'For anyone oblivious of the location of his own head and toes – the closest few objects in the world – is surely oblivious of the civic landmarks that lie outside of his disintegrated bedroom' (30). And Bishop describes the dreamer as a 'not very bright', 'uninquiring' and 'an altogether representative Western man' (38–9).

It is the contention of my *Reading Joyce's 'Ulysses'* (1987) that Joyce wished the reader to experience an odyssey as he makes his way through the adventure of reading and that Joyce's use of the quest motif extends to the reader's often frustrated but finally partially fulfilled quest for unity and understanding. Gradually emerging as a traditional critic who wants to explicate the text for the reader, Bishop finally gives Derridians less comfort than first appears. Bishop's book enacts the principle that novels are by human authors for human readers and about human subjects. At times, indeed, he seems to be part of the recent and, to my mind, healthy movement to recentre the subject in humanistic and mimetic terms. Because he rescues the *Wake* from linguistic games in which one examines discrete passages without making sufficient connection to the whole and because he seeks principles of formal and thematic unity, his study becomes an important book for those advocating a dialogue between traditional humanistic criticism and more recent theory. In *Finnegans Wake* he takes the *ultimate text* and shows that reading it does not mean participating in a kind of parlour game in which we let the free play of polysemous signifiers make their own rules, but rather a text that holds out the possibility of responding to our sense-making and to tentative hypotheses of coherence and meaning:

> By structuring the mind of his sleeping hero in the indirect images of all these others, Joyce demonstrates how fundamentally, if unconsciously, individuals are deeply entangled members of one another. . . . Less egocentric than somatocentric, it depicts a hero void of identity and weirdly named 'Here Comes Everybody,' who lies 'refleshed' in the universally experienced condition of sleep, thinking in the form of poetic wisdom that flows out of the body and underlies the texts of dreams, whose mind is an introjected image of the universe and of the universe of people who made him. (212, 215)

By arguing that one must understand the condition of sleep that dominates our nighttime self, does not Bishop argue that *Finnegans Wake* is not merely about language but about anterior reality? If sleep itself is something that is represented, how can we say that *Finnegans Wake* is about language? For sleep is a withdrawal from this world and dreaming is – like the act of artistic creation – the beginning of a new world: 'As in dreams, all "landshapes" in *Finnegans Wake* originate in the body of the sleeper to whom they occur; and correlatively, all such "landshapes" inevitably reveal the nature of the body of the sleeper' (37). As Bishop acknowledges: 'For all the book's purported verbal instability, virtually every page of *Finnegans Wake* refers comparably to "bed" (5.20, 6.26), or to "night" (7.2), or to things associated with a night in bed: to "dusk" (4.12), "eve" (5.11), peaceful rest (6.35), "slumber" (7.12), "sunset" (9.2), even snoring and pillows (7.28, 6.24)' (27–8).

As Bishop knows, Joyce is a 'writer of strong realist allegiances' (43): 'Brief examination of any page of *Finnegans Wake* will begin to reveal Joyce's success in this endeavor: the book represents nothing; or, to modulate the phrase one degree, much of it represents much the same kind of nothing that one will not remember not having experienced in sleep last night' (43). Even while denying the consistency of character and the organic unity of texts, Bishop reverts to such standards in his explanation, as when he writes:

> Toward the waking end of *Finnegans Wake*, its reader meets a figure who is given to venting, usually with great moral urgency, alarming statements on the order of 'I'm the gogetter that'd make it pay like cash registers' (451.4–5) and '*I've a terrible errible lot todue todie todue tootorribleday*' (381.23–4). He represents, among much else, that part of the *Wake*'s sleeping mind whose anxiety about quotidian survival – making rational sound sense and tons of pounds and pence – is alarming him up into agony. (23)

Ironically, because we all are 'Living as we do in a world where there are all kinds of pounds and pence and sounds and sense to make' (23), our readings of the world – Joyce's, Bishop's, mine – depend upon the ground of our prior experience with texts and life.

In the name of critical sophistication and reason we have been urged by deconstruction to banish discussion of mimesis from our literary discourse and pretend that we read to discover rhetorical patterns, tropes, and signs, as well as gaps, fissures and enigmas. But the most compelling trope – a trope that most readers refuse to read as 'trace', 'difference', or 'absence' – is characterization that represents human behaviour. In a word, we experience *prosopopeia* quite differently than other tropes because we read to discover ourselves; we take the process of reading – discovering meaning – seriously because we feel a continuity between reading texts and reading lives. Ironically, recent interest in the sense-making of readers – which some, like Jonathan Culler (in *On Deconstruction*), mistook as the triumph of deconstruction – returns interest, through the back door, to how humans behave. Is not the recent interest in how readers respond an inevitable result of some critics' efforts to banish authors and characters?

Fortunately, Bishop's own narrative is much easier to follow than Joyce's. In a way each of Bishop's chapters constitutes a separate reading:

What follows, then, is a primer, an illustration of a *process* that any reader might go through in 'reading [the] Evening World'. . . . On one level, it will simply be moving through the paragraph – and others along the way – very slowly, particle by particle, ultimately to read them in some depth. But at the same time, because it will be tracing long chains of association out of such paragraphs and throughout the entire book, it will be reading *Finnegans Wake* over and over again, from cover to cover, coming to terms on each repeated reading with a distinct aspect of the whole. (40–41)

In his twelve chapters Bishop brilliantly imposes his own narrative or sense-making. Indeed, each chapter of Bishop's book gives us a different perspective on the *Wake*, or at least a different view of how the *Wake* is a dream. Bishop's book enacts how *Finnegans Wake* works in the terms of various kinds of thematic principles and structures of coherence.

Basically, Bishop is reading spatially, inducing central images and establishing them at the centre of a thematic constellation around which relevant details rotate in concentric circles of importance. Each chapter is an argument for an interpretive constellation. Thus, Chapter Eleven, 'The *Nursing Mirror*,' is based on the idea that dreams 'entail "infantile regression," a return to the state of mind of infancy, is a central tenet of almost all writing on the night' (317). His brilliant fourth chapter, 'Inside the Coffin: *Finnegans Wake* and the Egyptian Book of the Dead', not only shows how Joyce used this Egyptian prototype as a source, but demonstrates how Joyce's piecemeal learning *requires* us to recuperate his text by reference to historical contexts and anterior reading. In Chapter Twelve entitled ' "Anna Livia Plurabelle": A Riverbabble primer', he explains brilliantly how the 'Anna Livia Plurabelle' chapter – which Joyce called 'a chattering dialogue across a river by two washerwomen who as night falls become a tree and a stone'[2] – works; she is ALP to the male HCE, an echo of 'Eve and Adam' in the book's first line. 'Because the unconscious perception of the bloodstream and all the "meanam" associatively adhering to it constitute an incessant part of the "gossiple so delivered in [HCE's] epistolear" (38.23), its sonority spills out of "Anna Livia" into everything else in the *Wake*, enveloping it everywhere and ultimately giving the book its circular, recirculating form' (363).

In Chapter Ten, ' "Litters": On Reading *Finnegans Wake*,' Bishop argues for the legitimacy of his non-sequential mode of reading, that is, for a kind of reading that 'has required a flagrant abandonment of sequential progression along the printed line and instead has cultivated sense by a broad-ranging and digressive association whose only limits have been the covers of the book and the terms contained in it' (305):

> As for the objection that the words and traits of seemingly independent 'characters' like Shaun have been misattributed to HCE, it will help to recall that Joyce said 'there [were] no characters' in *Finnegans Wake*, where all 'traits featuring the *chiaroscuro* coalesce, their contrarieties eliminated, in one stable somebody' (107.29–30): 'every dream deals with the dreamer himself. Dreams are completely egotistical'. (306)

But do we – can we – read without assigning language to a speaking voice? When we read a text – even when we read *Finnegans Wake* – we hear the voice of a particular teller and examine his motives and values, just as we examine the motives and values of characters whose actions he describes and whose dialogue and thoughts he presents. I am not sure that Bishop quite convinces me that the passage on 4.18–20 ('Bygmester Finnegan, of the Stuttering Hand, freemen's maurer, lived in the broadest way immarginable in his rushlit toofarback for messuages before joshuan judges had given us numbers, or Helviticus committed deuteronomy') – or any passage – frees us from 'readable and legible structure' or 'that the language of the book, like the language of dreams and like language autonomically disrupted by the stutter, will operate in a manner unpredictably different from that in which rational language operates' (307).

For can we ever entirely suspend our mimetic expectations or our linear habit of reading? Reading in terms of archetypes is far more mimetic than reading discrete passages for verbal pyrotechnics; yet even archetypal reading that collapses the distinction between Finnegan, HCE, Adam, Osiris, and Finn MacCool is not fully satisfactory to those of us who take joy in the idiosyncrasies and differences of character. Can we simply say that 'the questionable assumption that *Finnegans Wake* might operate as narrative arises from a failure to think about Joyce's subject, the night' (311)? Indeed, is not Bishop's argument for the efficacy of *Finnegans Wake* based in part on how Joyce depends on modifying and discarding traditional expectations and habits? To be sure, Bishop is right that we are frustrated in our efforts to read *Finnegans Wake* as traditional narrative, but perhaps that frustration says something pejorative about *Finnegans Wake*:

> As our reading of the Evening World will have suggested, [passages], like *Finnegans Wake* as a whole, might better be treated as a rebus, a crossword puzzle, or a hardly comprehensible dream whose manifest elements are particles of trivia and nonsense that conceal latent and apocalyptic senses which lie not on the lines but between them, and not in any literal senses but in 'outlex'. (315)

For do not our minds continuously rely on our sense-making skills, as Bishop's own work indicates, to impose our own narrative on Joyce's text?

In Chapter Five, 'Identity of the Dreamer', when Bishop explains that HCE is quite different from our usual expectation of character, we see something of the Foucault influence derived from the Berkeley school of the New Historicism – for surely New Historicism is one of the interpretive communities to which he belongs:

> As HCE, then, the 'belowes hero' of *Finnegans Wake* is not at all a 'character,' possessed of reified properties like 'personality,' 'individuality,' and 'identity,' but a body, inside of which, 'tropped head,' there is no consciousness of anything much outside, except as it has been cargoed and reformed in memory; on top of and throughout which, in wakefulness, the man-made constructs of character, personality, individuality, identity, and ego have been layered. This is the case not simply because all of these concepts and terms are arbitrary constructions entertained in consciousness to describe conscious agents, but also because they are parochially modern and narrow fictions, and not trans-historical or innate human properties. Developed in that period of historical upheaval that saw, with the rise of the novel, the evolution of a sense of selfhood compatible with the urgencies of capitalism, terms like 'character' and 'personality' harness the human into kinds of self-'possession' – ones heavily invested with a sense of the 'proper' and 'propriety,' of 'ownership' and one's 'own' – that ensure adaptive survival within a system structured on the values of 'possession' and 'property.' (142)

Yet is not the New Historicism, too, part of a reaction to deconstruction, a reaction which recentres the subject and retains a focus on human actions and human history as the object of mimesis? I believe that as New Historicism extends its influence, it will have less and less a Marxist orientation and will more and more turn its synchronic perspective, its idea that history is as much a part of literature as literature is a part of history, and its focus on power relationships on problems of the individual psyche. After all, Stephen Greenblatt and Joel Fineman explore how the psyche defines its own coherence in the face of historical and political demands and show that human will plays a role in defining the self within a system of prior and traceable historical causes.

Those who want to argue that *Finnegans Wake* is not representational may take some comfort from Bishop's convincing discussion that the *Wake* resists visualization. But I am doubtful that even the most graphic descriptions in realistic novels are visualized by most readers in quite the same way as we visualize paintings, sculptures, and cinema. When we read, do we not 'see' differently from our usual visual experience, and do we not individually 'see' what we are told or what we read quite differently from our friends and colleagues? Indeed, do not writers present visual images more for the structure of effects than to give us a photographic image? Do we really know what Leopold Bloom's or Gabriel Conroy's faces look like? In Chapter Eight, 'Meoptics', Bishop discusses the lack of visual images, even while allowing that 'Consciousness is so firmly affixed to the human eye that one would find it difficult to write an extended sentence in English without agitating some aspect of vision' (217).

If, as Bishop argues, sounds take precedence over sight in *Finnegans Wake*, are not sounds as representational as sight? 'Anything like "objective" vision, not least, receives a sharp, dark, refractive twist and wrench in the humor-filled "meoptics" of the *Wake*'s "Oscur Camerad" (602.23); there especially, the imperious vagaries of "point of view," as practiced by the first person, come to all kinds of problematic dead ends' (262). Bishop convincingly argues that different parts of the *Wake* require different kinds of reading; thus, he focuses on 301.1–311.4 at the beginning of Chapter I, iii to 'illustrate particularly well the potent nocturnal sweep of Earwicker's e'erwakened ears' (274).

Indeed, the more we reread Bishop the more a representational text *Finnegans Wake* becomes. Bishop speculates how 'Shem the

Penman' writes on the 'tissue peepers' of the eyes with 'eyebrow pencil':

> According to one line of speculation inevitably issuing from the *Wake*'s study of 'meoptics,' we might therefore conceive of an agent internal to the body agitating the 'rods and cones of this even's vision' into wakefulness during visual dreams – and doing so not haphazardly, but with such weird precision as to etch there, graphically, people, scenes, and even alphabetic characters of a sufficiently credulity-gripping lifelikeness as to convince the dreamer of their reality. (248)

Bishop goes on to argue that from another perspective, '*Finnegans Wake*, as an "imitation of the dream-state", is also, and necessarily, a representation of the body rather than of a life observed (through the eyes), narrated (by the tongue), or imperfectly understood (by the brain)' (251).

In Chapter Seven, 'Vico's "Night of Darkness": *The New Science* and *Finnegans Wake*', Bishop not only speaks wisely of Joyce's debt to Vico, but shows how Joyce's debt to Vico is different from and similar to the Freudian influence: 'Well before the appearance of Hegel's *Phenomenology of Mind*, *The New Science* necessarily implied that human consciousness was an evolutionary variable, changeable with history and society, and that it depended on the whole human past for its definition' (176). In a chapter in which every sentence is pregnant with important distinctions, he shows how Vico, like Freud, was interested in the unconscious. Bishop's 'new historical' perspective discovers important parallels among Vico, Freud, and Joyce:

> Achieving an inclusiveness that Joyce claimed not to find either in Freud's theory of consciousness, or in the socialist and anarchist literature in which he was widely read, *The New Science* gave Joyce a vision of a recurring patterning in social history that at once respected the unique problems and conditions of successive social eras, yet also isolated, as Marx did, social forces that manifested themselves in different cultures, in different material settings, and in different periods of history. (179–80)

He stresses why Joyce looks to Vico as a precursor; after all, *The New Science* is, like *Finnegans Wake*, predicated on etymological studies. He reminds us that the third book of *The New Science*, 'Discovery of the True Homer', helps us to understand *Ulysses*. In *Finnegans Wake* and *Ulysses* Joyce's subject, like Vico's, is the disruption of *family* and the need for its restoration. Finally, Bishop argues that *Finnegans Wake* owes its prose style to Vico, 'whose texture is as dense, punning, and polyglottal as that of *Finnegans Wake*' (184).

What some may miss in Bishop is a coherent reading of the novel from page 1. For my tastes, Bishop could have made further efforts to recreate the process of reading – the odyssey of reading – and might have shown us how the first reading differs from a later reading. To be sure, both *Finnegans Wake* and Bishop's study teach us that to read we have to reread, but rereading in light of prior reading has a linear as well as a spatial dimension. Does not rereading depend on the way that the evolving text of a complex work changes as the rereader gradually (often over a period of years) becomes more equipped to read it? Is this not especially true of reading *Finnegans Wake*? Although Bishop's interpretive constellations spatialize the text, finally, they also help us to a linear reading of the text, a sense-making that is informed by our prior reading of *Finnegans Wake* and our reading of his book.

As an Aristotelian, I am sceptical of Joyce's own testimony that '*Finnegans Wake* really has no beginning or end. . . . it ends in the middle of a sentence and begins in the middle of the same sentence' (*L*, I, 246). Even if the story of *Finnegans Wake* does not begin on page 1, the discourse of *Finnegans Wake* does. Does not each book we read take us into its own imagined world, each with its own narrative conventions, voice, mode of mimesis, characterization, rhetoric, and linguistic systems? The idea that books might not have beginnings is undermined by our sense that each book has its own genesis; when we begin reading a text, it begins to create its own imagined world – with its conventions, physical setting, grammar of motives, history, and way of telling. In the beginning is always the Word, the primal voice of a particularized speaker. That speaker transforms the potential of language into actuality. To quote from Stephen's artistic theory in 'Scylla and Charybdis', telling is the author's way of finding 'in the world without as actual what was in his world within as possible'. Paradoxically, the more striking the imagined world, the more the author is referring – as Joyce so often does – to prior moments in his or her text. The more an author is actually investigating the form of the novel as he or she writes his novel, the more the reader is aware that for each text 'In the beginning was the Word' and that the word is a signifier in search of a signified that represents something beyond and transcendent.

When reading *Finnegans Wake*, as when reading all texts, we search for a presence, a theme, a structural principle to pull together odd sounds, strange syllables, indecipherable shards, and puzzling fragments. If the text we read is generating its own special and unique code, we strive desperately, as Bishop does, to describe it, and we look as he does to historical and literary parallels and sources, as well as to the author's life, works, and letters. To the extent that the most striking feature of (and most plausible objection to) *Finnegans Wake* is its originality – its ghostlier demarcations and keener sounds which are so different that they tend to be at times frustrating, obscure, off-putting – we must consider what and *if* we are reading. And, indeed, Bishop's own curiosity reflects an Aristotelian bent to discover what the effects of a particular passage are: Why does the text begin with 'riverrun'? Why does it flow 'past Eve and Adam'? Why do the last words complete or at least fulfil the expectations of the very first sentence fragment?

I would have liked Bishop to place more stress on how the words reflect the characters of Finnegan and Earwicker. When I cannot relate the obscure etymologies and neologisms to the central characters and cannot find consistent principles about how Joyce's metaphoricity works and what his polyglot puns mean in terms of narrators and characters, I become sceptical about *Finnegans Wake*'s human and aesthetic values – a concept that still has meaning for some of us. When we hear a sound, we ask where did it come from; when we read words, we want to know what they tell us about the speaker. As Paul Ricoeur puts it,

Whereas the signs in language refer only to other signs within the same system, and whereas language therefore lacks a world just as it lacks temporality and subjectivity, discourse is always about something. It refers to a world which it claims to describe, to express, or to represent. It is in discourse that the symbolic function of language is actualized. . . . Whereas language is only the condition for communication for which it provides the codes, it is in discourse that all messages are exchanged. In this sense, discourse alone has not only a world, but an other, another person, an interlocutor to whom it is addressed.[3]

If, as Bishop argues, it is our ears that receive the material that we turn into dreams, do we not seek to *hear Finnegans Wake* as both a literal event – spoken by a voice – and as a dream? Is it possible to read *Finnegans Wake* as a comprehensible text? If so, do we not have to try to recuperate it in representational terms, even while acknowledging how it resists our attempts? Recently, I heard a well-known post-structuralist talk about 'The Mookse and The Gripes' passage (*Finnegans Wake*, 152ff.) without commenting much about its echoes of prior Joyce, its continuity with other Joyce fables and bestiaries, or its place in the novel. While he was penetrating in discussing Joyce's linguistic phenomena – especially the puns and etymologies – he did not see how the Mookse's quest echoes that of Ulysses, HCE, Bloom, and how the garden in the passage takes us back to Adam's and Eve's fall and the opening of *Finnegans Wake*. Nor did he realize that Joyce ironizes the *agon* of the debate between the Mookse and Gripes – the archetypal debate between two positions that need not be so contentious as the participants make it – with: 'And bullfolly answered volleyball' (*Finnegans Wake*, 15).

Because Bishop takes diverse words and phrases from *Finnegans Wake* – particularly words that are open to wildly diverse interpretation – and puts them into radically new Bishopian contexts, do we not have Bishop's story of reading *Finnegans Wake*? No matter how brilliant, it is a story elegantly controlled by Bishop's discourse rather than Joyce's. Bishop would reply: 'To the objection that terms have been taken out of context the obvious reply is that they *are* the context' (305). While Bishop's uses of Joyce's phrases legitimately become the ground for his story of reading *Finnegans Wake*, do they not also obscure and deflect the possibility of counter-argument or alternative stories of reading? When Bishop takes bits and snips from diverse passages and weaves together a paragraph of discourse, is he not distorting Joyce's context and creating his own text? Is not his procedure somewhat different from the use of *substantial* quotations from traditional texts to 'prove' or 'establish' a reading? While all stories of reading reflect the sense-making of the teller, the critic of *Finnegans Wake* who discards linearity may be engaging in an activity that is not merely different in degree but different in kind from what we classify as 'close' reading of a text. Does *Finnegans Wake* inevitably make the critic – rather than an exegetical intermediary between text and reader – a kind of super-reader who finally disdains the text?

A few quibbles: Could Bishop have stressed the continuity between dreaming and artistic creation, particularly because it is an important theme of *Finnegans Wake*? Although Bishop briefly touches on recent sleep research, one might ask if he sufficiently explores the potential of that research. He might have done more with the text of *Finnegans Wake* as a dialogue among styles, perhaps exploring Bakhtin's conception of heteroglossia, a conception which valuably fuses stylistics and representational analyses. But I want to conclude by stressing Bishop's contribution to a humanistic poetics. In important ways, Bishop's study not only synthesizes past work on the *Wake*, but discovers the energy and joy of its imagined world. I believe this brilliant, elegant, appreciative, and beautifully written study will be read by generations of readers who will be indebted to Bishop for reclaiming *Finnegans Wake* both from the esoterica of the Joyce industry and from its consignment to the literary curiosity shop by those who are not privy to the secret lore of the *Wake*.

Notes

1. See my discussion of Auerbach in Chapter 6 of my *The Humanistic Heritage: Critical Theories of the English Novel from James to Hillis Miller*.
2. James Joyce, *The Letters of James Joyce*, Vol. I, ed. Stuart Gilbert (New York: 1957); quoted in Bishop, p. 347.
3. Paul Ricoeur, 'The Model of the Text: Meaningful Action Considered as a Text', reprinted in *Social Research: 50th Anniversary* 51:1 (Spring 1984), p. 187.

Selected Bibliography

I have included all the critical and scholarly studies cited in my text and notes plus a selection of works that are essential to a humanistic poetics as well as to the issues I discuss.

Abel, Elizabeth (ed.), *Writing and Sexual Difference*. Special issue of *Critical Inquiry* 8 (1981). See especially 'Editor's Introduction', 173–8; and Elaine Showalter, 'Feminist Criticism in the Wilderness', 179–205.

———, '(E)Merging Identities: The Dynamics of Female Friendship in Contemporary Fiction by Women', *Signs* 6 (1981), 413–35.

Abrams, M. H., *The Mirror and the Lamp: Romantic Theory and the Critical Tradition* (New York: Oxford University Press, 1953).

———, *Natural Supernaturalism: Tradition and Revolution in Romantic Literature* (New York: Norton, 1971).

———, 'The Deconstructive Angel', *Critical Inquiry* 4 (1977), 425–38.

———, 'How to Do Things with Texts', *Partisan Review* 46 (1979), 366–88.

Adams, Robert M., *Strains of Discord: Studies in Literary Openness* (Ithaca: Cornell University Press, 1958).

Aldridge, John W. (ed.), *Critiques and Essays on Modern Fiction 1920–51* (New York: Ronald Press, 1953).

Allen, Walter, *The English Novel* (London: Phoenix House, 1954).

Aristotle, *Poetics*, trans. Preston H. Epps (Chapel Hill: University of North Carolina Press, 1942; rpt., 1970).

Arnold Matthew, ed. Lionel Trilling (New York: Viking, 1962).

Atherton, James, S., *The Books at the Wake: A Study of Literary Allusions in James Joyce's Finnegans Wake* (New York: Viking, 1960).

Auerbach, Erich, *Mimesis: The Representation of Reality in Western Literature*. Trans. Willard Trask (Princeton: Princeton University Press, 1953).

———, *Literary Language and Its Public in Late Latin Antiquity and in the Middle Ages* (Princeton: Princeton University Press, 1953; orig. ed., 1946).

Bakhtin, Mikhail, *Problems of Dostoevsky's Poetics*, ed. and trans. Caryl Emerson (Minneapolis: University of Minnesota Press, 1984).

———, *The Dialogic Imagination*, ed. Michael Holquist, trans. Caryl Emerson and Michael Holquist (Austin: University of Texas Press, 1981).

Bakhtin: Essays and Dialogues on His Work, ed. Gary Saul Morson (Chicago: University of Chicago Press, 1986).

Barthes, Roland, 'Introduction to the Structural Analysis of Narrative', in *Image–Music–Text*, trans. Stephen Heath (New York: Hill & Wang, 1977), 79–124.

———, *The Pleasure of the Text* (New York: Hill & Wang, 1974).

———, *S/Z* (New York: Hill & Wang, 1974).

Batchelor, John, *The Edwardian Novelists* (New York: St. Martin's Press, 1982).

Beach, Joseph Warren, *The Twentieth Century Novel: Studies in Technique* (New York: Appleton–Century, 1932).

Beja, Morris, *Epiphany in the Modern Novel* (Seattle: University of Washington Press, 1971).

Benjamin, Walter, *Illuminations*, trans. Harry Zohn, 1968; rpt. (New York: Schocken, 1969).

Bialostosky, Don, 'Dialogics as an Act of Discourse in Literary Criticism', in *PMLA* 105:5, October 1986.

Bishop, John B., *Joyce's Book in the Dark: 'Finnegans Wake'*, (Madison: University of Wisconsin Press, 1986).

Blackmur, R. P. (ed.), *The Art of the Novel: Critical Prefaces by Henry James* (New York: Scribner, 1934).

——, *Eleven Essays in the European Novel* (New York: Harbinger, 1954).

Bloom, Harold, *The Anxiety of Influence: A Theory of Poetry* (New York: Oxford University Press, 1973).

——, *A Map of Misreading* (New York: Oxford University Press, 1975).

——, (ed.), *Romanticism and Consciousness* (New York: Norton, 1970).

Booth, Wayne, 'Between Two Generations: The Heritage of the Chicago School', in *Profession* 82, 19–26.

——, *The Company we Keep: An Ethics of Fiction* (Berkeley: University of California Press, 1988).

——, *Critical Understanding: The Powers and Limits of Pluralism* (Chicago: University of Chicago Press, 1979).

——, *Now Don't Try to Reason With Me: Essays and Ironies for a Credulous Age* (Chicago: University of Chicago Press, 1970).

——, *The Rhetoric of Fiction* (Chicago: University of Chicago Press, 1961; revised ed. 1983).

——, 'The Rhetoric of Fiction and The Poetics of Fiction', *Novel* 1:2 (Winter 1968), 105–13.

——, *The Rhetoric of Irony* (Chicago: University of Chicago Press, 1974).

Bornstein, George (ed.), *Romantic and Modern: Revaluations of Literary Tradition* (Pittsburgh: University of Pittsburgh Press, 1977).

Bové, Paul, *Intellectuals in Power: A Genealogy of Critical Humanism* (New York: Columbia University Press, 1986).

Bradbury, Malcolm, *Possibilities: Essays on the State of the Novel* (New York: Oxford University Press, 1973).

Bradley, F. H., *Appearance and Reality*, 2nd edition (London: 1908).

Brooks, Cleanth, *The Well Wrought Urn* (New York: Harcourt Brace, 1947).

Brooks, Peter, *Reading For The Plot* (New York: Knopf, 1984).

Burke, Kenneth, *The Philosophy of Literary Form* (New York: Vintage, 1957).

Cain, William E., *The Crisis in Criticism: Theory, Literature, and Reform in English Studies* (Baltimore: Johns Hopkins University Press, 1984).

Calderwood, James L. and Harold E. Toliver, *Perspectives on Fiction* (New York: Oxford University Press, 1968).

Chase, Richard, *The American Novel and Its Tradition* (Garden City, NY: Doubleday, 1957).

Chatman, Seymour Benjamin, *Story and Discourse: Narrative Structure in Fiction and Film* (Ithaca: Cornell University Press, 1978).

Clayton, Jay, *Romantic Vision and the Novel* (Cambridge: Cambridge University Press, 1987).

Cohn, Dorrit, *Transparent Minds: Narrative Modes for Presenting Consciousness Fiction* (Princeton: Princeton University Press, 1978).

Crane, R. S., 'The Concept of Plot and the Plot of *Tom Jones*', in *Critics and Criticism*, ed. R. S. Crane (Chicago: University of Chicago Press, 1957).

Criticism in the University. Tri-Quarterly Series on Criticism and Culture, No. 1, ed. Gerald Graff and Reginald Gibbons (Evanston: Northwestern University Press, 1985).

Culler, Jonathan, *On Deconstruction: Theory and Criticism After Structuralism* (Ithaca: Cornell University Press, 1982).

_____, *The Pursuit of Signs: Semiotics, Literature, Deconstruction* (Ithaca: Cornell University Press, 1981).

_____, *Structuralist Poetics: Structuralism, Linguistics and the Study of Literature* (Ithaca: Cornell University Press, 1975).

Daiches, David, *The Novel and the Modern World* (Chicago: University of Chicago Press, 1939; revised ed., 1960).

De Man, Paul, *Allegories of Reading: Figural Language in Rousseau, Nietzsche, Rilke and Proust* (New Haven: Oxford University Press, 1979).

_____, *Blindness and Insight: Essays in the Rhetoric of Contemporary Criticism* (New York: Oxford University Press, 1971).

_____, *The Resistance to Theory* (Minneapolis: University of Minnesota Press, 1986).

_____, *The Rhetoric of Romanticism* (New York: Columbia University Press, 1979).

_____, *Responses on Paul de Man's Wartime Journalism*, ed. Werner Hamacher, Neil Hertz, and Thomas Keenan (Lincoln and London: University of Nebraska, 1989).

_____, *Wartime Journalism, 1939–43*, eds. Werner Hamacher, Neil Hertz, and Thomas Keenan (Lincoln and London: University of Nebraska Press, 1988).

Demetz, Peter, *Marx, Engels, and The Poets*, trans. Jeffrey L. Sammons (Chicago: University of Chicago Press, 1967).

Derrida, Jacques, *Writing and Difference* (Chicago: University of Chicago Press, 1978).

_____, *Of Grammatology*, trans. Gayatri Chakravorty Spivak (Baltimore: Johns Hopkins University Press, 1974).

_____, 'Like the Sound of the Sea Deep Within a Shell: Paul de Man's War', *Critical Inquiry* 14 (Spring 1988), 590–652; see *Critical Inquiry* 15:4 for responses to Derrida's essay.

Diacritics, Special issue: 'Cherchez La Femme: Feminist Critique/Feminist Text' 12:2 (Summer 1982).

Donoghue, Denis, 'Deconstructing Deconstruction', *New York Review of Books* 27:10 (12 June 1980), 37–41.

Eagleton, Terry, *Literary Theory: An Introduction* (Minneapolis: University of Minnesota Press, 1983).

_____, *Marxism and Literary Criticism* (London: NLB, 1976).

Eco, Umberto, *The Name of the Rose*, trans. William Weaver (New York: Wayne Books, 1983).

Edel, Leon, *The Psychological Novel 1900–1950* (London: Rupert Hart-Davis, 1961).

Eisenstein, Hester and Alice Jardine (eds), *The Future of Difference* (Boston: G. K. Hall, 1980).

Eliot, T. S., *Selected Essays*, new ed. (New York: Harcourt, Brace & World, 1960).

——, 'Ulysses: Order and Myth', *Dial* (November 1923), rpt. in *James Joyce: Two Decades of Criticism*, ed. Seon Givens (New York: Vanguard Press, 1948).

Ellmann, Richard, *The Consciousness of Joyce* (New York: Oxford University Press, 1977).

——, *Eminent Domain* (New York: Oxford University Press, 1967).

——, *James Joyce* (New York: Oxford University Press, 1984).

——, *Oscar Wilde* (New York: Knopf, 1988).

——, *Ulysses on the Liffey* (New York: Oxford University Press, 1972).

Ellmann, Richard and Charles Feidelson, Jr. (eds), *The Modern Tradition: Backgrounds of Modern Literature* (New York: Oxford University Press, 1965).

Felman, Shoshana, 'Rereading Femininity', *Yale French Studies* 62 (1981), 19–44.

Fetterley, Judith, *The Resisting Reader: A Feminist Approach to American Fiction* (Bloomington: Indiana University Press, 1978).

Finlayson, Iain, *The Sixth Continent: A Literary History of Romney Marsh* (New York: Atheneum, 1986).

Fish, Stanley, *Is There a Text in the Class?* (Cambridge: Harvard University Press, 1980).

Fogel, Aaron, *Coercion to Speak: Conrad's Poetics of Dialogue* (Cambridge: Harvard University Press, 1985).

Ford, Boris (ed.), *The Modern Age*, Volume 7 of *The Pelican Guide to English Literature*, Third Edition (Baltimore: Penguin, 1973).

Forster, E. M., *Aspects of the Novel* (New York: Harcourt, Brace & World, 1954, orig. ed., 1927).

Foucault, Michel, *Language, Counter-Memory, Practice: Selected Essays and Interviews*, trans. Donald F. Bouchard and Sherry Simon (Ithaca: Cornell University Press, 1977).

Frank, Joseph, 'Spatial Form in Modern Literature', *Sewanee Review* 53 (1945), 221–40, 435–56, 643–53.

——, 'Spatial Form: An Answer to Critics', *Critical Inquiry* 4 (Winter 1977), 231–52.

——, *The Widening Gyre: Crisis and Mastery in Modern Literature* (New Brunswick, NJ: Rutgers University Press, 1963).

Freud, Sigmund, *Civilization and Its Discontents*, trans. James Strachey (New York: Norton, 1962).

Friedman, Alan, *The Turn of the Novel* (New York: Oxford University Press, 1966).

Frye, Joanne S., *Living Stories, Telling Lives: Women in the Novel* (Ann Arbor: University of Michigan Press, 1985).

Frye, Northrop, *Fearful Symmetry* (Princeton: Princeton University Press, 1947).

——, *Anatomy of Criticism: Four Essays* (Princeton: Princeton University Press, 1957).

_____, *Fables of Identity: Studies in Poetic Mythology* (New York: Harcourt, Brace & World, 1963).

Gallop, Jane, *The Daughter's Seduction: Feminism and Psychoanalysis* (Ithaca: Cornell University Press, 1982).

Garner, Shirley Nelson, Clarie Keohane and Madelon Sprengnether (eds), *The (M)other Tongue: Essays In Feminist Psychoanalytic Interpretation* (Ithaca: Cornell University Press, 1985).

Gelley, Alexander, *Narrative Crossings* (Baltimore: Johns Hopkins University Press, 1987).

Genette, Gerard, *Narrative Discourse: An Essay in Method*, trans. Jane E. Lewin (Ithaca: Cornell University Press, 1980).

Gilbert, Sandra M., 'Costumes of the Mind: Transvestism as Metaphor in Modern Literature', *Critical Inquiry* 7:2 (Winter 1980), 391–417.

_____, and Susan Gubar (eds), *The Madwoman in the Attic: The Woman Writer and the Nineteenth-Century Imagination* (New Haven: Yale University Press, 1979).

_____, and Susan Gubar (eds), *Shakespeare's Sisters: Feminist Essays on Women Poets* (Bloomington: Indiana University Press, 1979).

Girard, Rene, *Deceit, Desire, and the Novel: Self and Other in Literary Structure*, trans. Yvonne Freccero (Baltimore: Johns Hopkins University Press, 1965).

Gordon, Lyndall, *Virginia Woolf* (New York: Norton, 1984).

Graff, Gerald, *Literature Against Itself: Literary Ideas in Modern Society* (Chicago: University of Chicago Press, 1979).

Graham, Kenneth, *Indirections of the Novel: James, Conrad, and Forster* (Cambridge: Cambridge University Press, 1988).

Greene, Gayle and Coppelia Kahn (eds), *Making a Difference: Feminist Literary Criticism* (London: Methuen, 1985).

Gross, Beverly, 'Narrative Time and the Open-Ended Novel', *Criticism* 8 (Fall 1966), 362–76.

Guerard, Albert, *Conrad the Novelist* (Cambridge: Harvard University Press, 1958).

Harari, Josue (ed.), *Textual Strategies: Perspectives in Post-Structuralist Criticism* (Ithaca: Cornell University Press, 1979).

Hardy, Barbara Nathan, 'Toward a Poetics of Fiction: An Approach Through Narrative', *Novel* 2:1 (Fall 1968), 5–14.

_____, *The Appropriate Form: An Essay on the Novel* (London: University of London, Athlone Press, 1964).

_____, *Tellers and Listeners: The Narrative Imagination* (London: Athlone Press, 1975).

Hartman, Geoffrey, *Wordsworth's Poetry, 1787–1814* (New Haven: Yale University Press, 1971).

_____, *Beyond Formalism: Literary Essays 1958–1970* (New Haven: Yale University Press, 1970).

_____, *Criticism in the Wilderness* (New Haven: Yale University Press, 1980).

_____, *Saving the Text: Literature, Derrida, Philosophy* (Baltimore: Johns Hopkins University Press, 1981).

_____, 'The Culture of Criticism' *PMLA* 99:3 (May 1984).

Harvey, W. J., *Character and the Novel* (Ithaca: Cornell University Press, 1965).

Heilbrun, Carolyn and Margaret R. Higonnet (eds), *The Representation of Women in Fiction* (Baltimore: Johns Hopkins University Press, 1983).

Hirsch, E. D., *The Aims of Interpretation* (Chicago: University of Chicago Press, 1976).

——, *Validity in Interpretation* (New Haven: Yale University Press, 1967).

Hofstadter, Douglas, *Godel, Escher, Bach: An Eternal Golden Braid* (New York: Basic Books, 1979).

Holdheim, W. Wolfgang, 'Auerbach's *Mimesis*: Aesthetics as Historical Understanding', *CLIO* 10:2 (1981), 143–54.

Holland, Norman, M., *The Dynamics of Literary Response* (New York: Oxford University Press, 1968).

Howe, Irving, *Politics and the Novel* (New York: Horizon Press & Meridian Books, 1957).

Hyman, Stanley Edgar, *The Armed Vision* (New York: Alfred A. Knopf, 1948).

Iser, Wolfgang, *The Implied Reader: Patterns of Communication in Prose Fiction from Bunyan to Beckett* (Baltimore: Johns Hopkins University Press, 1974).

——, 'The Act of Reading: A Theory of Aesthetic Response (Baltimore: Johns Hopkins University Press, 1978).

Jacobus, Mary, 'Is There A Woman In This Text?' *New Literary History* XIV (1982/83), 117–41.

——, *Reading Woman: Essays in Feminist Criticism* (New York: Columbia University Press, 1986).

——, (ed.), *Women Writing and Writing About Women* (New York: Barnes & Noble, 1979).

James, Henry, 'The Art of Fiction' (1884), in *Theory of Fiction: Henry James*, ed. James E. Miller (Lincoln: University of Nebraska Press, 1972).

——, *The Art of the Novel: Critical Prefaces* ed. R. P. Blackmur (New York: Charles Scribner's Sons, 1934).

——, *Notes on Novelists* (New York: Charles Scribner's Sons, 1914).

Jameson, Frederic, *The Political Unconscious* (Ithaca, NY: Cornell University Press, 1981).

——, *Marxism and Form* (Princeton: Princeton University Press, 1972).

Joyce, James, *Dubliners: Text, Criticism, and Notes*, ed. Robert Scholes and A. Walton Litz (New York: Viking, 1969).

——, *The James Joyce Archives, Ulysses* vols, ed. Michael Groden (New York: Garland Publishing, Inc., 1978).

——, *Letters*, Vol. I. ed. Stuart Gilbert (London: Faber and Faber, 1966).

——, *A Portrait of the Artist as A Young Man*, 1916 text corrected by Chester G. Anderson and edited by Richard Ellmann (New York: Viking, 1964).

——, *Selected Letters of James Joyce*, ed. Richard Ellman (New York: Viking, 1975).

——, *Stephen Hero*, 1944, rev. ed. Ed. Theodore Spencer (New York: New Directions, 1963).

——, *Ulysses*, 1922, rev. ed. (New York: Modern Library/Random House, 1961).

——, *Ulysses: A Critical and Synoptic Edition*, ed. Hans Gabler with Wolfhard Steppe and Claus Melchior (New York and London: Garland, 1984).

Kennan, George, 'The Buried Past', *The New York Times Review of Books* 35:16 (27 October 1988).

Kermode, Frank, *The Genesis of Secrecy: An Interpretation of Narrative* (Cambridge: Harvard University Press, 1979).

———, *Romantic Image* (London: Routledge & Kegan Paul, 1957).

———, 'Secrets and Narrative Sequence', in *On Narrative*, ed. W. J. T. Mitchell (Chicago: University of Chicago Press, 1981).

———, *The Sense of an Ending: Studies in the Theory of Fiction* (New York: Oxford University Press, 1966).

———, 'Sensing Endings', *Nineteenth Century Fiction* 33 (June 1978), 144–58.

———, *The Art of Telling: Essays on Fiction* (Cambridge: Harvard University Press, 1983).

Kettle, Arnold, *An Introduction to the English Novel* (2nd edition) Vols 1 and 2 (New York: Harper, 1960; orig. ed., 1951).

Kiely, Robert, *The Romantic Novel in England* (Cambridge: Harvard University Press, 1972).

———, *Beyond Egotism* (Cambridge: Harvard University Press, 1980).

Kolodny, Annette, 'Dancing Through the Minefield: Some Observations on the Theory, Practice and Politics of a Feminist Literary Criticism', *Feminist Studies* 6 (1980), 1–25.

———, 'A Map for Rereading: Or, Gender and the Interpretation of Literary Texts', *New Literary History* 11 (1980), 451–67.

Krieger, Murray (ed.), *Northrop Frye in Modern Criticism* (New York: Columbia University Press, 1966).

———, *Theory of Criticism: A Tradition and its System* (Baltimore: Johns Hopkins University Press, 1983).

Lacan, Jacques, *Feminine Sexuality*, eds J. Mitchell and J. Rose (London: Macmillan, 1982).

Langbaum, Robert, 'The Epiphanic Mode in Wordsworth and Modern Literature', *New Literary History* 14:2 (Winter 1983).

———, *The Poetry of Experience: The Dramatic Monologue in Modern Literary Tradition* (New York: Norton, 1957).

———, *The Modern Spirit: Essays on the Continuity of Nineteenth and Twentieth Century Literature* (New York: Oxford University Press, 1970).

Lanser, Susan, *The Narrative Act* (Princeton: Princeton University Press, 1981).

Lawrence, Karen, *The Odyssey of Style in Ulysses* (Princeton: Princeton University Press, 1981).

Leavis, F. R., *The Common Pursuit* (New York: Penguin, 1962, orig. ed., 1952).

———, *The Great Tradition: George Eliot, Henry James, Joseph Conrad* (London: Chatto & Windus, 1948).

———, *Revaluations* (London: Chatto & Windus, 1936).

Leitch, Vincent B., 'The Lateral Dance: The Deconstructive Criticism of J. Hillis Miller', *Critical Inquiry* 6:4 (Summer 1980), 593–607.

Lentricchia, Frank, *After the New Criticism* (Chicago: University of Chicago Press, 1980).

———, *Criticism and Social Change* (Chicago: University of Chicago Press, 1983).

Lester, John, *Conrad and Religion* (New York: St. Martin's Press, 1988).

Levine, George, *The Realistic Imagination: English Fiction from Frankenstein to Lady Chatterley* (Chicago: University of Chicago Press, 1981).

Lodge, David, *Language of Fiction: Essays in Criticism and Verbal Analysis*

of the English Novel (New York: Columbia University Press, 1966).
——, *The Modes of Modern Writing: Metaphor, Metonymy, and the Typology of Modern Literature* (Ithaca: Cornell University Press, 1977).
——, *Working with Structuralism: Essays and Reviews on Nineteenth- and Twentieth-Century Literature* (London: Routledge & Kegan Paul, 1981).
Lubbock, Percy, *The Craft of Fiction* (New York: Viking, 1957, orig. ed., 1921).
Lukàcs, Georg, *Studies in the European Novel* (New York: Grossett & Dunlap, 1964).
Mack, Maynard and Ian Gregor (eds), *Imagined Worlds: Essays in Honour of John Butt* (London: Methuen, 1968).
Marks, Elaine and Isabelle de Courtivron (eds), *New French Feminisms: An Anthology* (Amherst: University of Massachusetts Press, 1980).
Martz, Louis L. and Aubrey Williams (eds), *The Author in His Work* (New Haven: Yale University Press, 1978).
McConnell-Ginet, Sally and Nelly Furman (eds), *Women and Language in Literature and Society* (New York: Praeger, 1980).
McKeon, Richard, *Thought, Action, and Passion* (Chicago: University of Chicago Press, 1954).
Meyerhoff, Hans, *Time and Literature* (Berkeley and Los Angeles: University of California Press, 1955).
Miller, D. A., *Narrative and its Discontents: Problems of Closure in the Traditional Novel* (Princeton: Princeton University Press, 1981).
Miller, James E. (ed.), *Theory and Fiction: Henry James* (Lincoln: University of Nebraska Press, 1972).
Miller, J. Hillis, *The Disappearance of God: Five Nineteenth-Century Writers* (Cambridge: Harvard University Press, 1963).
——, 'Ariadne's Thread: Repetition and the Narrative Line', *Critical Inquiry* 3 (1976), 57–78.
——, 'A "Buchstabliches" Reading of *The Elective Affinities*', *Glyph* 6 (1979), 1–23.
——, 'Deconstructing the Deconstructors', *Diacritics* 5:2 (1975), 24–31.
——, *The Ethics of Reading* (New York: Columbia University Press, 1986).
——, *Fiction and Repetition: Seven English Novels* (Cambridge: Harvard University Press, 1982).
——, *The Form of Victorian Fiction* (Notre Dame: University of Notre Dame Press, 1968).
——, 'Narrative and History', *ELH* 41 (1974), 455–73.
——, *Poets of Reality: Six Twentieth-Century Writers* (Cambridge: Belknap Press of Harvard University Press, 1965).
——, 'Ariadne's Broken Woof', *Georgia Review* 31 (1977), 44–60.
——, 'The Critic as Host', *Critical Inquiry* 3 (1977), 439–47.
Miller, Nancy K., 'Emphasis Added: Plots and Plausibilities in Women's Fiction', *PMLA* 96 (1981), 36–48.
Millett, Kate, *Sexual Politics* (New York: Doubleday, 1979).
Mitchell, W. J. T. (ed.), *On Narrative* (Chicago: University of Chicago Press, 1981). Rpt. of articles from *Critical Inquiry* 7:1 (Autumn 1980) and 7:4 (Summer 1981).
——, (ed.), *The Politics of Interpretation* (Chicago: University of Chicago Press, 1983).

_____, (ed.), Against Theory: Literary Studies and the New Pragmatism (Chicago: University of Chicago Press, 1985).

Moi, Toril, Sexual/Textual Politics: Feminist Literary Theory (London: Methuen, 1985).

Moser, Thomas, Joseph Conrad: Achievement and Decline (Cambridge: Harvard University Press, 1957).

Muir, Edwin, The Structure of the Novel (London: Hogarth Press, 1954; orig. ed., 1928).

Newton, Judith and Deborah Rosenfelt (eds), Feminist Criticism and Social Change: Sex, Class and Race in Literature and Culture (New York: Methuen, 1985).

Norris, Margot, Beasts of the Modern Imagination: Darwin, Nietzsche, Kafka, Ernst, and Lawrence (Baltimore: Johns Hopkins University Press, 1985).

_____, The Decentered Universe of Finnegans Wake (Baltimore: Johns Hopkins University Press, 1976).

Nuttal, A. D., A New Mimesis: Shakespeare and the Representation of Reality (New York: Methuen, 1983).

Paul, Janis, The Victorian Heritage of Virginia Woolf: The External World of Her Novels (Norman, OK: Pilgrim Books, 1987).

Phelan, James, Worlds from Words: A Theory of Language in Fiction (Chicago: University of Chicago Press, 1981).

_____, Reading People, Reading Plots: Character, Progression and the Interpretation of Narrative (Chicago: University of Chicago Press, 1989).

Plato, Symposium, trans. Walter Hamilton (New York: Penguin, 1951).

Poulet, George, 'Phenomenology of Reading', New Literary History 1:1 (October 1969), 53–68.

_____, 'Criticism and the Experience of Interiority', The Structuralist Controversy: The Languages of Criticism and the Sciences of Man, eds Richard Macksey and Eugene Donato (Baltimore: Johns Hopkins University Press, 1970).

Pratt, Mary Louise, Towards A Speech Act Theory of Literary Discourse (Bloomington: Indiana University Press, 1977).

_____, 'Interpretive Strategies/Strategic Interpretations: On Anglo-American Reader-Response Criticism', in Postmodernism and Politics, ed. Jonathan Arac (Minneapolis: University of Minnesota Press, 1986).

Price, Martin, Forms of Life: Character and Moral Imagination in the Novel (New Haven: Yale University Press, 1983).

Rathburn, Robert C. and Martin Steinmann, Jr. (eds), From Jane Austen to Joseph Conrad: Essays Collected in Memory of James T. Hillhouse (Minneapolis: University of Minnesota Press, 1958).

Richards, I. A., Principles of Literary Criticism (New York: Harcourt, Brace & World, 1925).

_____, Practical Criticism (New York: Harcourt, Brace and World, 1929).

Richter, David H., Fable's End: Completeness and Closure in Rhetorical Fiction (Chicago: University of Chicago Press, 1974).

_____, 'Closure and the Critics', Modern Philology (February 1983).

Ricoeur, Paul, 'The Model of a Text: Meaningful Action Considered as Text', Social Research: Fiftieth Anniversary 51:1 (Spring 1984).

Riffaterre, Michael, 'Interpretative and Descriptive Poetry: A Reading of Wordsworth's "Yew-Trees"' *New Literary History* 4 (Winter 1973).

Rosenbaum, S. P. (ed.), *The Bloomsbury Group* (Toronto: University of Toronto Press, 1975).

——, *Victorian Bloomsbury: The Early Literary History of the Bloomsbury Group* Vol. 1 (New York: St. Martin's Press, 1987).

Rosenblatt, Louis M., *The Reader, the Text, the Poem: The Transactional Theory of the Literary Work* (Carbondale: Southern Illinois Press, 1978).

Rosmarin, Adena, *The Power of Genre* (Minneapolis: University of Minnesota Press, 1986).

Ruppert, Peter, *Reader in a Strange Land: The Activity of Reading Literary Utopias* (Athens: University of Georgia Press, 1986).

Russo, John Paul, *I. A. Richards: His Life and Work* (Baltimore: Johns Hopkins University Press, 1989).

Sabin, Margery, *The Dialect of the Tribe: Speech and Community in Modern Fiction* (New York: Oxford University Press, 1987).

Sacks, Sheldon, *Fiction and the Shape of Belief* (Berkeley and Los Angeles: University of California Press, 1967).

——, (ed.), *On Metaphor* (Chicago: University of Chicago Press, 1979).

Said, Edward, *Beginnings: Intention and Method* (New York: Basic Books, 1975).

Salusinszky, Irene, *Criticism in Society* (New York: Methuen, 1987).

Scholes, Robert (ed.), *Approaches to the Novel* (San Francisco: Chandler Publishing Co., 1961; rev. ed., 1966).

Scholes, Robert and Robert Kellogg, *The Nature of Narrative* (New York: Oxford University Press, 1966).

Schorer, Mark, et al. (eds), *Criticism: The Foundation of Modern Literary Judgement* (New York: Harcourt, Brace; rev. ed. 1958).

——, *The World We Imagine* (New York: Farrar, Straus, Giroux, 1968).

——, 'Technique as Discovery', *Hudson Review*, 1948. Rpt in *Perspectives on Fiction*, eds. James L. Calderwood and Harold E. Toliver (New York: Oxford University Press, 1968).

Schwarz, Daniel R., *Conrad: 'Almayer's Folly' to 'Under Western Eyes'* (London: Macmillan; Ithaca: Cornell University Press, 1980).

——, *Conrad: The Later Fiction* (London: Macmillan; New York: The Humanities Press, 1982).

——, *The Humanistic Heritage: Critical Theories of the English Novel From James to Hillis Miller* (London: Macmillan; Philadelphia: University of Pennsylvania Press, 1986).

——, *Reading Joyce's 'Ulysses'* (London: Macmillan; New York: St. Martin's Press, 1987).

——, *The Transformation of the English Novel, 1890–1930* (London: Macmillan; New York: St. Martin's Press, 1989).

——, 'The Ethics of Reading: The Case for Pluralistic and Transactional Reading', *Novel* 21:2 and 3 (Winter/Spring 1988).

——, 'The Narrator as Character in Hardy's Major Fiction', *Modern Fiction Studies* XVIII (1972), 155–72.

Searle, John, R., *Speech Acts: An Essay in the Philosophy of Language* (London: Cambridge University Press, 1969).

_____, *Expression and Meaning: Studies in the Theory of Speech Acts* (Cambridge and New York: Cambridge University Press, 1979).

_____, Rev. of *On Deconstruction*, by Jonathan Culler, *New York Review of Books* (27 October 1983), 74–9.

Seidel, Michael, *Exile and the Narrative of Imagination* (New Haven, CT: Yale University Press, 1986).

Showalter, Elaine, *A Literature of Their Own: British Women Novelists from Brontë to Lessing* (Princeton: Princeton University Press, 1977).

_____, 'Critical Cross-Dressing: Male Feminists and the Woman of the Year', *Raritan* 3:2 (Fall 1983), 130–49.

_____, (ed.), *The New Feminist Criticism* (New York: Pantheon, 1985).

Smith, Barbara Herrnstein, 'Narrative Versions, Narrative Theories', in *On Narrative*, W. J. T. Mitchell, ed. (Chicago: University of Chicago Press, 1981).

_____, *Poetic Closure: A Study of How Poems End* (Chicago: University of Chicago Press, 1968).

Stanford, W. B., *The Ulysses Theme* (Oxford: Blackwell, 1954).

Stevens, Wallace, *Collected Poems* (New York: Alfred A. Knopf, 1965).

Sturrock, John, *Structuralism and Since: From Levi-Strauss to Derrida* (Oxford: Oxford University Press, 1979).

Suleiman, Susan, and Inge Crosman (eds), *The Reader in the Text: Essays on Audience and Interpretation* (Princeton: Princeton University Press, 1980).

Tave, Stuart M., *Some Words of Jane Austen* (Chicago: University of Chicago Press, 1973).

Thickstun, William, *Visionary Closure in the Modern Novel* (New York: St. Martin's Press, 1989).

Thornton, Weldon, *Allusions in Ulysses: A Line-by-Line Reference to Joyce's Complex Symbolism* (Chapel Hill: University of North Carolina Press, 1968. Rpt New York: Simon and Schuster, 1973).

Todorov, Tzvetan, 'Structural Analysis of Narrative', *Novel* 3:1 (Fall 1969), 70–76.

_____, *The Poetics of Prose*, trans. Richard Howard (Ithaca: Cornell University Press, 1977).

Tompkins, Jane P. (ed.), *Reader Response Criticism* (Baltimore: Johns Hopkins University Press, 1980).

Torgovnick, Marianna, *Closure in the Novel* (Princeton: Princeton University Press, 1981).

Trilling, Lionel, *The Liberal Imagination* (New York: Viking 1950).

_____, *The Opposing Self: Nine Essays in Criticism* (New York:Viking, 1955).

Van Ghent, Dorothy, *The English Novel: Form and Function* (New York: Harper & Row, 1953).

Watt, Ian, *The Rise of the Novel* (Berkeley and Los Angeles: University of California Press, 1957).

_____, *Conrad in the Nineteenth Century* (Berkeley and Los Angeles: University of California Press, 1979).

White, Hayden, 'The Value of Narrativity in the Representation of Reality', in *On Narrative*, ed. W. J. T. Mitchell (Chicago: University of Chicago Press, 1981).

Williams, Raymond, *The English Novel from Dickens to Lawrence* (New York: Oxford University Press, 1970).

——, *Marxism and Literature* (Oxford: Oxford University Press, 1977).

——, *Politics and Letters* (London: NLB, 1979).

Wilson, Edmund, *Axel's Castle: A Study in the Imaginative Literature of 1870–1930* (New York: Charles Scribner's Son, 1959).

Wimsatt, William K., Jr and Cleanth Brooks, *Literary Criticism: A Short History* (New York: Vintage, 1967; first ed., 1957).

Winner, Anthony, *Culture and Irony: Studies in Joseph Conrad's Major Novels* (Charlottesville, University of Virginia, 1988).

Woolf, Virginia, 'Mr. Bennett and Mrs. Brown' (1924), in *The Captain's Death Bed* (New York: Harcourt, Brace & Co., 1950).

——, *A Room of One's Own* (New York: Harcourt, Brace & World, 1957; original ed. 1929).

Index